# Money Minds

# Money Minds

## Helping Kids Make Smart Choices with Money

Eli Shepherd

Mindful Pages

Published in 2025

ISBN: 9789371775946 (PB)
ISBN: 9789371773874 (eBook)

*Published by*

**Mindful Pages**
*Imprint of Alpha Editions LLC*
312 W. 2nd St #1834
Casper, WY 82601, USA


This book was developed using advanced writing tools to support the drafting and ideation process. All content has been thoughtfully curated, refined, and reviewed to ensure quality and relevance.

# Content

# Introduction
# The Silent Curriculum of Money

Walk through any supermarket with a child and you're not just running errands—you're entering a living classroom of economics, one without a syllabus yet overflowing with lessons. Every pause before reaching for the store brand, every card swipe without comment, every weary "we can't afford that" teaches something. These small, unguarded moments transmit more than arithmetic; they shape outlooks. A child watching isn't learning facts, but frameworks—narratives about how the world of money works, and how it feels to live within it.

Children are learning about money constantly, whether or not we mean to teach them. The messages we send—through our habits of spending, saving, giving, and even worrying—form the foundation of their understanding. While schools might offer definitions of "budget" or "interest," the deeper education unfolds in the home, in the car, at the till, and in the quiet spaces between paydays. It isn't lectured; it's modelled. It seeps in through tone, timing, and gesture. This is the unspoken curriculum of money.

We often imagine financial literacy as a checklist of skills—like learning to tie shoelaces or ride a bike. But the truth runs deeper. Real financial literacy isn't a discrete subject; it's a worldview, a psychological and moral scaffolding that matures alongside a child's sense of self. To teach money well is not to train accountants—it is to raise thinkers, citizens, and human beings who can navigate a world where money is everywhere yet explains very little.

Money, after all, is rarely just about currency. It's about control, fear, freedom, love, and identity. It holds the fingerprints of our anxieties and our ambitions. It can deepen intimacy or fracture trust. For children, money soon becomes bound up with fairness, belonging, and self-worth. So, when we talk about "teaching" money, we are really stepping into an ongoing conversation—one they've already been having, quietly observing us all along.

Of course, we adults bring our own unresolved stories to this table. Many of us inherit confused or conflicting beliefs about money. We might speak of prudence while spending impulsively. We might preach independence yet hover protectively over every financial choice. We might say money doesn't matter—only to fight about it in hushed tones. These contradictions don't make us hypocrites; they make us human. But if left unexamined, they also make us unreliable teachers.

*Money Minds* begins by naming these tensions—not to induce guilt, but to illuminate them. It is not a manual of quick fixes or tidy formulas. It is a developmental map, built on behavioural science and parenting psychology, designed to help children understand not only how money works, but how *they* work in relation to it.

The urgency of this work is undeniable. We are raising children in an economy engineered for impulse. From YouTube unboxings to app-store microtransactions, the world they inhabit rewards immediacy and comparison. Patience, restraint, and empathy have to swim against the current. These environments are not neutral—they are persuasive. They whisper that saving is pointless, that work is optional, that generosity is secondary to display.

In such a climate, raising financially grounded children is not a luxury—it's an act of protection. Age alone will not confer wisdom. A teenager who has never earned, budgeted, or given meaningfully can reach adulthood functionally literate yet emotionally naïve. Habits of autonomy, purpose, and delayed gratification need practice, not just instruction.

But this can't be achieved through rigidity. We must teach both prudence and courage; both boundaries and freedom. Children should understand that money is a tool—capable of creating choices, shaping futures, and expressing values. Yet they must also see that money cannot secure love, integrity, or contentment. Our task as parents is not to choreograph every decision but to cultivate the soil in which sound judgement can grow.

A child's financial development mirrors their psychological one. What a five-year-old perceives about money differs profoundly from what a fifteen-year-old can reason through. Expecting maturity too soon—or denying responsibility too long—breeds confusion and defiance.

Teaching must meet children where they are: the toddler grasping that coins can be traded, the adolescent beginning to see risk and consequence. *Money Minds* offers the scaffolding to match those stages, step by step.

Across these chapters, you'll learn how to:

- Notice and interrupt the hidden messages your actions send about money.
- Reflect on your own upbringing to uncover emotional inheritances around wealth and scarcity.
- Engage children in age-appropriate ways—from hands-on coin jars for the little ones to budgeting apps for teenagers.
- Reimagine allowance, chores, and early earnings as chances to build character, not merely commerce.
- Cultivate saving, spending, and giving habits aligned with emerging personal values, not parental anxiety.
- Navigate tricky conversations—from "Are we rich?" to "Why can't I have what they have?"—with openness instead of avoidance.
- Set healthy boundaries around digital spending and consumer exposure without shame or secrecy.
- Prepare children to earn, manage, and occasionally fail with money—within a safe, guided structure.

At its core, *Money Minds* invites a reimagining of financial education as a branch of cultural and ethical literacy. It doesn't offer perfection—because children will err, and parents will contradict themselves. The goal is not flawlessness, but integrity. Not control, but clarity.

We want our children to inherit more than competence. We want them to learn how to pause before purchasing, to give without resentment, to save with meaning, to earn with dignity. To understand that their worth is never measured in currency—but that every pound spent, saved, given, or wasted reflects something of what they value.

To reach that point, money must come out of hiding. The unsaid must become spoken. The mysterious, explained. The passive, intentional. Home, in this light, is not merely a backdrop—it is the first and most formative classroom for financial life. Not because it provides the most data, but because it transmits the deepest meaning.

This book will walk you through that classroom. Within it are stories, strategies, research, and reflection points—but above all, a way to relate to your child that reflects not just your knowledge, but your values and your vision for who they might become.

Because the real aim is not to raise children who are merely *good with money.*
It is to raise people who are good with choices. Good with responsibility. And—perhaps most importantly—good with enough.

# Chapter 1
# Why Kids Struggle with Money

It's tempting to think that when children stumble with money, it's simply because no one has explained the mechanics—how a budget balances, how interest works, how to calculate what's left after a purchase. But that's only the surface. Their difficulty rarely stems from ignorance alone. More often, it grows from the quiet confusion of the financial world they inhabit: a tangle of mixed messages, unspoken tensions, and inconsistent examples. Long before a child learns to count coins, they've already drawn conclusions about what money *is*—what it means, what it signals, and how it behaves in the lives of those around them.

This learning happens beneath the radar, through what educators might call the hidden curriculum—the lessons that are never formally taught, but constantly demonstrated. It lives in our habits, in our tempers, in the small inconsistencies that children observe but we hardly notice. It seeps through when we mutter about bills, or fall silent at the mention of debt. It's there in the tightness of a parent's jaw at the checkout, the resigned swipe of a card, or the weary justification, *"I've earned this."* To an adult, these are fleeting moments. To a child, they are data points, carefully catalogued.

Children are extraordinary witnesses. They might not yet grasp compound interest or mortgage rates, but they are fluent in emotion. They sense the unease that hovers when bills arrive. They notice the sigh after a purchase or the quick change of subject when money is mentioned. And because children crave safety, they seek patterns in these emotional cues. If every mention of money carries stress, then money must be perilous. If giving is rare, generosity must be risky. If spending is impulsive, restraint must be unnatural. Slowly, unconsciously, they construct a worldview.

To understand why children falter with money, we must first recognise that they've been learning all along—just not always from us, and not always what we meant to teach.

Their difficulties are magnified by the worlds they move through, which are meticulously designed to fuel desire and shorten attention spans. The marketplace no longer sits in the high street; it lives in apps, games, and social feeds. Each "free" download is a disguised shopfront. Each unboxing video whispers want. Even play has been monetised, reshaped into a constant rehearsal for consumption. The lines between playtime, advertising, and identity are almost gone.

Expecting children to resist this pull is wishful thinking. Their brains are still under construction—their prefrontal cortex, the seat of judgement and self-restraint, matures painfully late. Meanwhile, their reward systems are already on overdrive, making every offer of "instant" gratification feel irresistible. In such an environment, asking a child to self-regulate without guidance is like sending them to sea in a paper boat.

There is another, subtler problem: the vanishing link between work and reward. In many homes, particularly those cushioned by convenience, money has become invisible. Food appears, lights glow, packages arrive—yet the connection between labour and outcome is rarely seen. For a child, money can seem more like weather than effort: it simply happens. When something costs nothing to obtain, it risks costing nothing to waste.

Without personal experience of earning or contributing, children find it difficult to locate money within any moral or practical frame of value. Ten pounds handed over feels the same as ten pounds earned—though research tells us otherwise. Money that's worked for is more often saved, managed, even cherished. To teach respect for money, one must let a child *feel* its weight, not merely spend its sum.

And then, of course, there's the silence. The great cultural hush that surrounds money talk. In many families, it's the one subject that remains unspoken, cloaked in euphemism or avoidance. We say we're "tight this month" or "managing fine," but we rarely explain what those words mean. Sometimes it's to protect children from worry; sometimes it's because we were never taught how to talk about it ourselves. Yet silence doesn't neutralise the subject—it mystifies it.

Children, ever curious, will fill that void with their own theories. Without context, imagination takes over: money is scary, or endless, or unfair. And when parents avoid honest discussion, children turn to their peers or—more perilously—to the internet. TikTok influencers now teach "financial literacy" with the same confidence once reserved for adults, blurring the boundary between advice and advertisement. What children used to glean slowly from observation, they now absorb instantly from monetised screens.

So why, truly, do children struggle with money? Because the world around them trains them to spend, not to pause.
Because the systems that surround them are designed for extraction, not education.
Because their brains are wired for the present, while money demands patience.
Because our discomfort too often keeps us silent.
Because every sigh, indulgence, or omission teaches them something—whether we intend it or not.
And perhaps most of all, because we forget how early this learning begins.

This chapter examines those forces in turn. We start with the hidden curriculum—the quiet, everyday lessons that flow from our behaviour more than our words. We look closely at what children infer from our inconsistencies, our arguments, our tone. Then, we dissect the machinery of impulse culture: how consumer design exploits human psychology, and why developing minds are its easiest prey. We'll also revisit the concept of work and effort, and what happens when children grow up in a world where labour is invisible. Finally, we'll confront the silence around money itself—why we avoid these conversations, and what is lost when we do.

What we uncover is not a story of failure, but of mismatch. The issue is not intelligence or discipline; it's context. And when the context changes, the learning changes. Not through lectures or punishment, but through modelling, dialogue, and steady, transparent participation.

By the end, you'll see that a child's confusion about money isn't a personal shortcoming. It's an invitation—to clarify, to engage, to teach with empathy rather than fear. Because children don't need perfect households or flawless examples. They need constancy. They need adults who can narrate rather than conceal; who can explain instead of evade; who can welcome them into the conversation rather than wall them off from it.

The problem has never been that children don't understand money. The problem is that we too rarely recognise *why*. When we do—when we name the conditions honestly—we gain the power to reshape them. Not just to fill gaps in knowledge, but to cultivate wisdom. Not just to manage behaviour, but to build understanding. Not merely to protect, but to prepare.

## The Hidden Curriculum

A child can recite the cost of their favourite toy before they can explain what money actually is. They might mimic tapping a credit card on a reader or parrot the phrase "we can't afford that" without understanding what it means. But beneath these surface behaviours lies something more enduring: the internal architecture of belief, attitude, and emotion that will shape their lifelong relationship with money. What they think about money—its role, its power, its danger, its meaning—is not taught directly. It is modelled, absorbed, and inferred. This is the hidden curriculum of money: the unintentional syllabus written by every parental action, omission, and reaction. It is not housed in lectures but in life, and its influence often outpaces even our most carefully planned financial lessons.

Children learn to speak money long before they learn to manage it. From a young age, they begin decoding adult behaviour for clues about what matters. They notice tone, observe habits, and draw conclusions from patterns. A parent who grimaces when paying bills communicates something different from one who does it with calm. A child who hears arguments after every credit card statement absorbs more than the figures—they absorb fear, secrecy, maybe shame. If a parent refuses to discuss prices or household budgets, the child learns not neutrality, but taboo. In this way, financial norms are not inherited through formal instruction. They are downloaded through daily exposure.

Consider a child growing up in a household where money is spoken of only in moments of stress. The car breaks down. The rent is due. There's a layoff. Tension spikes, voices rise, decisions get made behind closed doors. The child may not understand income or interest, but they understand mood. They sense when the atmosphere thickens. Over time, they begin to link money with instability. Or fear. Or silence. They may vow never to be "bad with money," even if they have no idea what that means. Alternatively, they may disengage altogether, adopting an unspoken family rule that money is dangerous or best avoided. This is not rare. It is common. And it is formative.

Equally formative—but less often acknowledged—is the indulgent silence of affluence. In higher-income homes, children may grow up with abundance but little context.

They receive without contributing. They want, and the want is met. Not always from a place of spoiling, but often from convenience, guilt, or love. The hidden lesson here is that money appears easily, that desires should be fulfilled quickly, and that choice is an entitlement rather than a privilege. These children are no less vulnerable to the distortions of the hidden curriculum—they simply inherit a different distortion.

Both scarcity and abundance can miseducate when left uninterrogated. In one, the child may learn fear; in the other, entitlement. In both, they miss the chance to develop what behavioural economists call "mental accounting"—the sense that money has source, purpose, and limit. And the problem is not income level per se, but the absence of reflection. Without dialogue, modelling, or boundaries, children form their own narratives in the dark. And the narratives stick.

One of the most persistent distortions of the hidden curriculum comes from inconsistency. Parents who alternate between strict frugality and impulsive splurging confuse their children not just financially but psychologically. A mother who insists on budgeting every grocery item but buys luxury handbags without explanation leaves a child unsure what money *ought* to mean. A father who tells his children to save but constantly complains about taxes or blames others for financial hardship transmits mixed values. And children, being natural sense-makers, will attempt to resolve these contradictions—usually by adopting the more emotionally charged message.

Behavioural science tells us that humans learn not only from rules, but from outcomes. If every spending decision is followed by stress, money becomes a source of anxiety. If spending is unrestrained and never contextualised, it becomes a route to emotional regulation. In both cases, the child absorbs not just information, but *affect*—emotional associations that form the bedrock of future habits. These affective associations often override later cognitive input. This is why an adult who knows how to budget can still sabotage their own finances under emotional strain. Early emotional encoding runs deep.

The hidden curriculum also governs how children perceive earning. When work is invisible—when children do not see or hear about the time, effort, or trade-offs involved in bringing money into the household—money loses context. A parent disappears to a job and returns home with bags of shopping. The link between effort and reward is abstract. And in an increasingly digital world, where money is often exchanged via taps, transfers, and subscriptions, that abstraction intensifies. For a child watching an adult tap a phone to buy something, the causal chain of labour → income → decision → outcome is reduced to a single, frictionless gesture. The process becomes opaque, the inputs disappear, and only the gratification remains visible.

Even in households where work is discussed, the tone matters. If parents speak about work only in terms of drudgery, exhaustion, or resentment, children may absorb a belief that earning is suffering. If, instead, they hear about work as meaningful, disciplined, or skill-based, they develop a different internal script. Work becomes an identity, a contribution—not merely a sacrifice. These subtle differences shape not just financial understanding, but broader life orientation: toward entitlement or effort, passivity or agency.

Silence is often mistaken for protection. Many parents refrain from discussing money with children to preserve their innocence or shield them from stress. But this silence can be counterproductive. When children are excluded from financial conversations—especially ones that affect them directly—they often sense that something is being withheld. In the absence of information, they generate their own explanations. A parent says "we can't afford that," but offers no further context. Does it mean they are poor? That the child has done something wrong? That asking was selfish? Without scaffolding, the message can easily warp.

Transparency need not be total to be effective. Children do not need to know the specifics of mortgage rates or pension plans. But they *do* benefit from understanding principles: how trade-offs work, why choices are made, what values are prioritised. Saying, "We're choosing not to spend on that right now because we're saving for something more important," teaches far more than "We can't afford it." The former invites children into a value conversation. The latter shuts the door.

Children also observe our emotional reactions to others' wealth. If we sneer at someone's expensive car, they learn that money is a source of judgement. If we speak with envy about wealthy relatives or disparage people who "waste" money, they internalise that money is status—but status to be resented. These meta-messages are powerful. They shape whether a child views wealth as aspiration, corruption, luck, or burden. Often, these narratives persist unchallenged into adulthood.

What makes the hidden curriculum so challenging to correct is precisely its invisibility. It is easier to change what we can name. But these lessons operate below the level of conscious awareness. They are inferred, not declared. They emerge from tone, frequency, omission. And they are shaped not just by what we teach, but by what we *repeat*. Children are pattern-recognition machines. If generosity is discussed once but frugality is practised daily, the implicit message is that generosity is ornamental, while frugality is essential. If we say we value saving but indulge in retail therapy as self-care, the child will likely privilege the action over the claim.

The hidden curriculum also interacts with culture in complex ways. In some households, money talk is seen as gauche. In others, it is a constant presence. Cultural scripts about class, gender, and worth often influence how parents model financial behaviour. A mother might feel pressure to appear financially secure, even when struggling. A father may avoid admitting financial mistakes to maintain authority. These pressures reinforce the silence or distortion, even when intentions are good.

To surface the hidden curriculum requires both awareness and humility. It asks parents to examine not only what they say, but how they act under pressure. It invites us to look at how we react to bills, windfalls, losses, gifts, tips, negotiations, and purchases. It challenges us to reflect on what our children might be learning—not from what we *intend*, but from what we *do*.

This is not a call for perfection. Children do not need financially flawless parents. But they do need *coherent* ones. They need modelling that aligns with values, explanations that match actions, and access to age-appropriate truths. They need to be allowed into the conversation—not all at once, but progressively, with care. And they need to see that money, like any human construct, is not static or sacred. It can be talked about, shaped, re-evaluated.

In truth, the most powerful financial education a child will ever receive is already happening. It is not scheduled. It is ambient. It is you. The way you speak, decide, withhold, explain, and react—these are the textbooks they are reading. They are learning whether you notice or not. The task, then, is not to begin the education. It is to take authorship of it.

To step out of the shadows of the hidden curriculum is to say: this matters enough to name. And in that naming, we begin to replace the unintended with the intentional. Not by rewriting the past, but by showing up differently—today, tomorrow, and in all the mundane, unremarkable moments where the real teaching happens.

## Impulse by Design

A child does not need to step foot in a shopping centre to be marketed to. They do not need to understand price tags or credit to engage in transactional behaviour. By the time a child reaches primary school, many have already been exposed to hundreds of in-app purchase prompts, unboxing videos masquerading as entertainment, and influencer content that blurs the line between friendship and persuasion. These aren't incidental exposures—they are engineered systems optimised to provoke one consistent response: impulsive consumption. The problem facing today's parents is not simply that their children are exposed to consumer culture, but that this culture has become *interactive, immersive,* and *neurologically targeted*. What was once passive advertising is now a participatory environment, built to bypass reflection and accelerate action.

Impulse is no longer a by-product of poor decision-making; it is the design objective of modern commerce.

To understand why this matters so profoundly for children, one must first grasp the neurodevelopmental landscape. The prefrontal cortex, the region of the brain responsible for executive functions such as planning, impulse control, and long-term thinking, is not fully mature until the mid-twenties. Meanwhile, the limbic system—the brain's reward centre—develops much earlier and operates with far greater intensity during childhood and adolescence. This creates a predictable mismatch: *an underdeveloped brake system paired with an overactive accelerator*. It is not simply that children are impulsive; they are *wired* for immediacy. This biological predisposition is not a flaw—it is part of the natural maturation process. But in a consumer environment that exploits this imbalance, it becomes a vulnerability.

Today's digital ecosystems do not merely allow impulsivity—they cultivate it. Game designers, app developers, and social platforms routinely employ persuasive technology principles to maximise user engagement. One of the most prevalent techniques is the use of "variable rewards"—a mechanism borrowed from behavioural psychology and casino design. In games and apps, this takes the form of loot boxes, mystery rewards, or algorithmically timed "bonuses" that drop unpredictably. The brain, when exposed to intermittent reinforcement, becomes hyper-attentive. The uncertainty is what makes it addictive. Children, with their nascent cognitive control systems, are particularly susceptible. They learn, without ever being explicitly taught, that waiting is irrational and that the next click might bring gratification.

Influencer culture intensifies this dynamic. Children are not just observing celebrities from a distance; they are forming parasocial relationships with YouTubers, streamers, and social media personalities who speak directly to them, often in the tone of friendship or mentorship. When an influencer promotes a product—whether it's a limited-edition hoodie, a game currency pack, or a DIY toy kit—it is received not as advertising but as *social proof*. The logic becomes simple: if someone I admire, trust, or aspire to be is using it, it must be good. And if I do not have it, I must be behind. The impulse to purchase becomes entangled with identity formation, status anxiety, and a desire for inclusion.

The consequences of this design are not abstract. A study published by the UK's Behavioural Insights Team found that children as young as six could recognise brand logos at high rates and that brand affinity strongly influenced their perceptions of peer popularity. Meanwhile, research by the Children's Commissioner for England highlights how in-app purchasing systems—especially in free-to-play games—exploit the social dynamics of peer comparison, making it difficult for children to participate without spending. In one striking case, children described being mocked or excluded for using "default" avatars, a term that has become shorthand for those who do not spend money in digital spaces. Here, we see the direct connection between monetised impulse and social belonging.

And it's not limited to games or influencers. E-commerce platforms have adapted to this psychology as well. "Buy now, pay later" schemes, one-click purchasing, and limited-time countdowns are designed to compress the space between desire and decision. For adults, these tools can strain budgets and delay consequences. For children, they obliterate the already fragile mechanisms of pause and reflect. The architecture of these environments assumes financial literacy, while actively undermining the cognitive conditions necessary for it to develop.

Parents often find themselves bewildered by the velocity and intensity of these dynamics. A child who begged for a new skin in a game yesterday may now be obsessed with a toy brand discovered through a viral TikTok. Attempts to say no may be met with disproportionate emotional responses—not because the child is spoiled, but because the systems they are engaging with are designed to provoke urgency, FOMO (fear of missing out), and emotional saturation. This creates a fraught domestic atmosphere where parents must not only enforce boundaries but also counteract the persuasive infrastructure of billion-pound industries.

It is important not to romanticise the past, but the contrast is instructive. In previous generations, advertising was largely linear, broadcast-based, and unidirectional. Children encountered ads during Saturday cartoons or on billboards—static, recognisable, and easy to filter. Today, commercial content is algorithmically tailored, disguised as entertainment, and integrated into platforms where children socialise, play, and learn. The commercial message is no longer an interruption—it *is* the experience. And because many digital environments operate in private, personalised ways, parents often lack visibility into what their children are seeing or how it's being interpreted.

One of the most insidious aspects of this system is its reward loop. Children are praised—both digitally and socially—for consumption. Sharing hauls, reviewing products, and showing off virtual purchases all garner likes, views, and status. Meanwhile, there is little cultural reinforcement for restraint, delayed gratification, or mindful spending. The child who resists a purchase is not celebrated; they are often unnoticed. And so the feedback mechanisms that might cultivate self-control are structurally absent. Parents can attempt to compensate, but the broader environment is tilted steeply against them.

There is a philosophical tension at play here: should children be protected from these environments, or prepared for them? Total avoidance is unrealistic. The digital economy is not optional. Nor is it intrinsically negative. Games can teach strategy, collaboration, and perseverance. Online creators can inspire creativity, confidence, and community. The issue is not participation, but *unmediated participation*. Children need to engage with consumer environments *with a lens,* not in a fog. And that lens must come from adults who understand both the mechanics of impulse design and the developmental needs of young minds.

The first step is awareness. Parents must recognise that saying "no" to a purchase is not just a boundary-setting exercise—it is a corrective to a well-funded psychological system. Explaining *why* the answer is no, or *how* decisions are made, shifts the interaction from control to coaching. For example, discussing the real cost of a game purchase—not just the pound amount, but what else that money could do—helps restore context. Similarly, modelling one's own moments of restraint ("I really wanted that, but I realised I didn't need it") provides a narrative alternative to automatic consumption.

Children benefit from *seeing* the decision-making process, especially when it involves trade-offs. This helps them internalise that purchases are choices, not reactions. When a child is invited to pause, reflect, and evaluate their desire—rather than being told it is wrong—they begin to cultivate the capacity for self-regulation. Tools like waiting periods, personal budgets, or even "wish lists" (where items are recorded but not immediately bought) can slow the impulse cycle without demonising the desire itself.

Crucially, this approach requires consistency. A parent who lectures about digital purchases but indulges in late-night online shopping without comment sends a conflicting message. Children are not just listening to what we say—they are watching how we spend. If we are quick to tap, splurge, or cave to our own impulses, our financial lectures ring hollow. But when our actions demonstrate intentionality, restraint, and critical thinking, children begin to see those behaviours as viable—not just virtuous.

Education systems, too, must catch up. Current financial literacy curricula, where they exist, often lag behind the realities of children's lived experiences. Teaching children how to write a cheque is increasingly irrelevant if they are already navigating microtransactions and influencer marketing. A modern approach to financial education must include *digital spending literacy*—understanding not just budgets and savings, but persuasive design, algorithmic targeting, and the emotional strategies used in commercial content. Without this, we are leaving children underprepared for the economy they actually inhabit.

This is not cause for despair. It is a call for precision. Children are not helpless consumers. They are perceptive, adaptive, and capable of critical thinking—when given the tools. The task is not to eliminate desire but to situate it within a framework of choice, consequence, and self-awareness. When children understand *how* their impulses are being shaped, they can begin to reclaim agency. And when parents understand the systems at play, they can move from reactive discipline to proactive mentoring.

Impulse control is not something children either have or lack. It is a developmental process, one that can be nurtured or undermined depending on the environment. The consumer landscape children now inhabit is not neutral—it is designed to displace that process, to keep them in a state of reactive wanting. But with thoughtful intervention, clear modelling, and sustained dialogue, it is possible to reverse that tide.

We cannot slow down the commercial machine, but we can teach children how to walk through it with discernment. The first step is recognising that impulsivity is not a personal failing. It is, increasingly, a system response. And that insight alone reframes everything—from how we parent, to how we equip the next generation for a world where impulse is not a mistake, but a market strategy.

## When Earning Feels Abstract

A ten-year-old clicks a few buttons on a screen, receives virtual currency, and within moments is upgrading their avatar's wardrobe. No waiting. No effort. No visible cost. The digital transaction is clean, efficient, and emotionally frictionless. The parent might see a small charge on their card—£4.99 here, £2.49 there—but to the child, money has simply moved from nowhere to somewhere. No one built it, folded it, deposited it. It just *arrived*. This detachment is not limited to digital spaces. In many homes, the processes by which money is earned, managed, or even emotionally valued have become increasingly opaque. Children are growing up in a reality where outcomes are visible—purchases, privileges, possessions—but the inputs are concealed, compressed, or abstracted. And when earning feels abstract, so too does the value of what is earned.

To understand this growing disconnection, it is necessary to examine both structural and cultural shifts in how labour and reward are represented in children's lives. In previous generations, money was more tangible, time was visibly traded for goods, and children were often witnesses to the mechanics of effort: fathers coming home dusty from trades, mothers budgeting at the kitchen table, older siblings saving pocket money to buy their first bicycle. Even in middle- and upper-income households, the rhythms of earning and spending were more readily observable. Money was often counted physically. Labour had a visible arc. Sacrifice, when present, was easier to comprehend.

Today, many of those signals have vanished. As economies have become more knowledge- and service-based, much of the labour adults do is invisible to children. A parent working from home may appear to be merely staring at a laptop, occasionally speaking on the phone, then later buying groceries or paying bills with a quick card tap. There is little context for what that work involves, or why it warrants payment. Worse still, many children receive without asking how. Their devices update automatically, meals appear with a tap, parcels arrive the next day. The exchange of effort for outcome—the foundational premise of earning—becomes blurred, then irrelevant.

This abstraction has consequences. Without exposure to the logic of effort and trade-off, children may begin to regard money as an ambient resource, one that exists in fixed supply and flows according to mysterious, possibly arbitrary rules. In such a framework, entitlement is not a moral failure but a developmental inevitability. If one is constantly on the receiving end of outcomes, without insight into their production, it becomes reasonable to expect that provision is the norm and limitation is unfair. The child learns that asking should yield. That disappointment means denial. That being told "no" requires justification, preferably accompanied by an alternative.

This entitlement is rarely malicious. It is more often a sign of conceptual absence. The child lacks the schema to situate money within a narrative of work, cost, time, or complexity. The result is not only unrealistic expectations but fragile gratitude. If one cannot see how much something *cost* in terms of time or energy, one cannot fully appreciate what it *means*. Gratitude, then, becomes a performance of manners rather than a felt sense of valuation.

Parents often find themselves caught in the middle of this gap. They want to protect children from the stresses of adult financial life, yet also desire appreciation and responsibility. But the two goals are difficult to reconcile in the absence of transparency. Shielding children from the realities of earning might spare them momentary anxiety, but it also deprives them of crucial cognitive and emotional anchoring. And when the time eventually comes for them to earn their own money—through chores, jobs, or entrepreneurial efforts—the concept feels foreign, and often unfair. Why should I work for this, when so many other things have arrived freely?

This tension becomes especially pronounced when children transition from passive recipients to active earners. For many, their first encounter with structured earning—whether through an allowance, odd jobs, or entrepreneurial activity—brings a jolt of reality. The realisation that effort does not always yield immediate or proportionate reward can be disillusioning. If that process has not been scaffolded through years of observation and conversation, it can feel punitive rather than empowering. This is the paradox: children raised without exposure to earning often struggle more—not less—with the concept of effort.

Some parents attempt to address this by linking money to household chores, a practice with both proponents and critics. On the one hand, tying effort to reward reinforces the transactional logic that underpins adult economic life. On the other, it risks externalising contribution: a child may come to see any unremunerated effort as a loss, rather than a shared responsibility. The key distinction lies in how the relationship is framed. When money is positioned not as a bribe or threat, but as a tool for learning about choice, delay, and contribution, the dynamic shifts. A child who helps wash the car and is later walked through the cost of the supplies, the time invested, and the price someone else might have paid for the same service, begins to build a mental model. That model need not be perfect. But it must exist.

Even outside of paid chores, children can—and should—be invited into the economic life of the household. This does not mean disclosing every financial stress or burden. It means narrating the logic of decisions. "We chose to make dinner at home because we're saving for a trip." "Mum worked late today because she's on deadline, and that project helps cover the car insurance." "We're waiting until next month to buy that because it's not urgent, and we're being careful with our spending." These statements are not lectures. They are breadcrumb trails, each one linking outcome to effort, timing to priority, money to values.

Children who hear these things regularly begin to see money not as a fixed supply to be distributed by adults, but as a dynamic system that interacts with time, trade-offs, and personal agency. They begin to realise that money is earned in ways that are not always visible, but are nonetheless real. This changes how they approach both receiving and spending. They hesitate more. They ask better questions. They start to internalise the concept of "worth" not just as price, but as value relative to effort.

Of course, this understanding must be developmentally staged. A six-year-old cannot grasp tax brackets or overhead costs. But they *can* understand that time is limited, that some tasks are harder than others, and that choices come with consequences. When a parent says, "I worked an extra hour so we could buy this for your birthday," it gives the gift a deeper meaning. When a child spends money they earned themselves—no matter how small the sum—they often treat it with greater deliberation. These are not coincidences. They are cognitive milestones.

The rise of digital payments has further abstracted the experience of earning. When parents transfer allowance via banking apps or let children pay with contactless cards, the loss of physicality matters. Research in behavioural economics consistently shows that people spend more freely with cards than with cash. The tangibility of money affects psychological restraint. For children, the absence of physical currency can reduce opportunities to learn about denominations, accumulation, and delay. A jar of coins filling slowly is not merely a container—it is a visual, tactile representation of progress. That progress means something. It is felt.

This is not to suggest that digital tools are inherently harmful. In fact, age-appropriate apps that visualise savings goals, categorise spending, or track earning can reinforce positive habits—*if* they are accompanied by parental involvement and contextual conversation. The problem arises when digital abstraction is layered upon developmental abstraction: the child does not understand where the money came from, *and* now cannot see where it's going. This compounds detachment and weakens feedback loops.

In some households, children are introduced to financial literacy through school programmes. While these can be valuable, they often focus on budgeting, saving, or consumer choices—topics downstream from the experience of earning. Without first understanding what it means to *generate* money, children may struggle to relate to the frameworks being taught. It's akin to teaching someone how to spend calories before explaining how the body produces energy. Earning is the first principle. And when children are detached from it, everything else becomes less meaningful.

There is also a moral dimension to this. When children are disconnected from the effort behind money, they may become less empathetic toward those who struggle financially. If earning is unseen, and provision is assumed, then lack of money is interpreted as irresponsibility, not circumstance. This can lead to a narrow and often judgmental worldview, one that is at odds with economic reality. Understanding the variability of work—its dignity, its complexity, its unpredictability—fosters humility. It tempers entitlement with perspective.

Ultimately, reconnecting children to the process of earning is not about instilling hardship. It is about cultivating respect—for time, for contribution, for the mechanics of provision. It is about giving children the tools to interpret the world not just through what is given, but through what is *built*. And that understanding, once formed, becomes the cornerstone of responsible financial behaviour—not out of fear or scarcity, but out of recognition.

When earning feels abstract, children are deprived of one of the most essential cognitive links in their development: the link between action and outcome, between choice and consequence. Rebuilding that link does not require a radical shift in parenting strategy. It requires attention, narration, and invitation. It requires letting children see more, do more, ask more. Not all the time. Not in every decision. But enough to shape their mental model of money into something grounded, graspable, and real.

## The Cultural Taboo of Talking About Money

Ask a child where babies come from, and you'll likely receive a carefully crafted answer delivered with varying degrees of anatomical honesty. Ask that same child how much their parents earn, and you're far more likely to encounter silence—either from the child, who was never told, or from the parent, who has taught, directly or indirectly, that such topics are inappropriate. Money remains one of the final frontiers of family silence, a subject that in many households carries more emotional weight than sex, politics, or religion. It is discussed in hushed tones, behind closed doors, or not at all. This silence is rarely malicious. It is often motivated by protection, propriety, or the simple inheritance of norms. But its consequences are profound, and its logic deserves closer scrutiny.

The taboo around money is culturally pervasive but unevenly applied. In some families, it is the subject never to be broached at the dinner table, even while children are exposed to a relentless stream of financial cues—luxury cars, private schools, holiday destinations. In others, money is the source of open conflict, but never of reflective explanation. There are also households in which money is flaunted but not contextualised, where the message is that wealth speaks for itself and needs no narration. In all these configurations, children are left to fill in the blanks. And children are rarely idle narrators. They piece together meaning from tone, from omission, from the reactions of adults when questions are asked. They learn quickly that money is powerful—but dangerously unspeakable.

The origins of this silence are layered. In Western societies, financial privacy is often seen as synonymous with dignity or discretion. Asking someone what they earn, owe, or have saved is treated as socially intrusive, bordering on offensive. Some of this is tied to status sensitivity: money reveals disparities we prefer not to name. Talking about it openly risks embarrassment, envy, or judgement. In family contexts, these risks are amplified by emotional complexity. A parent may fear that revealing too much will cause worry, rebellion, or entitlement. Others may not fully understand their own financial picture and would rather avoid exposing that gap. There are also gendered legacies at play—mothers historically excluded from financial decision-making may still carry uncertainty or discomfort discussing money with authority, while fathers may feel pressure to project control even when anxious or unsure.

But silence is not neutral. It is a form of instruction. When a child asks, "How much did that cost?" and is met with "That's not something you need to know," they don't simply drop the question. They internalise a rule: *money is private*. When a teenager inquires, "Are we rich?" and the parent bristles or deflects, the unspoken lesson is that *money talk creates discomfort*. These responses do not protect children from stress. They initiate them into secrecy. And like all inherited silences, this one replicates itself across generations, growing heavier each time it is left unexamined.

The consequences of this taboo show up in children's financial literacy, but more importantly, in their *emotional relationship* to money. When children are excluded from financial conversations, they are more likely to view money through the lens of mystery or magic. They may grow up with exaggerated perceptions of their family's wealth—or poverty—based on incomplete or distorted cues. They may develop anxiety about money without knowing its source. They may, in adulthood, avoid financial planning, delay difficult conversations with partners, or conflate material worth with personal value. And crucially, they may carry into parenting the same silence they once received, believing that financial discretion means shielding rather than guiding.

It is worth noting that the silence is not always about numbers. Many parents avoid money talk not because they are unwilling to share amounts, but because they lack a language for values. They struggle to articulate why they spend where they do, or how they make trade-offs between needs and wants, generosity and self-care. Without this vocabulary, even well-intentioned transparency can fall flat. Telling a child what something costs is not the same as teaching them what it *means* to spend thoughtfully. And for that, parents must first feel comfortable examining their own financial scripts—scripts they may not have written, but which they have certainly rehearsed.

These inherited scripts often take the form of binary beliefs: *Money is either security or risk. Talking about it is either vulgar or empowering. Saving is either virtue or deprivation.* But financial maturity lies in nuance. Children who are invited into nuanced conversations about money—conversations that acknowledge both its utility and its emotional charge—develop more adaptive frameworks. They begin to see that money is not just a resource, but a reflection of priorities. That budgets are not prisons, but expressions of values. That generosity is not just about giving, but about recognising sufficiency. These are not lessons that land in a single conversation. They require repeated exposure, gentle honesty, and a willingness to tolerate discomfort.

Some parents fear that opening up about money will burden their children. They worry about inducing guilt, fear, or performance anxiety. These fears are not unfounded. A child told too much, too soon—or in a tone of panic rather than planning—may indeed feel overwhelmed. But withholding everything is not the answer. The goal is not radical transparency, but calibrated inclusion. Children do not need to know how much is in the family's savings account, but they *can* be told, "We're saving up for something big, and that's why we're making different choices this month." A teenager does not need to manage the mortgage, but they *can* be involved in planning a holiday within a budget. These moments offer not just information, but participation—and participation fosters competence.

There is also a social cost to money silence. When families treat money as unmentionable, children are less likely to ask questions, seek help, or disclose mistakes. They enter adulthood with a fractured understanding of financial norms and a limited ability to compare notes with peers. This makes them vulnerable to predatory lending, debt cycles, or consumer manipulation. It also impairs their capacity for financial collaboration in relationships, where shared money management requires shared language. The irony is stark: in trying to protect children from the discomfort of money talk, we often send them into adulthood unarmed for the financial realities they must face.

Breaking the taboo is not merely about raising financially literate children. It is about raising *financially relational* children—young people who can talk about money without shame, ask for clarity without fear, and approach financial decisions as acts of alignment, not secrecy. This requires a redefinition of what it means to be "appropriate" in financial conversations. Respecting a child's developmental stage does not mean avoiding the topic altogether. It means choosing the *right entry points*. "We're choosing not to buy that now." "That's expensive for our family, so we save for it." "Some families spend differently because they have different incomes or priorities." These statements are accessible, honest, and grounded. They build literacy without undermining trust.

Educators have long noted that when students are exposed to taboo subjects in safe, structured ways, they become more thoughtful and less reactive. The same applies to money. Parents who demystify finance do not encourage greed or materialism. They encourage awareness. They signal that money is not off-limits. That curiosity is welcome. That questions are not dangerous.

None of this requires financial perfection. It requires presence. Children are not asking for expertise. They are asking to understand the world they inhabit, and money is a part of that world—whether we like it or not. When adults avoid the subject, children don't feel protected; they feel excluded. And exclusion, particularly when it occurs in a domain as consequential as money, is educational in its own right. It teaches that some truths are too difficult to discuss. That some knowledge must be earned through trial, error, and silence.

There is no script for these conversations. But there are principles: honesty over evasion, context over confusion, and inclusion over insulation. When families treat money as part of life rather than a separate sphere, they raise children who are not only better equipped to handle it, but who relate to it with confidence, clarity, and conscience.

The silence around money is not just a lack of speech. It is a missed opportunity—for connection, for learning, and for building a shared language around one of life's most consequential realities. Breaking that silence does not mean flooding the home with financial data. It means creating the space where a child's first question about money is met not with dismissal, but with dialogue. That shift, quiet though it may be, is where true financial education begins.

# Chapter 2
# The Parent's Mirror

Most parents want to raise children who are thoughtful, resilient, and anchored in values that endure. When the topic turns to money, that hope sharpens into something more specific: to raise children who treat money neither carelessly nor worshipfully, who know the difference between enough and excess, between generosity and indulgence. Yet, despite good intentions, many parents find themselves replaying the very patterns they once swore to abandon—or quietly modelling beliefs they would never endorse aloud. The lapse is rarely deliberate. It is the inevitable echo of what was learned long ago, the inheritance of unexamined habits passed through generations like family heirlooms no one thought to question.

Before a parent can teach wisely about money, they must first turn the lens inward. Parenting is not merely a forward-facing act of guidance; it is also a backward glance, a transmission of everything unresolved and unspoken. And few things pass more easily—or more invisibly—than our own unhealed money stories.

Financial behaviour does not spring from nowhere. It's a tapestry woven from early experiences, emotional residue, and the scripts we absorbed without consent. A child raised in scarcity might grow into an adult who saves obsessively, haunted by the fear of loss even in times of plenty. Another, raised in abundance, may equate spending with affection, proof of worth or generosity. Others oscillate endlessly between restraint and indulgence, seeking balance but never quite finding it. These patterns are not usually dissected in real time—they simply *feel* right, or at least familiar. But to a child watching from the wings, they are instruction. Children do not invent financial beliefs; they inherit them through tone, context, and repetition. If parents fail to interrogate where their instincts come from, those same instincts will be quietly transmitted—complete with contradictions.

This chapter begins at the obvious but often neglected truth: you cannot teach what you have not first understood. To raise a child with a healthy relationship to money, a parent must confront their own. That confrontation is not indulgence; it's groundwork. It asks difficult questions: What did money *mean* in your childhood home—comfort, control, shame, affection? Which behaviours were celebrated, and which were met with silence or scorn? Were you granted transparency about financial decisions, or kept on the outside? How did your parents or caregivers speak about wealth, success, debt, or those with less? These aren't abstract reflections—they're diagnostic tools. Without them, history repeats itself not out of malice, but inertia.

Still, understanding one's own story is only half the task. The greater challenge is alignment: bringing what we *believe* into harmony with what we *do*. Parents often declare the values they want their children to embody—responsibility, generosity, independence—but their habits tell a different tale. A mother who praises thrift but indulges in impulsive buys sends one signal; a father who preaches restraint but splurges under stress sends another. Children notice. Always. They are decoding constantly: how we tip, how we speak about the wealthy or the poor, whether we treat money as private or performative. These micro-lessons form their financial consciousness long before we sit them down for "the talk."

The gap between professed values and lived rules is often where confusion begins. Families declare principles—"We live within our means," "We prioritise experiences over possessions," "We believe in giving back"—yet the daily practice may undermine them. A family that claims to value modesty but floods birthdays with luxury gifts, or one that praises hard work but shields children from any form of contribution, teaches inconsistency more effectively than honesty. Children rarely interpret that as hypocrisy; they read it as chaos. And chaos breeds compliance, not conviction.

Beneath these contradictions runs an emotional current—scarcity. Many parents still carry the residue of scarcity scripts learned in households where money was limited or unpredictable. "We can't afford it." "Don't ask for too much." "Be grateful for what you've got." These phrases, though practical in context, embed emotional codes. They teach that wanting is dangerous, that plenty is temporary, that financial safety is always conditional. Adults raised in such climates often feel guilt when spending, or hoard "just in case," or live in perpetual low-grade anxiety regardless of actual stability.

At the opposite extreme lies guilt spending—a more modern phenomenon. Here, parents use money as apology. The parent who works too long, who feels the ache of absence, compensates with excess: toys, trips, treats. Another, heavy with guilt after a divorce or move, tries to buy back emotional equilibrium. Such gestures come from tenderness, but they reshape meaning. Money becomes balm, rather than boundary; comfort, rather than clarity. The child learns not to link money with value-based choices, but with emotional repair.

These patterns are rarely visible to those living them. Parents don't aim to confuse their children. But intentions are only the preface; outcomes are written in action. Children crave consistency—the sense that the world, and the adults who run it, make sense. When that coherence falters, they adapt. They learn to read the family's emotional weather, to mimic or manipulate accordingly. Those adaptive scripts, forged in childhood, become the architecture of their adult financial lives.

Which is why modelling remains the most profound—and underestimated—teaching tool a parent possesses. Not the performative kind, but the quiet, daily modelling of thoughtfulness and transparency. The parent who pauses before spending and explains the pause; who admits an error; who shows that trade-offs exist and must be weighed—this parent teaches something invaluable. The lesson isn't perfection. It's deliberation. Money becomes not a mysterious force but a mirror for values, for limits, for priorities.

Modelling also extends beyond the household balance sheet. When children hear how parents speak about others—those richer, poorer, luckier, or struggling—they absorb moral cues as well as financial ones. A careless remark about "people who waste money" or "those who don't work hard enough" quietly instructs. Over time, such remarks sculpt a child's moral relationship with fairness, generosity, and humility. It's not enough to avoid prejudice; one must practise curiosity and empathy when speaking about financial difference. That, truly, is the beginning of economic ethics.

This chapter is not an indictment, but an invitation. Every parent inherits a mix of money beliefs—some useful, others outdated, defensive, even harmful. The task is not to erase them, but to examine them. To choose consciously which to keep and which to release. Through that reflection, parents shift from unconscious transmitters to intentional guides—less interested in perfection than in clarity.

The mirror, admittedly, can be unkind. But it is essential. Because children do not learn about money from lectures or rules. They learn from the texture of our lives—the choices, contradictions, and confessions they witness daily. Before we can offer them a healthier framework, we must first recognise the one we are already handing down, often without a word.

## Understanding Your Own Money Story

Most people believe they are teaching their children about money through what they provide: allowances, savings jars, spending limits, perhaps the occasional lesson on budgeting. But in truth, the most formative financial education a child receives has less to do with what is taught, and everything to do with what is *lived*. Every reaction to a bill, every sigh at the supermarket, every argument behind closed doors, and every silence at the dinner table becomes part of the child's developing money consciousness. The behaviours and emotions parents express around money don't appear in a vacuum—they are echoes of older patterns, often going back generations. Before any parent can teach wisely, they must first ask: *What story am I already telling?*

Every adult carries a money story, though few have paused to articulate it. It is not a single narrative, but a composite—built from childhood observations, adolescent experiences, cultural assumptions, and adult adaptations. This story shapes how we spend, save, give, and talk about money. It determines whether we feel safe or insecure, generous or guarded, worthy or anxious. And crucially, it informs how we respond when our children interact with money—whether they ask for it, waste it, question it, or show no interest at all.

To understand your money story, begin not with your current habits, but with your earliest memories. Was money a source of stress in your home, or was it rarely discussed? Were your caregivers generous to others, or quietly anxious about every purchase? Were you encouraged to earn, or simply expected to be grateful? Did you feel guilty for asking, or empowered to contribute? These memories may seem trivial, but they are foundational. Research in developmental psychology confirms that children begin forming financial scripts by age seven, based largely on the behaviours they witness rather than the lessons they are taught. These scripts persist well into adulthood, often guiding decision-making without conscious thought.

For example, a child raised in a home where money was scarce but never explained may internalise a deep sense of financial anxiety. As an adult, they may hoard resources, avoid financial risk, or equate spending with danger—even if they have achieved material stability. Conversely, someone raised in an affluent home where everything was provided but nothing was discussed may grow up feeling entitled or ill-equipped to manage financial trade-offs. These individuals might struggle with budgeting, delay financial planning, or conflate money with identity or self-worth. The behavioural expressions differ, but the common thread is the absence of reflection. In both cases, *the emotional inheritance* was passed down, unnamed and unchallenged.

Money stories are not inherently rational. They are emotional narratives, often governed more by fear, pride, shame, or longing than by spreadsheets or interest rates. They emerge in statements like, "We don't talk about money," or "I work hard, so I deserve this," or "I never want my kids to feel the way I did." Each of these statements signals a deeper belief system—one that may or may not serve the child who is now learning through observation. For instance, a parent who overcompensates for their own frugal childhood may find themselves indulging their children without limits. Another, determined to instil work ethic, may withhold too much, confusing discipline with detachment. These reactions are understandable. But when left unexamined, they can perpetuate the very confusion they seek to avoid.

To disrupt these patterns, it is not enough to identify what went wrong in one's upbringing. The more useful question is: *What did money mean in my family?* Was it linked to freedom, power, sacrifice, secrecy, conflict, or silence? Who had control over it, and how was that power expressed? Was success measured by income, possessions, education, or status? Or was it measured in stability, contribution, or restraint? These meanings may have been implied rather than declared, but their influence is no less potent.

Once these inherited meanings are made visible, parents can begin to revise them with intention. This does not mean rejecting everything that came before. Some financial habits and attitudes passed down from earlier generations are deeply valuable—discipline, delayed gratification, a healthy respect for earning. But others may be outdated or reactive: chronic scarcity thinking, avoidance of financial planning, or equating self-worth with net worth. Revising one's money story is not about perfection. It is about coherence. It is about ensuring that what you model aligns with what you believe, and that what you teach is not contradicted by what you unconsciously transmit.

The process of reflection also requires attention to cultural and societal scripts. Class, race, religion, and national identity all shape how money is perceived and managed. In some cultures, talking about money is taboo; in others, it is a marker of openness or savvy. In certain families, success is measured primarily in financial terms; in others, there is a suspicion of wealth, a valorisation of sacrifice. These cultural dynamics influence what parents feel is acceptable, admirable, or shameful around money—and, by extension, what children absorb. Recognising these layers can help parents differentiate between what is culturally inherited and what is personally endorsed.

Gender also plays a powerful, often unspoken role in the formation of money stories. Many women, particularly those raised before financial independence was widely encouraged, carry a sense of uncertainty or deferral when it comes to money management. Men, conversely, may feel pressure to perform financial competence, even when they lack experience or confidence. These gendered expectations can subtly influence how parents model financial roles in the home—who makes the decisions, who manages the accounts, who bears the burden of earning. Children, highly attuned to power dynamics, notice these distinctions even when no one is speaking about them.

Parenting from a place of financial awareness means making the implicit explicit. It means saying, "I grew up thinking money was something to fear, and I'm trying not to pass that on," or, "I tend to overspend because I was raised to associate love with gifts—let's talk about that." These admissions do not weaken authority. They strengthen it. They model self-reflection, humility, and growth. They show children that beliefs can be examined, habits can be changed, and meaning can be constructed—rather than inherited uncritically.

Understanding your money story also means recognising when past experiences are bleeding into present decisions. Are you saying no to your child because it's a healthy boundary, or because it triggers an old fear of indulgence? Are you giving freely because you value generosity, or because guilt is clouding your judgement? These are not simple questions, but they are essential ones. Because until you understand *why* you are reacting the way you are, your reactions will continue to operate from a place of reflex rather than reason.

There is also value in tracking your emotional state during money interactions. When does stress spike? When does avoidance set in? When do you feel empowered versus ashamed? These cues are diagnostic. They reveal the emotional architecture behind financial behaviour—architecture that children are studying closely, even if you believe you're hiding it. Parents often underestimate how perceptive children are when it comes to money. They may not know the specifics of an income or mortgage, but they can sense tension, inconsistency, and reactivity. And from that sensing, they begin to construct meaning.

Revising a money story is not a one-time act. It is an ongoing practice of awareness, inquiry, and reorientation. It involves learning from new inputs—books, conversations, partners, financial professionals—and integrating those insights into lived behaviour. It also involves forgiveness. Many parents feel shame or frustration when they begin to see how their own upbringing shaped them in limiting ways. But this work is not about blame. It is about agency. You may not have chosen your financial inheritance, but you *do* have a choice in how you reinterpret and redirect it.

Ultimately, the question is not whether you have a money story. You do. The question is whether you are aware of it, whether you have made it conscious, and whether it aligns with the values you hope to pass on. Children do not need financial experts for parents. They need models of clarity, intention, and humanity. They need to see that money is not just something we use—but something we think about, talk about, and take responsibility for. And that kind of modelling begins not with the child, but with the adult willing to look in the mirror.

## Values vs. Rules

A parent tells their child to save money. Not just occasionally, but consistently—after birthdays, after allowances, after holiday gifts. "Saving is important," they say. "You should always have something set aside." The rule is clear, repeated, perhaps even enforced. And yet, in that same household, the parent makes impulsive purchases, avoids discussing bills, rarely models delayed gratification, and doesn't articulate what saving is *for*. Over time, the child receives two messages: one spoken, the other demonstrated. And when the two contradict, the child—consciously or not—defaults to the louder lesson: behaviour. In families, values are aspirational. Rules are operational. The gap between them is where financial confusion, resistance, and mimicry quietly take root.

Every parent has a set of values they hope to instil in their children. These often include timeless virtues: responsibility, generosity, independence, discipline, gratitude. When it comes to money, most parents want their children to become competent stewards—not merely to understand budgets or interest rates, but to make thoughtful, value-aligned decisions. However, what parents *enforce* day-to-day often diverges from these broader aspirations. The child is told to save, but they see unexamined spending. The child is warned against greed, but also praised for designer clothes. The child hears, "Money doesn't buy happiness," yet watches adults tie worth to earnings or possessions. The contradiction is rarely deliberate. But for the child, it is formative.

This is not simply a matter of "practise what you preach." Children do not respond to abstract values alone—they learn through patterns. A rule repeated without clarity, without demonstration, and without emotional consistency becomes performative. "We value generosity" means little if family life centres around individual acquisition. "Money is not that important" rings hollow if status symbols are chased, celebrated, or envied. Children are sophisticated observers. They detect hypocrisy instinctively, even if they lack the vocabulary to name it. And when they detect it, they often withdraw—disengaging from financial teaching not out of defiance, but out of perceived incoherence.

Some of this conflict stems from the inherited scripts adults carry. A parent may say they want their child to be "financially secure," but what they actually model is avoidance, anxiety, or shame. Another may declare that "money should be used wisely," while treating purchases as emotional pacifiers. The value being professed is responsibility; the rule being enforced is emotional spending. In such environments, children don't just learn what to do with money—they learn what money *means*: control, escape, reward, proof. These meanings are never neutral. They are shaped not by single moments, but by repeated cues, especially during stress, conflict, or celebration.

It's tempting to rely on rules to impose discipline: no spending without permission, no toys unless earned, half of all money must be saved. But when rules are not grounded in clear, lived values, they quickly become transactional. Children comply to appease, not to internalise. They learn to perform the rule rather than understand its purpose. They may even learn to game the system—behaving well financially when watched, and reverting when not. This is not because children lack character, but because the system they are navigating lacks integration. Values, when consistently modelled and connected to rules, cultivate understanding. Rules without values produce compliance at best, confusion at worst.

A critical test for parents is to ask themselves: *What kind of financial adult am I trying to raise?* Do I want my child to be wealthy? Secure? Ethical? Autonomous? Minimalist? Philanthropic? And then: *Are the daily rules and responses I enforce aligned with that vision?* If a parent says they value autonomy but micro-manages every financial decision, the value is undermined. If they value generosity but shame their child for giving too freely, the lesson becomes self-protective. If they prize simplicity but reward material success with excessive praise, the child learns that materialism carries social capital. None of this happens in a vacuum. Children are forming identities—not just learning mechanics.

The modern consumer context compounds these tensions. Parents are bombarded with cultural contradictions: "Raise financially savvy kids" but "Let them be kids." "Teach them to save" but "Don't let them miss out." "Instil discipline" but "Don't shame desire." These tensions are not easy to reconcile. But they require clarity. If a parent tells their child to resist peer pressure while simultaneously capitulating to every consumer trend "to avoid embarrassment," the child will feel the cognitive dissonance—and eventually replicate it.

Values need not be perfect. But they *do* need to be visible. A parent who occasionally contradicts themselves but names the contradiction teaches something invaluable: that money is complex, that integrity matters more than image, and that thinking critically about decisions is more important than rigid adherence to dogma. Saying, "I know I just spent impulsively—that's something I'm working on," is more effective than pretending every action aligns with stated values. Children respect transparency, not perfection.

This is particularly important in moments of tension or conflict. If a child asks for something expensive and is denied with a flat "We don't waste money on things like that," they may interpret the rule as punitive. But if the refusal is framed within a shared value—"We're choosing to spend on things that bring lasting joy, and this doesn't quite fit that for us"—then the child learns not just what is being enforced, but *why*. Over time, they begin to internalise that financial decisions are not about arbitrary limits, but about consistent, reasoned alignment with principles.

This requires regular calibration. Values must be revisited, re-articulated, and reinforced—not in lectures, but in real-life moments. Family money discussions, if they exist, should include reflection: *Does this decision reflect who we say we are? What are we prioritising here—ease, joy, impact, appearances?* These are not abstract questions. They are vital frameworks for decision-making, both for children and for adults. And when children are included in these reflections—even in age-appropriate ways—they develop the capacity to evaluate choices through lenses beyond immediate gratification.

The deeper challenge, then, is not whether families have values. Most do. It is whether those values are truly operational—whether they guide decision-making, inform rules, and shape narratives. If not, they remain ornamental: inspiring to state, ineffective to teach. And ineffective values breed incoherence. A child raised with mixed signals about money may grow up deeply uncertain: Should I give or protect? Save or enjoy? Be modest or aspirational? Without consistent values, rules become battlegrounds—not because the child is disobedient, but because the context is unclear.

Parents who reflect honestly on these dynamics often discover that some of their own values were inherited unconsciously. Perhaps generosity was prized, but so was judgement. Perhaps security was preached, but so was fear. In revisiting these contradictions, parents can begin to curate a more integrated framework—not just for their children, but for themselves. Teaching a child that money is a tool for expressing values begins with knowing what those values actually are, and then living them out—consistently, even imperfectly.

Ultimately, the gap between values and rules is not a parenting failure. It is a visibility issue. Children can't internalise what they can't see. Closing that gap begins with noticing when actions drift from intentions, and with having the humility to narrate that drift. It is in the narration—in the daily modelling, in the transparent decision-making, in the unglamorous but consistent reinforcement—that children learn not just how to use money, but how to *think* about it. And that thinking, shaped by clarity rather than confusion, is what endures.

## Scarcity Scripts and Guilt Spending

A parent tells their child, "We can't afford that," with a tightness in their voice that signals more than budgeting—it signals fear. Later that same week, after a stressful day at work, the parent surprises the child with a new toy, meal out, or trip to the cinema. There's no explanation, no framework—just a surge of generosity that seems to erase the earlier restriction. To the parent, this may feel like balance, or perhaps emotional restitution. To the child, it is bewildering. What is money? Is it something limited or endless? Is it a reason to say no, or a tool to soothe discomfort? Without a consistent logic behind financial decisions, children internalise a fragmented view of money—one shaped not by clarity, but by reaction. And often, the root of these oscillations lies in two powerful, frequently unexamined forces: *scarcity scripts* and *guilt spending*.

Scarcity scripts are internalised belief systems developed in environments where money felt insufficient, unstable, or emotionally charged. These scripts are not always based on actual poverty; they emerge just as readily in middle-class households where financial conversations were laced with anxiety, secrecy, or control. A child who grows up hearing "We don't buy things like that" or "Money doesn't grow on trees" may absorb more than just caution—they may internalise a worldview in which financial security is always at risk, regardless of current circumstances. These beliefs persist not because they are objectively accurate, but because they become *emotionally true*. They shape default assumptions: that spending is dangerous, that pleasure must be justified, that provision is conditional.

These scripts often show up in adulthood as rigidity, reactivity, or avoidance. A parent may find it difficult to enjoy their own earnings, fearing they'll "jinx" their luck or become irresponsible. They may over-save to the point of denial, or scrutinise every household purchase with disproportionate intensity. Others may swing between deprivation and indulgence, creating an emotional rollercoaster for their children. What's crucial to recognise is that *children do not only inherit their parents' financial resources—they inherit their parents' financial emotions*. The child learns not just that money is tight, but that it is frightening. That asking for things is burdensome. That security is always temporary.

Scarcity scripts are powerful precisely because they are invisible to the person operating within them. A parent might believe they are simply being responsible, frugal, or "smart with money." But beneath the justification often lies an unexamined legacy of fear—fear that is unintentionally passed on to the next generation. And when this fear is combined with the natural guilt many parents feel (especially in the context of working long hours, shared custody, economic hardship, or personal overwhelm), the result is an erratic pattern of decision-making that children absorb in full.

Enter guilt spending. Guilt spending is not rooted in entitlement or indulgence—it is rooted in emotional compensation. A parent feels they've been too strict, too absent, too distracted, or too harsh, and seeks to repair the perceived rupture with a purchase. This may look like a surprise gift, a lifted restriction, or an unplanned outing. In the moment, it may feel generous, even loving. But when the pattern repeats—restrain, then release; deny, then indulge—it becomes a confusing operating system for the child. One day they are told money is tight; the next, it flows freely. One week they are instructed to save; the next, they are treated to excess. The result is not trust—it is *incoherence.* And incoherence, especially around money, breeds misunderstanding, entitlement, or insecurity.

There is also a subtler, but equally important, impact of guilt spending: it teaches children that love is expressed through material concession. That boundaries are negotiable if the emotional stakes are high enough. Over time, they may learn to escalate requests until the guilt mechanism kicks in, or they may struggle to distinguish between emotional generosity and financial permissiveness. The issue here is not the occasional gift or surprise—it is the underlying motivation and the absence of articulated logic. *When children do not understand the "why" behind a financial decision, they default to interpreting its emotional undertone.* If the undertone is shame, guilt, or compensation, they learn that money functions as a tool of repair, not a reflection of values or priorities.

These patterns are often reinforced by cultural scripts as well. Western consumer culture promotes two parallel myths: that withholding is cruel, and that spending is proof of love. Advertisements appeal not just to desires, but to identities: "You deserve it." "Give them everything." "Make it up to them." Parents are not immune to these narratives—especially those who feel they are working against a backdrop of financial struggle, divorce, limited time, or inherited hardship. The desire to give one's child "more than I had" is a noble impulse. But when it is expressed through inconsistent financial behaviour, it can produce the opposite of its intent. Children raised in such environments are often *more* confused about money, not less. They inherit not clarity, but contradiction.

The antidote to these patterns is not austerity. Nor is it emotional self-sacrifice. It is *intentionality*—the practice of aligning financial decisions with articulated values, and of communicating those values clearly and calmly. A parent who says, "We're choosing not to buy this because we're saving for something more important," is teaching discernment. A parent who acknowledges, "I know I've been spending more lately to make up for being busy—let's talk about that," is modelling self-awareness. These moments are not grand gestures; they are small acts of financial clarity that build a child's internal framework over time.

It also helps to reframe the relationship between money and emotion. Money decisions *will* always be emotional to some extent—but that doesn't mean they have to be reactive. A parent can feel guilt and *still* uphold a boundary. They can feel scarcity and *still* explain their choices in a way that affirms security. Children don't need parents who never waver; they need parents who narrate their choices with honesty and coherence. This narrative becomes the child's reference point—not just for spending, but for emotional regulation, prioritisation, and self-respect.

What's often missed in conversations about financial parenting is that *consistency is not about sameness—it's about predictability of logic*. If a child understands the framework—what matters, what the limits are, how trade-offs work—they are far more likely to respect financial boundaries, even when disappointed. But when decisions feel arbitrary, reactive, or based on adult moods, the child is left to guess. And guessing about money, especially in emotionally charged households, rarely yields healthy long-term habits.

Parents who reflect on their own financial upbringing can begin to spot these cycles. Was deprivation framed as virtue, or was it used to control? Was indulgence seen as generosity, or as guilt management? Were surprises used to reward behaviour, distract from conflict, or bypass difficult conversations? These are not easy questions, but they are transformative. They reveal not just what one learned, but *why* one learned it—and how those lessons are now being handed forward, often unintentionally.

Crucially, shifting these patterns does not require perfection. It requires presence. A parent who catches themselves veering into guilt spending and says, "I was about to buy this for you because I felt bad—I realise that's not the best reason," is doing powerful work. They are showing their child that self-correction is part of maturity, that money is not a tool to manage emotion, and that love does not require financial proof.

In families where scarcity scripts and guilt spending dominate, the path to healthier financial modelling begins with slowing down. Slowing down decisions. Slowing down reactions. Slowing down the automatic yes or the automatic no, and replacing it with a pause—a moment of intention. In that pause is the chance to say, *What do I want my child to learn from this?* Not what will make them happiest in the next ten minutes, but what will shape their clarity, confidence, and capacity to manage money over a lifetime.

Because ultimately, the goal is not to protect children from discomfort, or to replicate the financial extremes of the past. The goal is to raise children who understand money not as a symbol of fear or compensation, but as a tool—one that requires thought, boundaries, and above all, *emotional clarity*.

## The Example Is the Lesson

When a parent tips generously at a café, sighs audibly while paying a utility bill, or comments disparagingly on someone's flashy car, their child may not say anything—but they are learning. Not about decimal points or interest rates, but about *how money behaves*, how it feels, and what it says about a person. Children do not begin their financial education in formal lessons. They begin by watching. And what they watch is not abstract instruction—it is lived behaviour. A parent's financial habits, reactions, and rituals become the child's baseline for what is normal, appropriate, admirable, or suspect. Without ever needing to be stated, a value system is transmitted. And once embedded, that system is difficult to revise. It becomes the lens through which the child will later view their own earning, spending, giving, and saving. In this sense, *modelling* is not a secondary educational tool. It is the primary one.

This is not a sentimental claim. It is grounded in developmental psychology and reinforced by decades of behavioural research. Children are observational learners. Long before they can parse complex instructions, they learn by internalising what is modelled by the adults around them—especially their caregivers. Albert Bandura's seminal work on social learning theory, for example, demonstrated that children imitate not only the actions of adults but the apparent *meaning* of those actions. If a behaviour appears to elicit praise, approval, or emotional relief, the child is more likely to adopt it, regardless of what they have been told. If a parent says, "It's important to save," but models impulsive shopping, the lesson absorbed is not restraint—it's *performance*. Talk one way, act another.

This dissonance is particularly potent in the domain of money because so much of our financial behaviour is infused with emotion. A parent may not remember slamming the phone down after speaking with a debt collector, or nervously laughing about an overdraft fee. But the child notices. They notice the tension when the credit card statement arrives. They watch how generosity is extended—or withheld—depending on social context. They listen for cues about whether someone is "wasting money," "lucky," or "irresponsible." These impressions build quietly, piece by piece, into a working model of financial reality. Not a reality based on economic facts, but on emotional signals, relational norms, and subtle social codes.

Consider the act of tipping. It is a routine financial gesture, often unexamined. Yet when a child sees their parent tip well—without complaint, and with an acknowledgement of the service—they learn that money can be used to recognise effort, to reinforce fairness, to express gratitude. If, by contrast, tipping is done resentfully or withheld altogether, the child may learn that money is primarily transactional or a symbol of dominance. Similarly, if a child observes a parent speaking respectfully to someone in a low-income service role, they learn that wealth does not determine dignity. If they hear sarcastic remarks about those "who clearly don't know how to manage their money," they learn that financial status justifies judgement.

These moments may seem minor or incidental to the adult. But children, particularly in early and middle childhood, are exquisitely attuned to their caregivers' tone, body language, and emotional consistency. Research into parent–child communication has shown that *how* something is said often carries more weight than *what* is said. A parent may think they are "not discussing money in front of the kids," but if they routinely exhibit stress during financial transactions or visibly relax after spending, the message is clear: money is either a source of pressure or release. Rarely, in such dynamics, is it framed as neutral, deliberate, or values-driven.

This is where the concept of *financial modelling* becomes crucial—not as an abstract ideal, but as a practical framework. To model financial integrity means to behave in ways that align with what one claims to value, while acknowledging the inevitable inconsistencies along the way. It does not mean perfection. It means visibility. Children benefit less from being shielded from financial decisions and more from *being allowed to witness them responsibly*. A parent who says, "I'm thinking about how much to tip—this person was really attentive," is modelling discernment. One who says, "We're choosing to delay this purchase because we're prioritising something else," is modelling trade-offs. One who calmly says, "I made a financial mistake this month, and I'm figuring out how to correct it," is modelling resilience.

What is damaging is not the mistake itself—it is the refusal to narrate it. In the absence of narration, children fill in the gaps with emotion. They interpret financial conflict as instability, or secrecy as shame. This is especially true in households where children overhear arguments about money but are excluded from the subsequent resolution. The fight was witnessed; the repair was private. What remains is a skewed impression of financial life as unpredictable or combative.

Parents sometimes assume that by avoiding explicit financial talk, they are protecting their children. But avoidance is itself a form of modelling. It teaches that money is unfit for discussion—that it belongs behind closed doors, or that children are incapable of understanding its complexity. In reality, children are capable of understanding far more than they are often given credit for—so long as the information is scaffolded appropriately. Telling a seven-year-old how mortgage amortisation works is unnecessary. But involving them in a conversation about saving up for a shared family goal teaches delayed gratification, prioritisation, and collaborative decision-making—all without technical jargon.

Modelling also matters during high-stakes financial moments: job loss, unexpected expenses, windfalls. These are often the moments that most strongly shape a child's lifelong money attitudes—not because of the financial event itself, but because of how the adults around them *responded*. A parent who loses a job and tells their child, "This is going to change how we spend for a while, but we'll figure it out together," is modelling adaptability and transparency. A parent who receives a bonus and immediately spends it without context is missing an opportunity to model planning or generosity. These are the pivot points where financial values are either clarified or obscured.

Children also take cues from how adults talk about other people's money. Do we speak with envy about wealth, or with disdain? Do we praise frugality, or mock it as cheapness? Do we admire generosity, or question its motives? These comments, often tossed out casually, form the social backdrop of the child's financial worldview. They begin to develop internal metrics: What kind of spending is admirable? What kind is embarrassing? Who is to be emulated, and who is to be avoided? These judgments often carry into adulthood, influencing not just behaviour but identity. A young adult who grew up hearing that rich people are greedy may struggle with their own ambition. One who heard that frugality is a virtue may find it difficult to enjoy what they've earned.

This brings us to a deeper point: *financial modelling is never neutral, because money itself is never just about numbers*. It is always about meaning. The way a parent interacts with money reveals what they believe about freedom, safety, fairness, success, identity. And children are absorbing those beliefs—not just through explicit instruction, but through daily observation. The consistency—or inconsistency—between belief and behaviour is the crucible in which their financial ethics are formed.

The good news is that modelling is not performative. It doesn't require curated moments or perfect scripts. It requires awareness. It requires noticing the small decisions—how we handle waitstaff, how we respond to requests, how we speak when we're worried or proud or tired—and treating those moments not as background noise, but as the curriculum. Because they are. Whether or not we acknowledge it, *our example is the lesson*. The only question is whether we want that lesson to be accidental or intentional.

Intentional modelling means choosing to make our financial lives visible in developmentally appropriate ways, to speak aloud the logic behind our decisions, and to show our children that money is not something to be hidden or feared—but something to be understood, shaped, and used well. In doing so, we give them more than knowledge. We give them a template for coherence. And in a world where so many financial messages are distorted, commodified, or contradictory, that coherence may be the most valuable inheritance of all.

# Chapter 3
# Age-Appropriate Money Thinking

Ask a six-year-old where money comes from and you might hear, quite sincerely, "the bank" or "the card." By twelve, the answer matures slightly—"from work"—though if you press them for details, they'll likely shrug. A sixteen-year-old, proudly wielding their own debit card, may struggle to recall how much they've spent in the past month. These responses aren't failures of upbringing or evidence of indifference. They are developmental markers, each one reflecting the natural evolution of how young minds come to grasp value, exchange, and consequence. A child cannot understand compound interest any more than they can understand algebra before mastering arithmetic. Similarly, ideas like budgeting or ethical spending make little sense before a child has first internalised the tangible workings of money—what it is, where it goes, and why it matters. True financial education, then, is not a single conversation or checklist of rules; it is a slow, responsive process that tracks the child's growing mind and emotional capacity. Yet, too often, parents miss the rhythm—expecting too much too soon, or too little too late. The result is not ignorance but disconnection: children swamped by information they cannot yet process, or insulated from lessons they're perfectly ready to learn.

The premise of this chapter rests on one essential truth: money understanding must align with brain development. What a five-year-old can absorb about coins and choices bears little resemblance to what a teenager must learn about digital payments or delayed gratification. When parents ignore these differences, learning doesn't just falter—it warps. Young children learn through their senses; they need to see, touch, count, and feel. Abstractions like "saving for later" or "value for money" mean nothing unless rooted in physical experience. Simply handing a small child a tap-to-pay card and calling it "financial education" skips the very stage that gives meaning to the concept. They need to feel the weight of coins leaving their hand, witness money diminishing and reappearing through effort. Without that sensory grounding, financial lessons float untethered—interesting perhaps, but not remembered.

This isn't, however, an argument for postponing the subject. In fact, quite the opposite. Children form impressions about money long before they can count it. By the age of three, they're already absorbing patterns; by seven, researchers suggest, their core attitudes toward saving and spending are largely set. These beliefs aren't taught formally—they are observed. They come from tone, from routine, from how adults behave. When a parent says, "We're buying food with this," or "We can't get that today—we're saving for something special," the child begins to understand cause, effect, and purpose. What looks like a mundane exchange at the till is, in truth, a powerful early lesson in patience, planning, and trust.

As children move into middle childhood—roughly ages seven to twelve—their reasoning capacities widen. They begin to see patterns, anticipate outcomes, and make sense of trade-offs. This is the ideal moment for small but meaningful financial experiments: chore-based allowances, visible savings goals, and limited spending autonomy. Yet many parents stumble here, either by shielding children from any real financial consequence or, conversely, by flooding them with complexity they cannot yet digest. A nine-year-old does not need to grasp interest rates, but they can certainly feel the difference between £10 earned through effort and £10 gifted without condition. They can experience the sting of spending their savings on something that breaks too soon—and, through that experience, build emotional durability. A parent who resists the urge to "rescue" in these moments, choosing instead to talk through what happened, lays the groundwork for genuine self-control and accountability later on.

Then comes adolescence—the most deceptive phase of all. Teenagers often appear financially fluent. They know prices, manage apps, perhaps even hold part-time jobs. But beneath that surface competence lies a neurological mismatch. The brain's planning centre, the prefrontal cortex, is still maturing, while the emotional core—the limbic system—is already in high gear, craving novelty, reward, and autonomy. This explains why a teen can know, intellectually, that spending their entire allowance on a festival ticket is unwise, yet still do it with gusto. It isn't rebellion—it's biology.

Parents who understand this developmental gap approach the stage differently. They trade control for collaboration, authority for guidance. Instead of dictating limits, they establish conditional freedoms: "This is your money to manage—let's check in together next week." The goal is not to prevent mistakes but to make them educational. This is the time to introduce budgeting, digital banking, and even ethical spending—but always through practice, never lecture. Let them plan a group trip, handle a subscription, or open a student account. Real-world engagement transforms abstract advice into lived competence. Yet one talk won't suffice; the lessons need revisiting, revising, reinforcing. Adolescence thrives on repetition wrapped in respect.

Still, financial education is not only about intellect. It's about the emotional and social realities that shape behaviour. A seven-year-old might intellectually understand saving, yet emotionally buckle under the wait. A teenager may grasp earning and spending, but struggle with the discomfort of inequality—seeing peers with more or less. Thus, the conversation must broaden beyond the "how" of money to include the "why." Why do we give? Why do we wait? Why do we choose what we choose? These are moral, even philosophical questions—and they are where true financial wisdom begins to form.

Parents often ask, almost anxiously, "When should I start teaching my child about money?" The honest answer is: right now. But with sensitivity to the child's stage. Financial literacy isn't a syllabus you deliver and tick off—it's an evolving dialogue, paced to the child's readiness. Too early, and it confuses; too late, and it leaves voids that will later harden into anxiety or ignorance. Children sense when adults misjudge them. They tune out when treated as incapable, and push back when overwhelmed. The art lies in pitching the challenge precisely—stretching, never snapping.

This chapter proposes a framework for that delicate calibration: aligning developmental stages with financial milestones, clarifying what children can grasp, when, and how. It respects the slow architecture of understanding, reminding us that early exposure should not be mistaken for early independence. Children need time. They need examples. They need the freedom to ask messy questions—

"Are we rich?" "Why do they have more than us?"—without the conversation turning defensive or dismissive. Those questions, after all, reveal emotional curiosity far more than greed.

To teach money well is to teach in rhythm with growth: not racing ahead, not lagging behind, but walking alongside. It means narrating choices, modelling values, and handing over responsibility inch by inch. Done with patience and honesty, it shapes more than numeracy—it shapes character. In the end, the goal is not merely to raise children who are financially competent, but individuals who see money not as a source of anxiety or status, but as a tool for living deliberately. Understanding how a mind learns to think about money is not a side lesson. It is the foundation upon which every other lesson rests.

## How Financial Understanding Evolves

Hand a three-year-old a shiny £1 coin and they may squeal with delight, captivated not by its purchasing power, but by its weight, its glint, its resemblance to treasure. Hand the same child a contactless card and the reaction is markedly different—detachment, confusion, or at best, imitation. The adult knows both objects represent value, but to the child, only one *feels* real. This divergence reveals a deeper truth: financial understanding does not emerge all at once, nor does it automatically track with exposure. It evolves through stages—cognitive, emotional, and social—that are predictable yet profoundly shaped by experience. And when parents misalign financial expectations with developmental capacity, they risk distorting the very lessons they hope to instil.

Financial cognition is not innate. It must be built, layer by layer, through direct experience and mediated interpretation. Children are not born knowing what money is, what it does, or why it matters. They construct these meanings gradually, drawing from what they observe, what they're told, and what they are allowed to try for themselves. Research in developmental psychology consistently shows that children form foundational money beliefs—about value, fairness, saving, and ownership—long before they can articulate them. By age seven, many of these beliefs are already entrenched. The implication is clear: financial education does not begin when a child opens a bank account. It begins the first time they witness a transaction, hear a comment about cost, or feel the sting of a denied request.

In early childhood, roughly ages three to six, money is primarily understood through *symbolic association*. A coin is not valuable because of what it can buy, but because it is given or withheld by adults, or perhaps stored in a colourful jar. At this stage, children grasp that money "buys things" but not why one item costs more than another, or why money is sometimes available and sometimes not. Their thinking is egocentric and literal. If the card "works" at the shop, then surely it can always work. If Mummy says she has no money but then buys something later, the child perceives inconsistency, not nuance. Abstract ideas like budgeting, opportunity cost, or debt are cognitively inaccessible. What they *can* understand, however, is tangible exchange: "I gave the man the coin and he gave me the apple." This is why physical money, however outdated it may seem to adults, plays a critical role in anchoring early financial intuition.

Children in this phase benefit most from experiences that involve concrete, visible outcomes. A clear jar to watch savings grow. A small coin purse to carry their own "spending money" at a shop. The ability to choose between two options and experience the satisfaction—or disappointment—that follows. These moments don't require instruction. They require proximity, patience, and repetition. When a parent says, "You can buy the crayons or the sticker book, but not both," and then stands back, the child is not just making a choice—they are rehearsing the mental structures of cost, trade-off, and consequence. No spreadsheet can replicate that.

As children move into middle childhood—typically ages seven to eleven—their cognitive capacity expands significantly. They begin to grasp sequencing, logic, and the basic arithmetic underpinning financial transactions. This is the golden window for introducing the mechanics of money: earning, saving, spending, and even giving. Children at this age can understand that money must be *earned*, that it can be *used up*, and that it often involves *waiting*. However, while they can perform calculations and make comparisons ("this toy is £5, that one is £10"), their emotional regulation is still developing. Impulse remains strong. The concept of saving for long-term goals is emerging, but fragile. Without reinforcement through practice, it does not stabilise.

This is where structured autonomy becomes essential. Allowances—whether tied to chores, freely given, or hybridised—offer a vehicle for children to *test* their understanding. Mistakes made with small sums teach lessons that lectures cannot. A child who spends all their money on sweets and later regrets not saving for a toy does not need a scolding—they need a conversation: "What did you notice? What might you do differently next time?" These reflective prompts build metacognition—the ability to think about one's thinking—which is the bedrock of financial reasoning. At this stage, children are also acutely sensitive to fairness. They compare their resources with siblings, friends, and peers. This creates an opening for conversations about equity, effort, and differing financial contexts—not in abstract terms, but grounded in everyday observations.

Adolescence introduces a paradox. Teenagers, especially from twelve onwards, *appear* financially competent. They can calculate, research, compare, even budget in short bursts. Many earn money through part-time work, babysitting, or entrepreneurial ventures. They may manage bank accounts, digital wallets, or online subscriptions. But beneath this surface competence lies a still-developing prefrontal cortex. The part of the brain responsible for long-term planning, impulse control, and consequence evaluation is under construction until the early twenties. This developmental lag explains the gap between what teenagers *know* and what they *do*. A sixteen-year-old may fully understand that they're overspending, but the reward circuitry in their brain—especially when influenced by peer validation or instant gratification—overrides that knowledge.

This stage requires a strategic recalibration from parents. Instead of micro-managing, the goal should be *scaffolding*—offering increasing responsibility with decreasing supervision, while maintaining regular check-ins and reflective conversations. A teen should be encouraged to manage their own budget for clothes, entertainment, or travel, but with parameters that promote foresight: "You have £50 for the month. How do you plan to use it?" Mistakes will happen. The key is not to prevent them, but to make space for debriefing. "What did you learn? Would you do anything differently?" These discussions build the internal compass that no app can provide.

It's also during adolescence that deeper questions begin to surface: *What does money say about me? Why do some families have more than others? Is financial success a moral achievement, a lucky break, or something else entirely?* These are not just economic queries. They are identity questions, shaped by exposure to social media, political discourse, and peer dynamics. Teenagers begin to connect money with status, autonomy, justice, and self-worth. Parents who treat these questions as nuisances miss an opportunity. Those who treat them as legitimate philosophical provocations create the space for ethical reasoning and value formation. A teen who is guided in thinking critically about advertising, inequality, and spending choices is not just becoming "financially literate"—they are becoming *financially conscious*.

Throughout all these stages, two principles remain constant. First, *experience precedes understanding*. Children must do before they can reflect. They must spend before they can budget, regret before they can restrain, give before they can grasp generosity. Second, *language shapes meaning*. The words adults use—"wasting," "spoiling," "deserving," "can't afford"—carry emotional weight and conceptual implications. A child repeatedly told "we can't afford that" may internalise scarcity, even in times of abundance. A child invited into conversations about trade-offs and priorities learns that money is not fixed or mysterious, but manageable.

Financial understanding is not a single "aha" moment—it is a slow accrual of insight, pattern recognition, emotional tolerance, and social context. It does not happen in classrooms alone, nor through osmosis. It requires thoughtful, age-attuned guidance, offered consistently across years, not weeks. And above all, it requires adults who are willing to meet children where they are—not where we wish they were, or fear they might be.

To truly prepare children for financial adulthood, we must first understand the terrain they are walking. Not all missteps are failures. Some are necessary calibrations. And when we align our expectations with their developmental stage—offering freedom matched with feedback—we don't just teach them how to use money. We teach them how to *think* about it, which is the only lesson with lifelong traction.

## Concrete Before Abstract

A child drops a coin into a piggy bank and hears the clink. Their eyes widen, their hand lingers on the cool metal. They do it again. It is a ritual both physical and symbolic—an act of cause and consequence, effort and accumulation. Now consider the same child watching a parent tap a contactless card. There is no weight, no sound, no tactile sequence—only a fleeting beep, a plastic gesture, and a bag to carry home. For the adult, this is efficiency. For the child, it is invisibility. And in a world where financial transactions are increasingly frictionless, this invisibility comes at a cognitive cost. Children's financial intuition is not built on explanation alone. It is built on experience—and that experience must be *concrete before it can become abstract*.

The prevailing assumption in many households is that young children are digital natives—savvy, adaptable, immune to confusion about non-physical systems. And in many ways, they are. A four-year-old may navigate a smartphone more fluently than their grandparents. But fluency is not the same as comprehension. Understanding how to *use* technology does not equate to understanding the *logic* behind what it does—especially when it comes to abstract systems like digital money. The developmental truth is that *young children think in tangible terms*. They grasp what they can touch, manipulate, and see. Abstract reasoning—about future value, symbolic exchange, or invisible flows—doesn't emerge in a meaningful way until middle childhood. To ask a six-year-old to understand that a plastic card represents a finite pool of stored labour, value, and trade-off is akin to asking them to visualise a mortgage. They can repeat the words. They cannot map them to lived meaning.

This disconnect matters because it undermines the foundation of financial learning. For a concept to become intuitive, it must be grounded in sensory experience. A child who watches money enter and exit their own hands begins to build a spatial and temporal sense of cost. They can *feel* that something is gone, or that something has grown. They learn that choices have weight—that spending means letting go of one thing to obtain another. This knowledge is not academic. It is embodied. And in early childhood, embodied knowledge is what sticks.

This is why many educators and developmental specialists recommend starting money lessons with coins and notes—not apps or digital wallets. Physical currency introduces several essential financial ideas in one compact experience: denomination (not all money is equal), exchange (money is traded for value), scarcity (money can run out), and accumulation (money can grow through saving). When children sort coins, they learn comparison. When they count change, they practise sequencing. When they hand over money and receive less in return, they begin to grasp the trade-off embedded in every purchase. None of these ideas require formal instruction. But they do require visibility—and visibility is lost when transactions occur entirely behind screens or through plastic.

Parents sometimes worry that physical money is outdated or confusing, especially when they themselves no longer carry cash. But introducing tangible currency to children is not about resisting technology—it is about respecting developmental sequencing. Just as we teach children to read with physical books before handing them e-readers, or to write with pencils before typing on keyboards, we must introduce money in ways that match the way young minds build understanding. Once the concrete is internalised, the abstract becomes not just accessible, but meaningful.

The problem is not digital money itself. It is the *premature reliance* on digital systems without the scaffolding that makes those systems intelligible. A child given a prepaid card or allowance app before understanding what money *is* may learn how to transact—but not how to think. They may know how to check a balance, but not how that balance connects to effort, choice, or limit. This is financial mimicry, not literacy. It produces behaviour that looks competent on the surface but lacks the underlying architecture to withstand real-world complexity.

Moreover, digital money introduces a cognitive illusion: frictionlessness. When money is spent with a tap, swipe, or click, the absence of physical interaction can lead children—and adults—to underestimate the loss. In behavioural economics, this is known as the "pain of paying" effect: we feel the financial loss more acutely when the payment method is tangible. The sharpness of handing over cash heightens awareness of cost. With digital payment, that pain is dulled, often to the point of disappearance. This is not a small matter. For a developing mind, *not feeling* the cost can result in a distorted sense of value. The child may assume that money is endless, or at least easily replenished. And when limits are imposed, they may perceive them not as economic facts, but as arbitrary parental restrictions.

This is especially important in families where digital spending is normalised through parental behaviour. When children see adults routinely tap to pay without commentary, or make large purchases with a few keystrokes, they absorb a money script of ease, not deliberation. Without the balancing experience of physical trade-offs, the child may conclude that money simply *exists*—not that it is earned, prioritised, or managed. Parents who say "money doesn't grow on trees" while spending invisibly create a cognitive gap that children cannot reconcile. And confusion is not neutral. It becomes the template upon which financial habits are later built.

To prevent this gap, financial education in early childhood must begin with the concrete. Not because children are fragile, but because they are building the cognitive and emotional infrastructure upon which all later financial thinking depends. Give them coins to sort, clear jars for saving, visual trackers for goals. Let them hand money to a cashier, count change, feel the delay of waiting for a purchase they want. Let them experience the mild regret of spending too quickly, and the satisfaction of reaching a savings target. These experiences don't require complex instruction. They require proximity, consistency, and patient narration.

Over time, as children mature, the focus can shift towards abstraction. A ten-year-old who understands cash flow in jars can begin using a child-friendly budgeting app. A twelve-year-old who's managed small purchases can start managing a digital allowance with real consequences. But even then, abstraction should never replace discussion. A parent might say, "Your balance went down because of the subscription—we'll talk about what that means for next week's spending." In doing so, they are making the invisible visible. They are connecting dots that, to the child, remain disconnected unless guided.

There is a temptation to treat digital fluency as financial maturity. But the two are not interchangeable. A child may be technologically adept and still financially naïve. They may know how to spend, but not why to wait. They may know how to track, but not how to interpret. And none of this is their fault. It is a function of how they've been introduced to money—not through intention, but through osmosis.

To build financial intuition that endures, we must start with what children can hold, sort, exchange, and lose. Only then can we responsibly introduce what they cannot see. The movement from concrete to abstract is not a step to be skipped—it is the path through which financial awareness becomes financial wisdom. And wisdom, unlike convenience, cannot be tapped into with a single gesture. It must be built, piece by piece, from what a child can see, feel, and understand.

## When Questions Begin

A six-year-old glances up during a car ride and asks, "Are we rich?" The question may sound innocent or even amusing, but for the parent in the driver's seat, it lands with a thud of complexity. Should you answer directly? Should you avoid the topic? Should you turn the question into a lesson? The impulse to deflect is common. Many adults grew up in families where money talk was taboo, or strictly need-to-know. But children today are growing up in a context saturated with cues about wealth, value, and status—from YouTube mansion tours to overheard conversations to the simple observation that some classmates always seem to have more. The questions come earlier than many parents expect. And how those questions are handled determines far more than just financial literacy. It sets the emotional tone of a child's relationship with money—whether they will grow up viewing it as a topic of clarity or confusion, honesty or evasion, openness or secrecy.

The curiosity stage usually begins between the ages of five and eight, when children are developing the cognitive capacity to notice patterns and ask comparative questions. They start to observe that some houses are bigger, some cars are newer, some toys are fancier. They ask about cost not to be rude or entitled, but to make sense of a world that is visibly unequal. "How much did that cost?" "Why can't we buy that?" "Do we have more money than them?" These are not tests of parental boundaries—they are developmental markers. They signal a child's growing awareness of difference and their attempt to locate themselves within the social landscape. If met with dismissiveness ("That's not for you to worry about") or vagueness ("It's complicated"), the child may stop asking. But the internal narrative doesn't stop—it simply becomes quieter, more private, more speculative.

It's important to recognise that these questions are not always about numbers. When a child asks, "How much do you make?" they may not be seeking a figure so much as a framework: *Are we safe? Are we enough? Am I allowed to ask?* The literal answer may matter less than the emotional tone of the response. A defensive or flustered reply can signal that money is a source of anxiety or shame. A calm and honest reply—matched to the child's level of understanding—teaches that money is a topic that can be approached with openness and care. The child isn't asking for a financial spreadsheet. They're asking for access to meaning.

This presents a challenge for many parents: how to be honest without being overwhelming, how to provide structure without projecting stress. The key is *contextual transparency*. This means offering truthful, age-appropriate answers that reflect both the facts and the values behind them. For example, if a child asks, "Are we rich?" a useful reply might be, "That depends on what you mean. We have enough for what we need, and we're lucky in many ways—but we also make choices about what we spend money on so that we can save for what matters." This kind of answer does several things at once: it validates the question, avoids binary thinking, introduces the idea of trade-offs, and sets the tone for future conversations.

Parents often worry that discussing money will burden children. But silence can be just as burdensome—especially when children sense that something is being hidden. When a child hears adults arguing about bills behind closed doors, or notices sudden changes in spending, their imagination fills in the blanks. They may assume the worst, or internalise a vague but persistent anxiety about financial insecurity. Conversely, when children are included in developmentally appropriate conversations—"We're being careful with money this month because we had some unexpected expenses"—they learn that money is manageable, not mysterious. They learn that challenges are part of life, and that stability is built through planning and prioritisation, not silence.

The curiosity stage also presents an opportunity to introduce the concept of *relative wealth*. Children naturally compare themselves to peers: "Why does she always have new clothes?" "Why do they go on so many holidays?" Without guidance, these observations can calcify into simplistic conclusions—*we're poor, they're rich, we're unlucky, they're lucky*. But parents can intervene not with defensiveness or denial, but with nuance. "Different families spend money in different ways. Some people like to spend more on holidays, others on their home, or hobbies, or education. Just because you see something doesn't mean you know the whole story." These statements teach that appearances are not always accurate indicators of financial reality—and that wealth is not the same as worth.

It's also essential to address the philosophical questions behind money curiosity. When a child asks, "How much do you make?" they may be trying to understand power, responsibility, or possibility. A parent might respond, "I make enough to take care of us and to save for what's important. My job isn't just about money—it's about what I do, who I help, and what I'm learning." This reframes income as one part of a larger life structure, and subtly shifts the child's attention from numbers to purpose. It communicates that earning is meaningful not just in its quantity, but in its context.

Children at this stage are also increasingly exposed to consumer messaging. Advertisements, influencers, and peers shape their perceptions of what money should be used for—often emphasising acquisition, speed, and prestige. This makes parental responses even more significant. When a child says, "My friend has the new iPad—why don't I?" a reactive "Because we're not wasting money on that" may end the conversation, but it also ends the learning. A more constructive approach might be: "That's a big purchase. We've chosen to spend money on other things this year. If it's something important to you, let's talk about a savings plan." In this way, the conversation becomes an entry point into budgeting, delayed gratification, and personal values.

Some parents fear that being open about money will lead to entitlement or greed. But the evidence suggests otherwise. Children who grow up in homes where money is discussed openly—alongside values like generosity, responsibility, and planning—are more likely to develop healthy financial behaviours as adults. They are also less likely to attach shame, secrecy, or identity to wealth. Openness breeds competence, not entitlement—*provided that it is matched with modelling and moral clarity.*

At times, a child's questions may hit emotional pressure points for the adult. A parent who feels insecure about their income may experience shame when asked about it. One who grew up in financial hardship may be tempted to withhold information out of a protective instinct. These reactions are understandable—but they are also informative. They reveal the emotional residue of the parent's own money story. Rather than shutting down the conversation, they can become a moment of modelling vulnerability and reflection. "That's a good question—and it's one I didn't grow up being allowed to ask. I'm learning how to talk about money more openly, too." These admissions are not signs of weakness. They are signs of strength, signalling that financial education is not about having all the answers, but about engaging with complexity.

As children grow, their questions will evolve. But what matters most is not the precision of the parent's answer—it is the atmosphere in which the question is received. Curiosity should be met with receptivity. Uncertainty should be met with honesty. Interest should be met with context. In doing so, parents raise not just children who are "good with money," but children who are *comfortable talking about money*—a trait that, for many adults, remains elusive well into midlife.

The beginning of financial inquiry is not a threat to be managed—it is a gift to be nurtured. It is an invitation to teach, to model, and to co-construct meaning. It is the moment when money shifts from being something children observe to something they begin to *think about*. And that shift, handled with intention, can lay the groundwork for a lifetime of clarity, competence, and confidence.

## Teen Brains and Risky Spending

Hand a teenager £50 and a day of unstructured freedom, and the money is often gone by nightfall—spent on impulse purchases, food deliveries, fast fashion, or entertainment. When questioned later, the teen may shrug, deflect, or express genuine confusion about where it went. "It didn't seem like that much." "It just added up." "I'll be more careful next time." From an adult's perspective, this kind of spending can look careless, entitled, or irresponsible. But from a developmental standpoint, it's none of those things. It's predictable. And unless parents recognise *why* it happens—and how to respond strategically rather than reactively—they risk turning every money conversation into a power struggle that reinforces defensiveness instead of growth.

To understand teenage spending, we must start with neuroscience, not character judgement. The adolescent brain is in a state of reconstruction. The prefrontal cortex—the region responsible for reasoning, planning, and impulse control—is still maturing, typically into the early twenties. Meanwhile, the limbic system, which processes reward, emotion, and social cues, is highly active. This developmental mismatch creates what researchers often describe as a "fast engine with weak brakes." Teenagers are biologically wired to seek novelty, take risks, and respond intensely to short-term rewards—precisely the kind of conditions under which impulsive spending thrives.

Combine this with the external pressures of adolescence—peer influence, identity formation, social status dynamics—and money becomes more than a medium of exchange. It becomes a mirror of self. A way to belong, differentiate, experiment, or signal autonomy. A hoodie isn't just a hoodie; it's a social cue. A spontaneous delivery isn't just convenience; it's control over time and gratification. When teenagers spend recklessly, they are not just "failing to budget"—they are navigating a terrain where emotion, identity, and neurobiology converge.

Yet many parents approach teen spending with outdated assumptions: that teens should already know better, that mistakes equate to defiance, that the solution is tighter control. This often backfires. Adolescents crave autonomy. When money becomes a battleground for authority, they are more likely to conceal, resist, or manipulate rather than reflect. The task, then, is not to clamp down, but to scaffold—to provide structured freedom, to set boundaries that teach rather than punish, and to stay engaged without micromanaging.

One of the most effective strategies is to shift from reactive to proactive framing. Instead of intervening after the fact—"Why did you waste your money on that?"—parents can preface financial autonomy with a collaborative plan: "Here's your monthly amount. You're free to decide how you use it, but let's set a time each week to look at how it's going." This model respects the teen's agency while still embedding reflection. It teaches that money is not just about permission—it's about *process*. Mistakes are expected, but they're not exempt from scrutiny.

The tone of these reflections matters. If teens sense judgement, they will withdraw or become defensive. If they sense curiosity—"What were you hoping that would give you?" "Was it worth it in the end?"—they're more likely to engage. The goal is not to shame poor decisions, but to build *meta-cognition*—the ability to think about one's own thinking. A teenager who can articulate why they spent impulsively is one step closer to delaying gratification next time. But they won't reach that step without safe, consistent space for dialogue.

It's also important to model consequence without catastrophe. If a teen spends their allowance in the first week of the month, resist the urge to bail them out. Offer empathy, not rescue. "That's tough. What do you want to do differently next month?" This teaches resilience and accountability. Over time, they learn that scarcity isn't fatal—it's instructive. They learn to forecast, prioritise, and delay not because they were told to, but because the experience became real.

Of course, not all impulsive spending is benign. Sometimes it signals deeper issues: anxiety, social exclusion, low self-esteem, or even compulsive behaviour. A teen who consistently overspends to fit in or soothe stress may need support that goes beyond budgeting tools. This is where financial parenting intersects with emotional attunement. Ask not just "What did they buy?" but "What need were they trying to meet?" Behaviour is always communicative. Understanding the emotional drivers behind spending helps parents respond with relevance rather than rigidity.

It's also worth acknowledging that today's teens are operating in a uniquely challenging consumer environment. Digital platforms don't just enable spending—they *engineer* it. Algorithms optimise for temptation, social media normalises excess, and microtransactions—especially in gaming and app ecosystems—blur the line between virtual and real-world value. A teenager might spend £30 across six apps in one afternoon and barely register the loss. These ecosystems are designed to bypass reflective thought. Without intentional counter-strategies, even financially aware teens can find themselves overextended or desensitised to cost.

Parents must therefore go beyond the "budget talk" and begin teaching *digital financial literacy*. This includes understanding subscription traps, distinguishing between needs and wants in online contexts, tracking digital spending over time, and even discussing the psychology of advertising and social comparison. These conversations may feel advanced, but they are essential. A 15-year-old navigating TikTok trends and digital wallets faces a vastly different money landscape than their parents did at the same age. Financial education that ignores these dynamics risks being obsolete on arrival.

One effective approach is to conduct shared reviews of digital statements. "Let's look together at where your money went this week. What surprised you? What felt worth it? What might you change?" This process teaches tracking, self-auditing, and adaptive decision-making. It also strengthens trust—when parents treat teens as financial thinkers rather than rule-breakers, teens rise to the level of that respect. They begin to internalise that money isn't just a thing to *use*—it's a thing to *manage*.

Crucially, parents must resist the fantasy of full control. No system can eliminate every mistake. No rule can replace experience. The objective is not to produce a teenager who never errs, but one who learns quickly, owns their choices, and seeks guidance without fear of reprisal. That growth happens not through lectures, but through *scaffolded autonomy*—the gradual release of responsibility, paired with ongoing support. It is the same principle used in academic learning, driving instruction, and emotional development. Money is no different.

By adolescence, the groundwork has been laid. The child has seen how money works, heard how it's talked about, and now begins to experience what it *feels* like to make independent choices. If parents step back entirely, they abdicate their influence. If they overstep, they stunt the teen's capacity for growth. The balance is delicate. But when struck well, it produces not just financial competence, but financial *agency*—the internalised belief that one can think critically, choose deliberately, and adjust responsibly. In a culture that prizes instant results, that kind of slow, grounded growth is revolutionary.

And it begins with recognising that teens are not broken adults. They are forming humans, with brains in flux and values in motion. Their mistakes are not personal affronts—they are developmental necessities. Our job is not to prevent them from falling. It is to ensure that when they do, they understand what happened, why it matters, and how to try again—with steadier footing and greater clarity next time.

# Chapter 4
# Earning with Effort

A child who earns £10 for washing the car experiences that money quite differently from one who simply receives the same note at week's end. The distinction lies not in the currency itself, but in the process that precedes it—the wet sponge, the dripping hose, the slow rhythm of labour and completion. Through that sequence of small, physical acts, an abstract idea begins to take shape: this is what it means to earn. Strip away that experience, and money risks becoming untethered—appearing and vanishing without reason, governed by adult decisions or the flicker of an app. And when money loses its context, it loses its meaning. Children sense this instinctively. They may not articulate it, but they feel the difference—deeply—between what is given and what is earned. The only way for that understanding to take root is through repetition and direct experience. Effort, far from being an outdated moral exercise, remains a psychological and developmental necessity for building a coherent sense of value.

This chapter turns its gaze to the act of earning made visible—not merely the wage, but the work that gives it substance. For children and adolescents alike, participation in even modest forms of work—structured, safe, and age-appropriate—is one of the most formative financial lessons available. It teaches that value is not dispensed; it is created. That money doesn't simply circulate, but must be generated, exchanged, and considered. Through such experience, abstract notions like scarcity, cost, and trade-off acquire weight and texture. Effort translates theory into something lived.

At its core, earning is not just about income—it's about identity. A child who weeds a neighbour's garden for a fiver is not merely learning arithmetic. They are discovering that their actions can be of use, their time holds worth, and consistency yields return. That emotional equity—"I did this, I made this happen"—instils discernment and self-respect. It shapes the internal calculus from "Can I have this?" to "Is this worth what I worked for?" It's a quiet, powerful shift—from consumption to evaluation, from entitlement to agency.

Yet the way we frame earning matters. Not all systems of pocket money or chores communicate the same message. Some cultivate pure transaction—"I only help if I'm paid." Others create dependency—"Money simply arrives." The true lesson lies in the structure's logic and its storytelling. Whether parents link allowances to chores, give them unconditionally, or adopt a mixed model where some tasks earn payment while others are communal expectations—what counts is clarity and intent. What does this arrangement teach about responsibility, effort, and fairness? The answer to that question shapes far more than the child's budget.

Parents often find themselves caught between two instincts. They want children to contribute as members of the household, but they worry that attaching payment will erode altruism. They want to teach earning, yet resist turning family life into an economy. The tension is genuine, but it's only problematic if the two ideas—earning and contribution—are seen as opposites. They aren't. Children can and should help without pay as a matter of belonging, while still being given paid opportunities for tasks that require initiative or persistence. The key is narrative:

"Everyone helps with the basics because this is our shared home. But when you take on extra work, we discuss what fair compensation looks like." Such framing honours both cooperation and independence, teaching that value is recognised in different ways, depending on context.

This question of monetisation grows even more complex in today's world, where children encounter notions of entrepreneurship and digital income before they've even opened a bank account. They see peers earning through TikTok sponsorships, gaming streams, handmade crafts, or online resales. Earning, once local and linear, has become global, digital, and—often—disproportionate. While this landscape can inspire creativity, it also distorts perception. Effort and reward no longer always correlate. And so, modern financial education must extend beyond "how to earn" toward "what earning means." What does it demand? What does it cost? Where should it fit in one's hierarchy of values? Without that guidance, children risk absorbing skewed ideals of success, productivity, or self-worth.

In exploring this theme, the chapter turns to real-world examples of earning done well—families who have crafted thoughtful, practical systems. From mini home enterprises and service projects to simple household initiatives, these stories demonstrate that financial learning doesn't require grandeur. A child who conceives an idea, follows it through, and receives recognition—monetary or otherwise—internalises a lesson no lecture could replicate: effort has consequence. Completion has meaning. Ownership, even in miniature, breeds maturity.

But there is another side to earning that must not be ignored: the value of work done without pay. Not every act of labour should be monetised. In fact, some of the most important human lessons—responsibility, empathy, humility—arise from unpaid contribution. Helping a sibling, tidying a communal space, volunteering for a cause—these acts teach that worth is not always transactional. They remind children that significance need not be measured in currency. In an age that prizes monetisation as the ultimate validation, this distinction becomes radical. If everything turns into a "gig," we risk raising children who ask not "Is this right?" but "Is this worth it?"

This is not a plea for austerity or moral lecturing. It's an argument for balance, for intention. Children should understand how to earn—and why some things should remain outside that logic. They should see that money motivates, yes, but that contribution, pride, or solidarity can do so too. Sometimes the reward lies not in the wallet but in the moment—the satisfaction of completing a task, the gratitude of another, the quiet pride of a job done well. Such experiences don't just create savvier earners. They create steadier people.

Teaching children to earn with effort is not preparation merely for employment—it's preparation for living. Life requires sustained effort without constant reward. It requires patience when outcomes lag, and resilience when results disappoint. Those who have learned to connect work with worth, rather than wealth alone, navigate such realities with steadier footing. They understand that while money can arrive from many directions, its true significance lies in how it's obtained.

This chapter, then, offers more than advice on pocket money or chores. It proposes a framework for cultivating financial agency through meaningful effort. It argues that earning is not just economic participation—it is psychological ownership, emotional grounding, and moral calibration. In a world where money often appears with a tap and vanishes with a swipe, to teach a child that value is made, not given, is to hand them an anchor. And anchors, once set, hold fast for life.

## The Value of Work, Not Just Wages

A child who scrubs a muddy pair of football boots for ten minutes, dries them carefully, and hands them over with a faint sense of pride does not just complete a task. They cross an invisible but significant developmental threshold: they connect effort to outcome. If that work is recognised—not necessarily with cash, but with acknowledgement, trust, or some form of reciprocal investment—they begin to understand that value is not something given, but something *generated*. That moment, repeated over time in various forms, is how the emotional architecture of financial literacy is built. Not through lectures or allowances alone, but through *effort made visible*. And yet, modern childhood is increasingly designed to remove friction, automate labour, and sever the link between work and reward.

The experience of earning is not just about accumulating money. It is about anchoring money to *meaning*. When we say a child "needs to earn to understand money," what we really mean is that they need to feel the *weight* of effort. The sensation of time passing as they work. The discomfort of persisting through a boring task. The surprise of discovering that some things take longer than expected. These experiences cannot be downloaded. They must be *lived*. And they must be scaffolded by adults who understand that the goal isn't just income—it's *insight*. That insight doesn't arrive automatically with a payslip. It arrives through repetition, reflection, and reinforcement. The point is not to raise small-scale capitalists. It's to raise people who grasp that effort and value are often entwined in subtle, non-linear ways—and that the more attuned you are to that relationship, the wiser your financial decisions become.

Too often, adult discourse around children and money treats work in purely transactional terms. The question is framed as: "Should I pay my child for chores?" This is the wrong starting point. A better question is: *What are we trying to teach about the nature of effort, contribution, and reward?* In some households, children receive payment for helping with the washing up; in others, chores are simply expected as part of family life. Neither model is inherently superior. What matters is the *narrative logic* behind the system. When children understand *why* certain tasks are expected and *why* others are compensated, they can make sense of their role in both family life and the broader economic world. Ambiguity breeds confusion. Clarity breeds agency.

There is a philosophical tension here worth unpacking. On one side is the argument that linking chores to payment undermines intrinsic motivation. If children are paid to make their beds, will they ever do so out of respect, routine, or a sense of shared responsibility? On the other side is the pragmatic view: if the real world pays people for work, why shouldn't children start learning that system early? Both views contain truths. The challenge for parents is not to pick one side, but to *integrate* both perspectives into a coherent practice. Children can be expected to contribute to family upkeep—without pay—as part of their communal responsibility. And they can also be given opportunities to earn by taking on tasks that go above and beyond. When this distinction is made explicit, it teaches that *not all work is transactional*, and that *some work is a contribution to something larger than oneself*. That is not just a moral lesson. It's a lesson in how value systems function—an essential skill in both personal finance and civic life.

In this context, household tasks become laboratories for financial and emotional development. A child who vacuums the living room every Saturday for a month, receives £5, and later debates whether to spend it on a snack or save for a toy, is engaging in complex internal reasoning. They are learning cost-benefit analysis, delayed gratification, self-regulation, and projection. If a parent narrates this back to them—"You chose to wait and now you have enough for something more meaningful"—the child not only feels seen, they also begin to develop *meta-cognition*: the ability to think about their own thinking. This skill—widely linked in developmental psychology to academic and life success—is rarely associated with money.

But it should be. Money management is a fundamentally metacognitive activity. We don't just spend—we *reflect* on spending. We forecast, prioritise, regret, revise. All of these processes are cognitive muscles. Earning strengthens them by giving the brain something real to work with.

This emotional dimension of earning is too often overlooked. When a child earns their own money—through labour that requires effort, repetition, or public accountability—the money feels different. It carries *emotional equity*. A child who weeds a neighbour's garden for two hours and earns £10 will often think harder about spending that money than one who receives it in a birthday card. Not because one source is morally superior, but because the *investment of self* alters the psychological frame. Money that comes through effort is felt more deeply. And that depth of feeling becomes a buffer against impulsivity, entitlement, and disengagement.

Real-world examples illustrate this principle powerfully. Consider a 10-year-old who starts walking neighbourhood dogs after school. At first, the motivation may be novelty or peer imitation. But over time, patterns emerge. They must negotiate schedules, show up consistently, manage expectations, and sometimes deal with disappointment—such as being underpaid or replaced. Each of these experiences embeds lessons far more durable than any spreadsheet. They learn that work is not always fair, that effort doesn't always correlate perfectly with reward, and that managing relationships is often as important as doing the task well. These are not side effects. They are *the curriculum*. And they build precisely the kind of emotional resilience and cognitive agility that later supports adult financial competence.

Contrast this with a more passive form of income: a weekly allowance given without explanation or condition. While well-intentioned, this model can sometimes teach the wrong lessons. Children may come to see money as an inevitable entitlement, untethered from behaviour or effort. They may spend without reflection, or come to believe that financial flow is controlled entirely by external forces. This doesn't mean unconditional allowances should be scrapped. But they must be accompanied by *conversation*. "Here's your weekly amount. We trust you to manage it. Let's check in on how it's going." In this way, even passive income becomes a site for reflection and learning.

As children grow older, the lessons must evolve. Teenagers, in particular, need exposure to environments where effort is visible, evaluated, and sometimes *unrewarded*. Part-time jobs, internships, volunteering—these are all arenas where the abstract lessons of early childhood gain complexity and consequence. A teenager who serves customers in a café, cleans up after closing, and receives a payslip with deductions for tax begins to understand that money is never just money—it is time, tax, tension, and sometimes tedium. These insights are not glamorous. But they are *grounding*. And they prepare young people for the psychological reality of adult financial life far more effectively than lectures or budgeting apps.

The deeper philosophical insight here is that *earning builds identity*. Children who experience earning—not just receiving—begin to see themselves as capable contributors. This shift in self-perception is subtle but profound. They become more confident in their ability to navigate complexity, more resilient in the face of delay, and more discerning about value. These traits are not just financially useful. They are *life skills*. And they begin with something as mundane as drying dishes or mowing grass.

In an age where children are increasingly bombarded with messages about wealth without work—viral fame, online monetisation, lucky breaks—it is more important than ever to anchor their understanding of money in *effort*. Not as punishment, but as perspective. Not as toil, but as training. When children learn that their actions create outcomes, that their effort produces options, and that their work carries meaning beyond the wage, they develop a financial compass that no economic fluctuation can dislodge. They begin to ask better questions. They begin to make wiser choices. And they begin to understand that money is never just what you *get*—it's also what you *give* of yourself to earn it. That understanding is the true value of work. And it lasts far longer than the money itself.

### Allowances: Earned, Gifted, or Hybrid?

How a family handles allowances is rarely just a logistical matter. It is a living expression of values, expectations, and worldviews—one that children absorb long before they can articulate its deeper logic. Whether a parent insists that every pound be earned, gifts money unconditionally, or blends the two approaches, they are doing more than managing a child's spending power. They are shaping a child's understanding of effort, entitlement, fairness, and autonomy. In other words, an allowance is never just money. It is a message. And that message—whether intentional or not—sets the tone for how young people will relate to money long after the pocket money stops.

At the centre of the allowance debate are three dominant models: the *earned allowance,* the *gifted allowance,* and the *hybrid* approach. Each is grounded in a different set of assumptions about what children need to learn and how they best learn it. But none is neutral. Every model signals something—about work, value, power, and responsibility—and children are astute readers of these signals. They notice when a system is consistent or arbitrary, when rewards are tied to contribution or withheld without explanation. And over time, they internalise not just the mechanics of the system, but its philosophy.

The *earned allowance* model ties money to chores, tasks, or measurable output. Children are paid for vacuuming, doing the dishes, mowing the lawn, or completing a set list of duties. The core premise here is behavioural: if you want to teach children that money is earned, not given, then they must have to work for it. Proponents argue this builds discipline, mirrors the real-world relationship between effort and reward, and helps children link work with value. On a practical level, it provides an immediate feedback loop—effort in, money out—which can be highly motivating, especially for younger children just beginning to understand the concept of earning.

However, the earned model comes with philosophical risks if not handled carefully. It can encourage transactional thinking: "What's in it for me?" becomes the default lens through which children assess tasks. Basic family contributions may be viewed as optional if they don't carry a monetary incentive. Parents often find themselves in a bind when children refuse to complete unpaid tasks, claiming, "That's not on the chart." And in moments of stress or negotiation, allowances can become a form of leverage or control, diluting the spirit of shared responsibility and relational trust. The child may come to believe that all effort should carry a price tag—a perspective that, if unchallenged, can lead to fragile intrinsic motivation and a diminished capacity for unremunerated contribution later in life.

The opposite approach is the *gifted allowance*—a fixed amount given regularly without direct ties to behaviour or task completion. This model assumes that children benefit most from having predictable access to money to manage, spend, save, and learn from. The rationale here is not about teaching the value of work per se, but about giving children autonomy and responsibility over a fixed financial domain. The idea is that the learning happens *after* the money is received: in the choices made, the consequences felt, and the conversations that follow. A child receives £5 a week not as a reward for obedience, but as a tool for practice. It's the financial equivalent of giving a child their own book to mark up—something to own, reflect on, and experiment with.

This approach aligns well with research in developmental psychology that emphasises the importance of *autonomy-supportive environments*. When children are trusted with responsibility, they often rise to it. Regular, unconditional allowances can foster budgeting skills, delay of gratification, and self-regulation, especially when paired with open-ended dialogue: "How did you decide to spend your money this week?" or "What are you saving for next month?" Importantly, the gifted model decouples money from obedience, reducing the risk of power struggles and reward-based manipulation.

But it too has limitations. Without accompanying structure or modelling, some children may come to view the allowance as a guaranteed entitlement, disconnected from effort, contribution, or the family's broader financial reality. Parents who gift allowances without discussion risk reinforcing passive consumption habits—especially if the child is never asked to reflect on their spending or to connect financial behaviour to underlying values. In families where money is tight or unevenly distributed among siblings of different ages, the gifted model can also lead to resentment if it's perceived as arbitrary or unfair.

The *hybrid model* attempts to bridge these gaps by combining elements of both approaches. Typically, a baseline allowance is provided as a tool for money management, while additional earnings can be made through extra tasks, projects, or responsibilities. This structure allows for both predictability and variability, encouraging a dual understanding: that some forms of money come through stewardship, others through initiative. A child might receive £5 per week to manage independently, but have the option to earn another £2 by washing the car or helping with a sibling's homework.

Done well, this model teaches layered lessons. It respects children's need for autonomy while still reinforcing the link between effort and reward. It models the adult world more accurately—where salaries often cover the basics, and bonuses, commissions, or entrepreneurial income reward initiative and extra labour. It avoids the trap of monetising every household task, while still recognising that paid opportunities can be motivating and instructive. It also creates natural openings for reflection: "You chose not to take the extra job this week—how did that affect your weekend spending?" or "Was the extra work worth the reward?"

Still, the hybrid model requires the most ongoing maintenance. It demands parental clarity, consistency, and intentional communication. Without clear guidelines, it can become confusing—children may not know which tasks are paid, when payments will happen, or what counts as "extra." Moreover, if incentives are inconsistently applied or too easily negotiated, the model can drift into a manipulative space, where children attempt to monetise every act of help and parents resort to money as a bargaining chip.

Across all three models, what ultimately matters most is not the *system*, but the *signals*. Children don't just learn from how much they receive, or when. They learn from how parents talk about money, how they frame rules, how they respond to mistakes, and whether they themselves model the behaviours they want to instil. If allowances are given begrudgingly, used punitively, or withheld unpredictably, the lesson becomes one of stress, control, or arbitrariness. If, on the other hand, allowances are integrated into a broader ethos of transparency, fairness, and shared reflection, they can become powerful vehicles for learning—not just about money, but about trust, maturity, and family culture.

This raises a final point: *allowances teach what we choose to prioritise*. A system that rewards effort teaches one kind of lesson. A system that nurtures autonomy teaches another. A system that acknowledges both teaches both—but only if it does so consciously. Allowances are not morally neutral tools. They shape the contours of a child's relationship to money, effort, power, and accountability. To design them well is to engage in the quiet work of culture-making, shaping not just how children spend, but *how they think*. That is the true currency in play—and one whose value will compound far beyond the childhood years.

## Work Without a Paycheck

A child clears the dinner table without being asked. A teenager helps a younger sibling with homework. A family dog is walked daily, not for payment, but because someone needs to do it. These acts are easily overlooked in the ledger of monetary reward, yet they play an essential role in shaping a young person's understanding of responsibility, contribution, and ethical citizenship. In a cultural climate where so much attention is given to monetisation—where children are encouraged to "hustle," to "monetise their passions," to turn every skill into a side business—it is more important than ever to articulate the enduring value of *non-monetised effort*. Not all work should be paid. Some of the most formative labour children engage in should remain outside the realm of commerce. This is not just a philosophical stance—it is a developmental necessity.

The challenge, of course, is that modern parenting often sits at the uneasy intersection of two opposing imperatives. On the one hand, there is the desire to prepare children for the financial realities of the world: that money is earned, that work has value, that effort should be rewarded. On the other hand, there is the equally vital aim of cultivating empathy, cooperation, and intrinsic motivation—none of which thrive when every task is viewed through the lens of compensation. If a child is paid for making their bed or loading the dishwasher, what happens when they are asked to do something without pay? What if they start calculating their worth solely by their income potential? What happens when a sibling needs help but there's no financial incentive to provide it?

This is where the concept of *work without a paycheck* enters with quiet urgency. It is the idea that some work carries *relational, communal,* or *character-building* value precisely because it is not monetised. It is work done in service of family, team, or community—work that teaches responsibility not through reward, but through meaning. And while this kind of effort does not contribute directly to a child's bank account, it contributes to something far more significant: their *identity*.

In families where every chore is monetised, children may come to view all domestic contribution as transactional. The implicit message becomes: effort is only valuable if it is remunerated. This undermines the ethic of shared responsibility that sustains family life. When a child tidies a common area, participates in meal prep, or cares for a pet, they are engaging in acts that maintain the ecosystem of daily living. These tasks are not "extra"—they are *essential*. And by performing them without compensation, children learn that being part of a system—be it a family, a classroom, or a society—requires effort that is not always acknowledged with money, but is no less valuable.

The developmental psychologist Edward Deci, one of the founders of self-determination theory, found that extrinsic rewards can sometimes crowd out intrinsic motivation. If a child is paid for reading a book, they may become less likely to read for pleasure. The same applies to household effort. If every act of help is tied to payment, the underlying motive may shift from care to calculation. This is not to romanticise unpaid labour or deny that children should be rewarded for initiative. Rather, it is to argue that *some domains of work must remain untouched by economic exchange if we are to preserve their moral and relational value.*

Consider the example of volunteering. When a teenager gives up a Saturday morning to serve meals at a community centre, they are not just helping others. They are gaining exposure to lives different from their own. They are learning humility, patience, and situational awareness. They are developing a sense of civic duty. These outcomes cannot be priced. Indeed, to monetise them would be to dilute their essence. The point is not that all volunteering is superior to paid work, but that *its value lies in being decoupled from personal financial gain*. It teaches children that worth is not always measured in currency—and that time, presence, and energy can be given generously without being diminished.

Parents can model and reinforce this ethos in subtle but consistent ways. When children help with non-paid tasks, they should be acknowledged—not with money, but with words, warmth, and respect. "Thank you for doing that without being asked. It helps everyone." This type of affirmation builds *moral memory*—the internal record children keep of their own helpfulness. When repeated, it becomes part of how they see themselves: someone who contributes. Someone reliable. Someone who understands that doing one's part is part of being in relationship with others.

There is also pedagogical value in helping children distinguish between different types of work. Some work is *paid because it is marketable*. Some is *unpaid because it is relational*. And some is *expected because it is responsible*. Parents who make these categories explicit help children locate their efforts within a broader moral economy. For example, "You're not paid to clean up your own room because that's part of looking after your space. But if you offer to clean the garage, which isn't your responsibility, that could be a paid task. And helping Grandma in the garden? That's something we do out of care, not for payment." These distinctions are not always easy to enforce, but they are deeply educational.

Critics may argue that in a capitalist world, teaching children to work without pay is naïve or counterproductive. But this conflates two separate functions. Yes, children need to learn how money works. They need to earn, save, budget, and spend. But they also need to learn that not every form of effort is—or should be—monetised. A society in which every action has a price is not one that builds ethical citizens. It builds contractors, not neighbours; consumers, not community members.

This is not to suggest that unpaid work is inherently virtuous or that children should be made to perform endless tasks without support or rest. Exploitation is exploitation, whether within a household or beyond it. The key distinction lies in *consent, context,* and *communication*. When children are invited into non-monetised work with clear rationale and fair expectations, they feel empowered, not exploited. When they see adults engaging in the same kinds of effort—tidying, volunteering, caring—they internalise that contribution is a shared value, not a punishment.

Real-world examples help bring this concept to life. A 12-year-old who regularly helps a younger sibling get ready for school is not simply "doing chores." They are practising empathy, time management, and reliability. A teenager who organises a school recycling programme is developing initiative and leadership. A child who visits an elderly neighbour, brings them books, or simply listens to their stories is not just "helping"—they are learning relational generosity. None of these efforts come with a wage slip. Yet all of them are the kind of work that builds durable character and prepares young people for meaningful adulthood.

Parents can support this growth by creating household cultures where both paid and unpaid contributions are valued—and distinguished. "This is a paid task, because it goes above your regular responsibilities." "This is an unpaid one, because it's part of caring for the people around us." "This is something we all do, because we live here together." When these messages are repeated and embodied, children stop asking, "How much will I get?" and begin asking, "What needs doing?"

That shift—from compensation to contribution—is not just moral. It is *pragmatic.* In every workplace, team, or relationship, there are tasks that go unrewarded but are crucial. Adults who succeed are often those who notice what's needed and step in, not because they are told to, but because they understand the ecosystem they're part of. Cultivating this mindset in childhood—through work without a paycheck—is not about nostalgia. It's about *preparation.*

Ultimately, teaching children to work without pay is not a rejection of economics, but an expansion of it. It invites them to recognise that value comes in many forms: financial, social, emotional, ethical. And that the richest lives are often built not just through earnings, but through effort freely given. Effort that says, "I see what needs to be done—and I'm someone who steps up." That is a lesson no allowance can buy. And once learned, it pays dividends for a lifetime.

## Real-Life Earning Scenarios

If financial literacy is to be internalised rather than merely instructed, children must move from abstract concepts to applied experience. Few avenues achieve this with more effectiveness than real-world earning scenarios—small-scale ventures initiated and operated by young people themselves, often under the thoughtful guidance of parents or mentors. These micro-enterprises not only introduce the mechanics of income generation but bring to life the invisible curriculum of effort, planning, risk, resilience, and self-reflection. The objective is not to manufacture mini-entrepreneurs for social media approval. It is to construct authentic developmental scaffolds where children learn, through practice, what money really represents: not just currency, but consequence.

One of the clearest insights to emerge from case studies across socio-economic contexts is that the most instructive ventures are not necessarily the most profitable. Rather, they are the ones where children are encouraged to own the *entire process*—from ideation to delivery, from failure to adaptation. Take the example of nine-year-old Maya in Sheffield, who during lockdown began baking simple chocolate chip cookies and selling them to neighbours through an old-fashioned flyer slipped into letterboxes. The enterprise was modest—£2 per dozen—but the exercise revealed a matrix of practical lessons: ingredient costing, inventory tracking, time estimation, client interaction, and quality control. When one batch was overbaked and a neighbour expressed disappointment, Maya didn't just apologise—she offered a refund and adjusted her next recipe. Her parents did not step in to shield her. They treated the feedback as an opportunity to reflect on consistency and accountability—principles that transcend business and touch on character.

Contrast this with the story of Jamal, a 14-year-old from Birmingham, who launched a mobile bike repair service after noticing several classmates commuting on poorly maintained bicycles. With minimal startup capital—basic tools bought with birthday money—he began offering tyre checks, brake adjustments, and chain replacements for a flat fee. His father, a mechanic by trade, provided guidance but deliberately refrained from intervening unless asked. Within months, Jamal had built a small customer base and was tracking weekly profits. But more importantly, he encountered the real-world friction of scheduling conflicts, client cancellations, and fluctuating demand. These experiences fostered adaptive thinking and patience. When interviewed later, Jamal didn't mention how much money he had made—he spoke about how he'd learned to stay calm under pressure and how good it felt to be trusted with something tangible.

Such anecdotes are not isolated. They represent a growing movement of parents who recognise that the most effective financial education occurs when *children are given room to try, stumble, recalibrate, and grow*. Not every child will gravitate toward selling goods or services. For some, earning begins within the household—taking on consistent responsibilities that extend beyond assigned chores. Twelve-year-old Aaliyah in Bristol began managing her family's grocery budget for the month as a homeschooling project. Her parents gave her £200 and the task of planning weekly meals, comparing store prices, and ensuring the family did not exceed the total. With a whiteboard calendar and spreadsheet, she tracked expenses, adjusted shopping lists, and negotiated with her younger siblings over snack preferences. It wasn't glamorous. But it was deeply educational. When the month ended with a £4 surplus, she didn't ask to keep it. She suggested rolling it over to the next month "for emergency chocolate." Her parents were struck not by the savings, but by her growing intuition for trade-offs.

Where these scenarios succeed is in their *embeddedness within real life*. They do not isolate money as a "subject" but weave it into the practical rhythms of household or community life. This integration is critical. When children see money as something that flows from their own efforts—rather than from adult benevolence or digital transactions—they develop a more grounded, less magical view of wealth. They begin to ask better questions: "Is this worth the time it takes?" "What happens if I underdeliver?" "How do I set a fair price?" These are not just financial inquiries. They are *ethical* and *relational* questions—the kind that lay the groundwork for thoughtful adulthood.

However, not all ventures succeed. Nor should they. Failure is a feature, not a flaw, of experiential learning. Consider the case of twins Alex and Sofia, aged 11, who attempted to sell handmade bracelets at a local car boot sale. They spent weeks designing, knotting, and packaging their products. But on the day of the event, sales were sparse. Rather than frame the day as a waste, their mother sat down with them afterwards to reflect. What had gone wrong? Were prices too high? Was the location poorly chosen? Was their booth too similar to another? The children re-examined their pricing model, redesigned their display, and pivoted to an online listing with better images. Slowly, sales trickled in. More than the money earned, it was the *post-mortem analysis* that made the difference. They learned that success is iterative, not instantaneous.

What unites these disparate cases is the presence of *adult scaffolding without adult domination.* In every instance, parents served as *facilitators,* not directors. They asked questions, provided access, helped connect dots—but resisted the urge to control outcomes. This balance is vital. A child who feels micromanaged will not internalise ownership. One who is abandoned to figure it out alone may become discouraged. The sweet spot lies in what psychologist Lev Vygotsky termed the "zone of proximal development"—that critical space where the task is just beyond what a child can do alone, but achievable with guided support. Earning scenarios, when properly designed, operate precisely within this space.

Importantly, these projects should not be treated as performance art. When parents feel pressured to turn every child's venture into an Instagrammable success story, the underlying lessons can be lost. The point is not visibility—it is *process.* A garden-minding gig for three neighbours may teach more than a viral lemonade stand. What matters is not the scale of the operation, but the depth of engagement. Children must feel the stakes. They must have something to lose and something to tweak. Otherwise, the project becomes yet another adult-driven simulation.

For children from under-resourced communities, earning opportunities may be harder to access—but this makes them *more* valuable, not less. When guided sensitively, they can become affirming experiences of agency in environments where economic power often feels distant. One 13-year-old from a housing estate in East London began offering digital tutoring to younger kids struggling with their reading. With a basic laptop and parent-supported scheduling, he earned a small income while strengthening his own literacy skills and sense of purpose. The ripple effects extended beyond the wallet: confidence, relational trust, and community connection all increased. He wasn't just earning—he was *becoming*.

These examples affirm a central truth: *earning is about more than income*. It's about the constellation of decisions, reactions, and responsibilities that orbit around the act of generating value. Whether a child sells artwork, dog-walks for neighbours, manages a family budget, or mentors peers, the outcome is not just financial. It is *formational*. Each project becomes a laboratory for autonomy, ethics, and resilience. And when embedded within a framework of adult support and reflective dialogue, these experiences become powerful contributors to a child's financial maturity.

The challenge for parents is not to invent perfect scenarios, but to *notice real ones*. Is there an unmet need in the neighbourhood? A task within the home that could be handed over? A passion that could be translated into a low-stakes service? The goal is not to professionalise childhood, but to activate it—to recognise that children, when trusted and supported, are capable of real contribution. And that when they earn on their own terms, they don't just learn about money. They learn about themselves.

# Chapter 5
# Saving Isn't Natural

Ask a child to choose between one sweet now or two in ten minutes, and chances are they'll seize the immediate treat—often before you've even finished speaking. This is not a lapse in character or a failure of parenting. It is biology in motion, psychology honed by evolution: human brains are wired to favour the immediate. In childhood, this impulse is amplified, and in our consumer-saturated world, it is constantly reinforced. Saving, then, is not intuitive. It is learned. More than that, it is felt—not as deprivation, but as meaningful choice.

Delayed gratification—the core of saving—is not a fixed trait but a muscle: pliable, responsive, and highly sensitive to context. Children are not born with the ability to defer desire; they are socialised into it. The classic "marshmallow test" was long misunderstood as a measure of innate self-control. Subsequent research revealed the real predictor: trust. Children who believed the adult would return with a promised second treat were far likelier to wait. Saving, then, is less about sheer willpower and more about environmental consistency. Children save when they trust the system, when the cues around them reinforce the connection between effort and reward, and when the promise of a future outcome is tangible and emotionally credible.

We must remember that children inhabit the present overwhelmingly. Cognitive development moves slowly from concrete to abstract, from immediate to deferred. Expecting an eight-year-old to save for something six months away—without scaffolding—is not a lesson in discipline; it is an invitation to frustration. Saving gains meaning when it is tangible. Jars, charts, stickers, and goal boards transform abstract future rewards into something a child can see, touch, and track. A transparent jar half-filled with coins is not just storage—it signals movement, agency, and progress. These simple cues, often dismissed as trivial, are neurologically aligned with how young brains perceive momentum. They bridge desire and patience.

Parents often overestimate the power of verbal explanation while underestimating environmental design. Money that vanishes into a digital wallet without any physical presence is less likely to be felt, less likely to be owned. Digital tools have their place, but they must complement, not replace, tangible experience. Early savings are cognitive rehearsals: practice in projecting forward, anticipating outcomes, and exercising control. Each small success reinforces neural pathways for foresight, emotional regulation, and impulse management.

Inevitably, children will stumble. They will spend impulsively, abandon goals, or tap into savings for fleeting desires. Here lies one of the most difficult parental disciplines: resisting the rescue instinct. Shielding a child from the natural consequences of spending may ease immediate discomfort, but it undermines the lesson. Saving becomes real only when non-saving carries weight. That disappointment—met with empathy rather than shame—teaches more than any lecture. The parent's role is to narrate and reflect: "That's frustrating—you were looking forward to that game. What might you do differently next time?"

Missteps must be normalised as part of the learning curve, not signs of failure. No child rides a bicycle without tumbles; no child learns fiscal foresight without occasional miscalculations. Reflection and recalibration are key: "What was the plan?" "What changed?" "Was the trade-off worth it?" These questions foster meta-cognition and establish a personal feedback loop—far more potent than correction alone.

Different goals demand different approaches. Short-term objectives—snacks, toys, birthday gifts—fit into a child's immediate horizon. Long-term aspirations—a concert, a high-value item—require structured scaffolding. Parents shift from observer to coach: breaking goals into increments, celebrating partial progress, and visualising milestones. This scaffolding is not indulgence; it recognises that the developing brain requires reinforcement to navigate deferred outcomes.

Consider Elias, ten, who wanted a mountain bike costing nearly £300—far beyond his weekly allowance. His parents did not dismiss his ambition. Together, they devised a plan: £5 weekly from allowance, seasonal jobs like dog walking, and matched contributions for every £20 saved. Nine months of small efforts, minor setbacks, and moments of temptation later, Elias had saved £160. Grandparents added the final £20. When he finally rode the bike, it was not merely ownership—it was earned pride, a deep satisfaction unmatched by a gift handed over.

At its essence, saving is not just financial; it is psychological: a belief that the future matters, that patience holds purpose, and that one can act with agency. These beliefs are cultivated, not innate. They flourish in environments where progress is visible, conversations are consistent, and mistakes carry material, not shameful, consequences. In such homes, saving becomes a rhythm rather than a rule.

This chapter examines why saving is difficult, the tools that make it achievable, and the developmental frameworks that allow children to succeed on their own terms. It differentiates between mechanical saving—tossing coins into a jar—and motivated saving, where children internalise the satisfaction of deferred reward. It also addresses subtle ways parents unintentionally undermine lessons: overcorrecting, overfunding, overprotecting.

Saving is not natural. That is precisely why teaching it is transformative. When a child learns to pause, plan, and prioritise, they are not merely managing money—they are developing foresight, patience, and the ability to construct a future. That, ultimately, is stewardship. And it begins with a single coin, deliberately set aside.

## The Psychology of Delayed Gratification

A child sits alone in a room with a marshmallow placed in front of them. They're told they can eat it now, or wait fifteen minutes and receive a second one. This deceptively simple setup, popularised by the Stanford "marshmallow test" of the 1970s, became one of the most widely cited experiments in behavioural psychology. For years, it was assumed that the ability to wait signalled superior self-control and predicted better life outcomes. Children who resisted the marshmallow, researchers claimed, were more likely to have higher SAT scores, healthier relationships, and greater professional success decades later. The story was compelling—but, as is often the case, the truth turned out to be more nuanced.

Subsequent studies revealed that the child's decision to wait was not merely a reflection of internal willpower. It was deeply influenced by trust. If the child believed the adult would follow through with the promise of a second marshmallow, they were far more likely to wait. In other words, *delayed gratification isn't just about patience—it's about belief in a reliable future.* This reframing has profound implications for how we teach children about saving, goal-setting, and long-term thinking. Because it suggests that before we can ask a child to delay gratification, we must first create an environment where delay is worth it.

Children, especially in early developmental stages, are neurologically tuned to the present moment. Their prefrontal cortex—the part of the brain responsible for planning, impulse control, and future-oriented thinking—is still under construction well into adolescence. What adults interpret as short-sightedness or impulsivity is often just developmental reality. The child who spends their pocket money ten minutes after receiving it isn't failing a test of discipline. They're operating from a brain that places a premium on immediacy and struggle to simulate long-term consequences. Expecting them to override this wiring without support is both unrealistic and unfair.

Yet delayed gratification is teachable—not as a moral virtue, but as a *cognitive skill set*. Neuroscience offers us promising insights. One of the most effective ways to build this capacity is through the use of *temporal framing*—helping children visualise the future not as a vague abstraction but as a specific, tangible experience. A child saving for a toy in six weeks is more likely to stay committed if they can picture that toy, chart their progress, and feel a sense of agency over the outcome. Concrete visual cues—jars filling with coins, countdown calendars, colour-coded charts—convert time into touchable progress. They activate the reward centres of the brain, bridging the motivational gap between now and later.

Equally important is the concept of *choice architecture*. When children are offered binary options—spend now or save for later—they often opt for immediacy. But when the options are scaffolded—spend some now, save some for next week, reserve a little for a larger goal—behaviour shifts. The introduction of structured flexibility transforms saving from a deprivation narrative into a self-authored decision. The child becomes not a passive follower of rules but an active planner of priorities.

Parents play a pivotal role in this process—not just as enforcers of discipline but as *modellers of delay*. A child who sees a parent postpone a purchase, budget over months for a holiday, or talk aloud about financial trade-offs is more likely to internalise the mechanics of delayed gratification. These micro-moments—how we respond to impulse, how we talk about waiting, how we narrate our decisions—form the implicit curriculum of self-control. Children are constantly decoding adult behaviour, not just for what is said, but for what is *valued*.

The challenge for parents is not to suppress a child's desire for immediacy, but to *channel* it. This means validating the emotional pull of the "now" while offering structures that make "later" feel real and achievable. For instance, instead of shaming a child for wanting to spend their allowance immediately, a parent might say: "It's exciting to have money—what are some things you could do with it this week, and what might you want to save for next month?" The tone shifts from control to collaboration. The child is not being told to wait—they are being *invited* to consider the future on their own terms.

Yet not all children respond in the same way. Socioeconomic context, temperament, and past experiences all play a role. A child raised in an environment where resources are unpredictable may develop a rational preference for immediate consumption. For them, delay may feel risky rather than prudent. In such cases, simply instructing them to save is unlikely to succeed. What's needed first is *predictability*: consistent routines, trustworthy systems, and adult follow-through. Once these are in place, the child can begin to see the value in waiting—not as a gamble, but as a strategy.

Philosophically, delayed gratification is a paradox. It requires us to resist something certain (pleasure now) for something uncertain (a larger reward later). To make this leap, the brain needs evidence that the future will deliver.

For children, this evidence is accumulated experientially. A child who saves for three weeks and successfully buys a coveted item now has a reference point—a felt sense that delay can work. The next time they're faced with a choice, the memory of that success provides motivational scaffolding. It becomes a story they can tell themselves: "I've done this before. I can do it again."

This is why one-off lectures or punitive restrictions rarely work. Telling a child "you should know better" after a spending impulse teaches little. Instead, *debriefing after the fact*—gently revisiting the moment, exploring what drove the decision, and considering what might be done differently next time—fosters introspection. It activates the same neural circuits involved in future planning and impulse regulation. The goal is not perfection but *progress*. Each decision becomes data for better decisions ahead.

One of the more powerful tools in cultivating delayed gratification is *co-saving*. When a parent or mentor agrees to match a child's savings, they transform delay into a relational act. The child is no longer waiting alone—they are collaborating. The promise of matching also adds incentive while modelling adult investment in long-term goals. The message isn't just "Save your money." It's "I believe in your goal—and I'm willing to back it."

Even setbacks offer rich teaching moments. When a child dips into savings impulsively and feels regret, the adult's response sets the tone. If the parent shames or rescues, the learning is lost. But if the parent invites reflection—"What happened there? Do you want to adjust your plan?"—the child begins to build a framework for *financial resilience*. Over time, these cycles of choice, error, and adjustment become internalised. They become less reactive and more deliberative. They begin to think not just about what they want, but *when* they want it—and *why*.

Ultimately, delayed gratification is not about suppressing desire. It's about *reframing desire across time*. When children begin to grasp that not all joy needs to be immediate—and that some of the most meaningful rewards are the ones we build toward—they step into a deeper form of autonomy. One that is not about rigid self-denial, but about strategic self-governance. It's a mindset that extends beyond money: into relationships, academics, health, and purpose. Because a child who can wait is not simply controlling a whim—they are shaping a life. And that is a skill worth building—day by day, coin by coin, choice by choice.

### The Magic of Visual Progress

A child places a coin into a clear jar and watches it clink to the bottom, landing atop a small but growing stack. The sound is satisfying, the accumulation visible, the purpose tangible. Without needing to explain inflation, compound interest, or the psychology of long-term planning, the child has engaged in a rudimentary form of savings that is not only intuitive but *motivating*. What the jar achieves—by virtue of being transparent, physical, and cumulative—is something that many sophisticated financial apps fail to deliver: *emotional engagement with progress*.

Humans, children especially, are visual creatures. The brain responds more strongly to what it can see, especially when that visual input signals growth or goal proximity. This has roots in our evolutionary wiring; detecting patterns and changes in our physical environment helped us survive. Today, this neural preference means that seeing progress triggers dopamine, the brain's reward chemical, creating a feedback loop of effort and reward. But while adults can often summon internal images of future rewards to sustain motivation, children need more than imagination—they need external prompts. *Visual tools translate abstract concepts into concrete experiences,* allowing children to experience savings not as a void or a delay, but as momentum.

This is precisely why physical tools—jars, thermometers, wall charts, sticker maps—remain remarkably effective, even in a digital economy. A child saving for a scooter who colours in a section of a savings tracker with each £5 deposit is not just marking time—they are *seeing themselves move.* This visual reinforcement creates a narrative of competence and control. Without it, savings can feel like a black hole: money disappears and nothing changes. With it, each small step becomes visible proof that the future is taking shape.

One particularly resonant example comes from a family in Edinburgh who developed a three-jar system for their two primary-aged children: one for "spend," one for "save," and one for "give." Each jar was clearly labelled, visually distinct, and physically handled by the children. Weekly pocket money was split among them according to pre-discussed proportions. The "save" jar, crucially, had a photograph taped behind the glass—a picture of the item each child was working toward. The visual cue anchored the savings goal in the child's mind, while the growing pile of coins made the journey feel real. Over time, the children began initiating conversations about adjusting the proportions, eager to reach their goals faster. The parents had not mandated this shift. It emerged organically, a by-product of *ownership through visibility*.

The cognitive load of saving is often underestimated by adults. For a child, the idea of giving something up now for a gain they cannot yet feel, touch, or enjoy is developmentally unnatural. Visual tools lighten that cognitive burden. They serve as scaffolding for memory, impulse control, and foresight. In effect, they say: *Look, this is working. Keep going.* This affirmation is especially crucial in the early stages of a savings goal, when the gap between desire and attainment feels widest. Just as a runner needs milestones to stay motivated in the first kilometre, a young saver needs proof that their effort is accumulating—even if the endpoint is still distant.

Digital platforms have begun to replicate these mechanisms with increasing sophistication: progress bars, coin animations, goal badges. But while these tools can be effective, they rely heavily on abstraction. A digital "coin" moved into a savings category may not carry the same visceral impact as a physical coin moved by a child's own hand. This is not a rejection of technology—rather, it is a call to *sequence it thoughtfully*. Younger children, especially those under ten, benefit from beginning with tactile systems that engage their senses and spatial reasoning. As they mature and develop greater cognitive flexibility, digital tools can then reinforce these habits with more nuanced metrics.

Not all visual systems are equally effective. The key is *personalisation and narrative*. A savings chart that a child co-designs—perhaps with markers, stickers, or drawings—is far more powerful than a generic printout. The process of making the tracker becomes an act of intention-setting. It invests the child in the goal, not just the method. Similarly, visual cues that are updated collaboratively—discussing progress at dinner, celebrating milestones with simple acknowledgements—deepen the motivational loop. What begins as a mechanical act becomes a story the child tells themselves: "I am someone who sets goals and achieves them."

There's also an emotional dimension to visual progress that often goes unspoken. For children who struggle with anxiety, perfectionism, or attention challenges, savings goals can feel overwhelming. A large goal with no markers can induce paralysis or avoidance. Visual systems break that paralysis. They chunk the goal into manageable increments and offer low-stakes wins along the way. Each step validated becomes a confidence builder. Importantly, these systems should be calibrated to the child's temperament. For a highly visual child, a colour-coded thermometer might be ideal. For a kinesthetic learner, physical tokens or manipulatives could work better. For a child with dyslexia or processing challenges, images might trump text. *The method should meet the child, not the other way around.*

Visualisation also supports the emotional intelligence of saving. As children watch their progress unfold, they begin to associate effort with outcome—not as a theoretical lesson, but as a lived experience. This reinforces agency, delayed gratification, and patience. It also fosters pride—a healthy pride born not of the thing purchased, but of the *process pursued*. When the goal is finally achieved, the memory of each marker—the jars filled, the chart completed, the stickers earned—creates a narrative thread that embeds the lesson far more deeply than a one-off reward ever could.

Of course, not every goal will be reached. Children may lose interest, spend prematurely, or shift their priorities. Visual tools serve here, too—not as evidence of failure, but as material for reflection. "What changed?" "Was the goal too big?" "Did something else become more important?" These are powerful developmental questions. They teach flexibility, introspection, and the art of re-setting. Saving, after all, is not just about reaching the target. It's about the evolution of thinking along the way.

In family systems, visual savings tools also offer a bridge between generations. When parents share their own progress charts—tracking a family holiday fund, a home improvement budget, or a debt payoff—they model not just transparency, but the practice of *collective visibility*. Children learn that adults, too, are working toward things. They learn that money is not a mystery, but a sequence of choices made visible over time.

The deeper truth is this: we move more confidently toward what we can see. A child who sees progress is a child who persists. A child who sees their effort accumulate is more likely to believe that their choices matter. And a child who internalises that belief carries it into every future decision, financial or otherwise. The jar, the chart, the coloured-in line—these are not gimmicks. They are anchors. They remind the child: *I'm getting closer*. And in a world that increasingly trades in distraction and instant gratification, such reminders are nothing short of magic.

## Short-Term vs. Long-Term Savings Goals

For a child holding their weekly allowance, the difference between saving for next Friday's trip to the toy shop and next summer's holiday activity is more than just a matter of time—it's a matter of cognitive reach. Adults often assume that children can generalise from small, immediate savings goals to longer-term ones with ease. In reality, these two types of goals sit on very different developmental planes. Understanding this difference—and teaching children how to navigate both—is essential for building a durable relationship with money. *Not all saving is created equal, and neither are all savers*. What we call "saving" may look similar across contexts, but the underlying mechanics, emotional drivers, and behavioural demands vary significantly depending on the time horizon.

Short-term savings goals align naturally with a child's psychological architecture. Young minds operate largely in the concrete and immediate. The gratification of buying a new book, football card pack, or small toy within the span of a few days or weeks provides enough proximity to be emotionally motivating and cognitively comprehensible. The cause-and-effect sequence is tight: I do X today, and I get Y soon. These goals are foundational because they offer children early success in delayed gratification—proof that saving works. Each short-term goal achieved creates a reinforcing loop: *saving results in reward; reward validates the saving behaviour.*

However, short-term goals alone do not cultivate the fuller spectrum of financial reasoning. A child who can save for a £10 toy over three weeks may not yet possess the patience or abstraction needed to save for a £200 instrument over nine months. Long-term goals are inherently more complex, both emotionally and strategically. They require the child to hold a vision that doesn't immediately offer sensory or social feedback. There's no quick dopamine hit, no peer validation in the schoolyard. The payoff lives in the far distance—an unfamiliar territory for a mind still learning to measure time in seasons rather than minutes.

This is where the adult role becomes essential. A parent who scaffolds a child's long-term goal—helping break it down into sub-goals, providing visual representations of progress, and celebrating milestones—does more than support a saving effort. They provide a bridge between the child's present and their imagined future. Without that bridge, long-term goals often collapse under the weight of abstraction. The child loses motivation not because they're lazy or impulsive, but because the goal has drifted out of their cognitive reach.

A practical example clarifies this divide. Consider two siblings: eight-year-old Ava and thirteen-year-old Leo. Ava wants to save £15 for a glitter slime kit. Her savings plan involves putting away £3 a week for five weeks. Each week, she colours in a square on her savings chart and receives a small sticker from her parents. Leo, by contrast, has set his sights on a £300 camera. He receives £10 weekly, but only if he completes certain household tasks. To stay on track, he needs to save consistently for six months. Without intervention, Leo might lose steam by week three. But with structured encouragement—monthly progress reviews, occasional matching contributions from relatives, and a printed image of the camera on his wall—the goal remains salient. *He begins to internalise the mechanics of deferred success*.

What Ava and Leo reveal is that *time horizon shapes the motivational strategy*. Short-term goals thrive on visibility and immediacy; long-term goals thrive on planning and pacing. Parents should therefore resist the temptation to treat all savings as the same lesson in patience. They should instead treat them as two distinct educational tracks—each building different muscles of self-regulation, foresight, and value alignment.

Another key variable is *emotional consistency*. Short-term savings often tie closely to impulse satisfaction—"I want this, and I'll wait a bit to get it." Long-term savings require the cultivation of a different mindset: goal fidelity. This is the ability to stay emotionally attached to a future objective even when distractions or temptations arise. It mirrors the discipline needed in adulthood for saving toward a house deposit, a degree, or a major purchase. Children don't come equipped with this skill—it must be modelled, coached, and rewarded. And perhaps most importantly, it must be *felt*. If saving for the long-term always feels like sacrifice without recognition, it will be abandoned. That's why celebrating intermediate progress—not just the final outcome—is crucial.

There's a philosophical tension here worth exploring: some argue that we should not ask children to save for long-term goals at all, suggesting that doing so imposes adult anxieties onto childhood. But this perspective underestimates children's capacity for vision and overestimates the fragility of their motivation. The key is not to avoid long-term goals, but to make them *developmentally appropriate*. A five-year-old saving for a school trip in six months will need vastly more hands-on support than a fifteen-year-old saving for a summer course. The lesson is the same—how to sustain effort over time—but the method must flex with maturity.

Importantly, the distinction between short-term and long-term savings also teaches a secondary but equally vital lesson: *prioritisation*. Children learn that not all desires carry the same weight. They begin to ask themselves not just "Do I want this?" but "Do I want this more than that?" This act of weighing, choosing, and sequencing builds critical thinking. It prepares them to make trade-offs later in life—not only between material goods, but between time, attention, and commitments.

Effective systems often divide savings physically or visually. Some families introduce dual jars or parallel digital categories: one marked "Soon," the other "Later." The language matters. "Soon" offers a sense of reward without the pressure of instant consumption; "Later" invites patience without suggesting indefinite delay. For older children, digital banking tools with partitioned goals or "buckets" can offer the same logic with more autonomy. The aim is to embed *structure within freedom*—a space where children can exercise agency, but with boundaries that guide rather than constrain.

This dual-goal framework also prepares children for the adult reality of *parallel financial objectives*. Adults do not save for just one thing at a time. They manage competing timelines: next month's rent, next year's holiday, long-term retirement. Teaching children early how to distinguish between near-term and far-term goals lays the groundwork for managing complex financial ecosystems later in life. It nurtures adaptability—the ability to shift focus without losing direction.

One final insight: the emotional reward of long-term saving, when achieved, is qualitatively different from that of short-term gratification. It is deeper, more sustaining. A child who buys a toy after three weeks feels joy. A child who purchases a concert ticket, a bicycle, or a first tablet after six months feels *pride*. And that pride, once felt, becomes a lodestar. It tells the child: *I can do hard things. I can delay today for something better tomorrow.* That belief—seeded in jars, tracked on charts, whispered in encouragement—shapes not just a child's financial behaviour, but their sense of self.

Teaching children to save is not about pushing them toward austerity. It's about showing them that money is not just a currency for spending—it's a language for planning. And when that language includes both short-term fluency and long-term vision, children begin to speak with clarity, purpose, and confidence. The future, once distant and vague, becomes theirs to design.

### When to Let Them Fail

Few instincts run deeper in parenthood than the urge to protect. It begins with physical safety—guarding against falls, burns, or stranger danger—and matures into emotional sheltering: shielding children from embarrassment, rejection, or disappointment. But as children grow, a subtler temptation arises—the desire to insulate them from the consequences of their own poor decisions, especially when it comes to money. A child wastes an allowance on something flimsy or impulsive, only to be disappointed the next day. A parent, watching the fallout, feels the tug to step in—to replace the item, offer more funds, or frame the loss as unfair rather than instructive. But these moments, however uncomfortable, are among the most potent teachers a child will ever encounter. *Failure, when allowed to run its course, can fertilise wisdom in ways success never could.*

Understanding when to let children fail financially—and how to do so responsibly—requires a shift in mindset. It asks parents to reframe their role not as rescuers, but as facilitators of resilience. It demands that we respect our children enough to let reality be their tutor, while remaining emotionally present and available as they process the lesson. Crucially, it calls for discernment: not all financial stumbles are created equal, and the art lies in distinguishing a productive misstep from a harmful derailment.

The first step is recognising that *natural consequences are not punishments*. They are the feedback loops through which all human beings—children and adults alike—learn to calibrate action with outcome. A seven-year-old who spends her entire allowance on sweets and has nothing left for the toy she was eyeing is not being punished by the system. She is being informed by it. That emptiness she feels is a cognitive moment of friction—an internal pause where reflection can enter. If the adult responds with "I told you so" or "I'll buy it for you this time," the lesson evaporates. In the first case, the child feels shamed. In the second, the consequence is neutralised. Either way, the learning is lost.

By contrast, when a parent responds with calm empathy—"That's disappointing. What do you think you'll do differently next time?"—they offer both validation and agency. They don't rush to fix, but neither do they abandon. *They hold space for discomfort, and in doing so, create the conditions for growth.*

Many parents fear that failure will discourage their children—that it will damage their confidence or diminish their motivation. But research in developmental psychology suggests the opposite: *well-managed failure is one of the most powerful drivers of competence*. When children experience the sting of a poor choice and then correct course, they don't become discouraged. They become empowered. They begin to trust themselves as learners, not just recipients of adult instruction.

The challenge, of course, is knowing where to draw the line. Not every financial error should be left to play out unmitigated. A five-year-old accidentally donating all his money to a YouTube scam deserves intervention. A teenager emptying a savings account on status symbols may need a conversation about boundaries and values. The parent's task is not to adopt a rigid "sink or swim" philosophy, but to *discern which failures are developmentally useful and which are developmentally harmful.*

A helpful test is to ask: *Is this a reversible mistake?* A small overspend, a lost receipt, or a regretful impulse purchase—these are the training wheels of adult decision-making. They're recoverable and rich with insight. But if the failure would leave the child financially paralysed, publicly shamed, or emotionally overwhelmed, adult guardrails are appropriate. The aim is not to teach through trauma, but through manageable tension.

This is especially relevant for adolescents, who sit at the intersection of two contradictory forces: surging autonomy and incomplete self-regulation. Teenagers crave independence. They want to make decisions on their own terms. But their prefrontal cortex—the brain's seat of planning and impulse control—is still under construction. This neurological mismatch means they will make flawed choices. The question is not how to prevent all of them, but how to structure space for those choices to *matter* without being catastrophic.

One strategy is to assign them "zones of ownership"—contexts in which they control spending and bear the consequences. For instance, a 14-year-old given a quarterly clothing budget learns to plan, prioritise, and reconsider. If they blow it all on one pair of shoes, they live with that choice. A parent might notice the discomfort, acknowledge it, but stop short of rectifying it. "It's not what I would've chosen, but I'm curious—what's your takeaway?" That approach respects the teen's agency while quietly nudging reflective thinking.

Parents can also model how failure functions in adult life. Sharing stories of financial missteps—missed deadlines, ill-considered purchases, investment regrets—normalises the reality that money mastery is iterative, not innate. It reassures children that learning through error is not a mark of inadequacy, but a feature of financial maturity. Done well, these disclosures don't glorify failure, but they humanise it. They communicate: *You are not alone. You are not broken. You are building something.*

An often-overlooked aspect of allowing failure is the emotional discomfort it stirs in adults. When a child suffers the consequences of their spending, the parent often feels helpless or guilty. "Was I too harsh?" "Should I have stepped in?" "Are they resenting me now?" These are legitimate fears—but they often reflect our own discomfort with uncertainty more than the child's inability to cope. In many cases, children move on from small financial setbacks far faster than their parents do. What they remember is not just the mistake, but how it was held. *A parent's calm containment teaches more than their correction ever could.*

Still, guidance matters. Allowing a child to fail doesn't mean offering no feedback. It means *delaying the feedback until the child is open to it*. Often, the best teaching moment is not in the heat of the mistake but in its aftermath. "What did you notice?" "What would you change next time?" "How did it feel, and how do you want it to feel next time?" These are scaffolding questions—not lectures, but invitations to growth. They teach reflection, pattern recognition, and future planning. Over time, they become internalised. The child starts asking them on their own.

A final caution: if a child fails repeatedly in the same way without apparent learning, that is not a sign of stubbornness—it's a sign of missing skills. Perhaps the task is too complex. Perhaps the emotional regulation isn't there yet. Perhaps the stakes feel too high. In such cases, the solution is not harsher consequences, but clearer support. Adults must ask not just "What went wrong?" but "What is this child ready to learn?" That question reframes failure as feedback, not just about the child, but about the system around them.

Letting children fail with money is not about tough love or cold detachment. It is about *respecting their capacity for growth*. It is about seeing mistakes not as threats to avoid, but as curriculum to embrace. And it is about holding our own discomfort long enough for our children to feel the edges of theirs—because that is where wisdom takes root. In the end, the goal is not to raise children who never fail with money. It is to raise children who fail wisely, recover quickly, and emerge more thoughtful, resilient, and capable every time.

# Chapter 6
# Spending with Intention

Every child learns to spend; the more pressing question is whether they learn to spend wisely. In a world designed for frictionless consumption—tap-to-pay apps, one-click purchases, constant digital temptation—thoughtful spending is far from instinctive. For children, desire and action blur easily; what they want often becomes what they have almost immediately. This chapter challenges that default pattern. It offers a framework for parents not merely to curb spending, but to cultivate discernment—helping children see money not as a reflex for gratification, but as a medium for signalling priorities, values, and measured restraint.

Spending is frequently presented as the simplest pillar of financial literacy: earn, save, then spend. Yet this neat sequence belies the complexity embedded in every transaction. Every purchase carries emotional, social, aesthetic, and functional weight, alongside opportunity cost. A child who spends £10 on a glittery keychain isn't merely acquiring a trinket; they are making a tiny, unconscious declaration about what they value, what brings them satisfaction, and what they are willing to forego. Guiding children to understand this interplay—financially and psychologically—is among the most potent lessons early financial education can provide.

At the core lies a deceptively simple practice: the pause. What I call the "Three-Second Rule" is more than a delay tactic—it is an invitation to reflection. Teaching children to halt briefly before reaching for a wallet creates space for questions: Do I genuinely want this? Will I still care tomorrow? What else could this money accomplish? These are not advanced economic queries; they are questions that even a six-year-old can be guided to ask. The objective is not indecision but intentionality: nurturing young consumers who treat spending as choice rather than impulse.

Pausing, however, is only the beginning. To foster true discernment, children need a framework that surpasses the tired "wants versus needs" distinction. That binary, though well-meaning, is too blunt to navigate the subtleties of modern consumption. A £3 comic book, revisited ten times, shared with friends, and sparking creative play, may deliver far greater value than a £20 toy that sits forgotten. This chapter proposes a richer lens—one incorporating frequency of use, emotional fulfilment, social context, and durability. Not all wants are wasteful; not all needs are wise. Children deserve a vocabulary robust enough to assess these nuances.

This language must also be anchored in evidence. The notion of an "Allowance Burn Rate"—the pace at which money disappears once in a child's hands—provides a measurable framework for self-observation. Like a miniature experiment, it allows children to notice patterns: which purchases vanish quickest, which bring regret or enduring satisfaction. When a fortnight's allowance evaporates over a weekend, children confront their own behaviours directly. Visibility empowers learning far more effectively than nagging; the evidence teaches where words often fail.

Yet the most insidious distortion of thoughtful spending is not ignorance—it is comparison. A child may be content with their choices until they see what another child possesses. Enter performative consumption: spending not for need or joy, but to signal status, belonging, or defiance. Branded trainers, the latest gadget, or a lavish birthday celebration can tempt children—and adults—to conflate authenticity with performance. Parents often respond with logic: "We can't afford that" or "That's unnecessary." Such statements address the item, not the impulse.

Navigating this terrain requires acknowledging the emotional currents beneath spending. Envy, insecurity, and the fear of exclusion are potent drivers that budgeting talk alone cannot neutralise. This chapter explores ways to surface these emotions without shame, equipping children with internal anchors: What truly matters to you? What is worth your resources? What is just noise? These form the foundations of a reflective spender.

Throughout, the aim is to shift control from external signals to internal values. We are not training children to obey rules but to consult themselves, to trust judgment shaped by reflection and thoughtfulness. This distinction is crucial: it moves conversations away from fear-based admonitions—"Don't waste your money!"—or controlling conditions—"You can only buy that if..."—toward a values-led dialogue: What does this choice say about you? How does it feel, now and later?

This process need not be abstract. It unfolds in queues, aisles, or app stores. It manifests in moments of choice: holding two items and deciding, resisting a purchase and feeling proud, selecting quality over quantity, or saving for a later desire. Each act is a small assertion of autonomy.

Spending becomes a medium for identity, not just inventory.

By the end of this chapter, parents will be equipped to help their children develop a personal ethic of spending. They will learn to embed small rituals that cultivate pause, reflection, and deliberate choice. They will gain language for framing post-purchase reflection in ways that foster insight rather than shame. And they will understand how to guide children through the emotional currents of peer comparison, status signalling, and the persistent pull of consumer culture.

If financial literacy teaches mechanics, intentional spending teaches meaning. It is how children discover that a pound is not merely currency—it is agency. It is how they practise weighing, valuing, choosing, and, when necessary, walking away. Each pound spent is a sentence in the story of who they are becoming—and, written thoughtfully, that story is one of both financial competence and character.

## The Three-Second Rule

It takes a child only a moment to want something—but it takes years to teach them how to question that want. In today's economy of speed, where transactions are designed to be frictionless and gratification is instantaneous, the simple act of pausing before spending has become a radical discipline. Enter the Three-Second Rule: a brief but deliberate pause that teaches children to stop, evaluate, and engage in micro-reflection before parting with their money. It's not a gimmick. It's the foundation for cultivating intentionality—arguably the most undervalued financial skill in a hyper-consumptive age.

The impulse to spend is not inherently irrational. At its core, spending is an expression of autonomy and preference. But in the absence of conscious inquiry, it quickly becomes reactive. Children, in particular, are neurologically primed for immediacy. The prefrontal cortex—the part of the brain responsible for decision-making and self-regulation—is still under construction well into adolescence. Meanwhile, the limbic system, which processes reward and emotion, is firing on all cylinders. This imbalance makes young people exquisitely sensitive to temptation and poorly equipped to delay gratification. The Three-Second Rule operates as a form of cognitive scaffolding, offering just enough space to engage higher-order thinking before action takes over.

What happens in those three seconds is subtle but profound. The pause interrupts the autopilot response and makes room for a question—sometimes unspoken, sometimes verbalised: *Do I really want this? Will I still care about it tomorrow? What else could this money do?* At first, children may need adult prompts to pose those questions. But over time, the pause becomes internalised, and with it, a habit of reflection that transcends money. The skill of evaluating choices before acting under pressure transfers directly to domains like digital media, peer influence, and time management. *Financial self-regulation is not an isolated trait—it is an extension of broader executive function.*

It is important, however, that the Three-Second Rule not be wielded as a disciplinary tool. If framed as a parental hurdle or a forced delay, children are likely to see it as obstructive rather than empowering. The key is positioning the pause as a superpower: something that gives them *more* control, not less. This means shifting the language from "Wait, do you really need that?"—which centres adult judgment—to "Take a second and check in with yourself"—which centres the child's developing discernment. When children feel that they are practising agency rather than obeying constraint, their engagement deepens and their learning sticks.

Practising the Three-Second Rule works best when it's embedded into low-stakes environments. A corner shop. A weekend market. An in-game store on a tablet. These are ideal spaces for experimentation, precisely because the costs are minimal and the lessons are immediate. A child might pause and decide to buy anyway. That's not a failure—it's the beginning of pattern recognition. The value of the exercise is cumulative. Over time, children begin to notice which purchases bring lasting satisfaction and which lose their appeal within hours. *Experience becomes data; reflection becomes calibration.*

This reflective loop—impulse, pause, choice, outcome—is the architecture of self-directed financial intelligence. It cultivates not only better decisions but deeper confidence. A child who can override impulse becomes a child who trusts their own judgment. This confidence is especially crucial in social contexts, where spending often becomes performative. The child who can pause in the presence of peer pressure is not simply resisting the object; they are resisting the collapse of their own values under external demand. The pause becomes a kind of psychological firewall.

But there's a further dimension to the Three-Second Rule that extends beyond individual behaviour. It is also a quiet act of resistance against the machinery of modern marketing. Today's children are growing up in an attention economy where urgency is manufactured. "Limited-time offer." "Only three left in stock." "Get it before it's gone." These cues are engineered not to inform, but to bypass deliberation. They exploit the immediacy bias hardwired into our evolutionary psychology—the tendency to overvalue the present and undervalue the future. Teaching children to pause is not merely a personal development strategy; it is an inoculation against systemic manipulation.

In this light, the Three-Second Rule takes on a moral texture. It is about reclaiming the space to think. And that thinking—especially when modelled and supported by parents—fosters not only wiser consumers, but more mindful humans. A parent who says, "I always give myself a moment before buying something on impulse" is not preaching—they're narrating a strategy. This kind of modelling reinforces the child's internal toolkit. They begin to see that adults, too, wrestle with want, and that wisdom often lies not in knowing what to buy, but in knowing when *not* to.

For younger children, the pause might be externalised through simple rituals: counting to three out loud, flipping a coin not to decide, but to delay, or setting a timer before clicking "buy." These mechanical pauses act as training wheels for cognitive delay. With teens, the practice becomes more internal. Encourage them to make private trade-off lists: "If I spend £20 now, what won't I be able to afford later this month?" This cultivates foresight—another key executive function—and links financial decisions to time horizons beyond the present.

One of the most powerful ways to reinforce the Three-Second Rule is through post-decision conversation. Not interrogation, but reflection. "How do you feel about what you bought yesterday?" "Would you make the same choice again?" These questions help build a narrative memory around spending that is richer than just price and product. They also help children encode satisfaction and regret as usable information. *The goal is not perfect decisions—it's cumulative wisdom.*

As with all habits, consistency matters more than intensity. One pause is not transformational. But a thousand micro-pauses, reinforced over months and years, build a disposition. Children begin to see themselves as choosers, not reactors. This identity shift—towards being someone who thinks before they act—will shape not only how they spend, but how they approach risk, relationships, and reward across the lifespan.

To be clear, the Three-Second Rule is not about cultivating frugality for its own sake. It is not about withholding joy or pathologising desire. Children should experience the thrill of spontaneous buying now and then. They should know what it feels like to act on delight. But they should also know what it feels like to *wait,* and to *choose,* and to feel proud of a purchase made on their own terms. That is the deeper satisfaction. And that satisfaction lasts longer than any fleeting novelty.

Ultimately, the discipline of pausing is a discipline of self-respect. It says: "My attention is not for sale. My choices are mine to consider. My money is not just to use—it's to *direct.*" When children internalise that message, they are not merely learning to spend less. They are learning to *spend well.* And that, more than any app or allowance system, is the mark of a financially literate mind.

## Wants vs. Needs Isn't Enough

The binary of "wants" and "needs" has long served as a foundational framework in financial education. It's simple, memorable, and appears logically sound: food is a need, sweets are a want; rent is a need, toys are a want. But while this dichotomy has pedagogical appeal, it collapses under the complexity of real-world decision-making. In truth, the question "Do I need this?" is not only insufficient—it's often misleading. It fails to account for use frequency, perceived value, emotional fulfilment, and even social context. If we want to raise financially literate children capable of navigating twenty-first-century markets and internal cues, we must move beyond a simplistic dualism. *"Wants versus needs" is a start, not a finish line.*

A more sophisticated model for evaluating purchases invites children to assess three key dimensions: *practical value, use frequency,* and *emotional impact*. These are not abstract economic concepts—they are intuitive markers that help children build a richer decision-making framework rooted in their lived experience. They shift the locus of judgement from external authority ("Is this objectively a want?") to internal clarity ("Is this worth it to me?"). And that shift matters, because when children begin to own their evaluation processes, their choices become not only more informed, but more consistent with their personal values and priorities.

Let's begin with practical value, the cornerstone of economic exchange. Not all wants are frivolous. A good winter coat, for instance, may not be emotionally exciting but delivers high functional value. A child may not "want" it in the same way they want a video game, but its purpose is durable. Yet even games—often dismissed as pure indulgence—can have high cognitive, social, or emotional utility, depending on how they're used. A blanket classification of games as "wants" may overlook their potential developmental or social return. This highlights a crucial nuance: *value cannot be judged purely by category—it must be judged by context*. Helping children ask, "What job will this item do for me?" or "What problem will this solve?" cultivates a utility-focused mindset rather than a consumption-based reflex.

Use frequency is the second dimension, and one that is often missing from traditional frameworks. Children are rarely encouraged to ask how often they will actually use the item they want. Yet frequency is a powerful predictor of satisfaction. An inexpensive item used daily often delivers far greater value than a high-cost item used once. That sparkly novelty pen might feel irresistible in the moment, but if it's forgotten in a drawer within a week, its real value is negligible. By contrast, a sturdy backpack that gets daily use over several years might be a "want" in theory, but a cost-effective investment in practice. Teaching children to consider use frequency moves their attention from the moment of acquisition to the *lifecycle of the object*—a much more realistic orientation.

Emotional impact—the third leg of the model—is where many traditional approaches falter, because emotions are often treated as suspect in financial reasoning. But this is a false dichotomy. Emotions are not irrational; they are data. Children's purchasing decisions are deeply intertwined with identity, aspiration, and affect. A pair of shoes may offer no more comfort than another pair, but may carry a sense of social belonging, confidence, or creative expression. We should not encourage children to ignore this dimension; we should help them *interrogate it*. Emotional resonance becomes problematic only when it overrides all other considerations. Asking "How will I feel after buying this?"

or "Will I still like this once the thrill wears off?" invites children to distinguish between lasting emotional satisfaction and fleeting excitement. That's not anti-emotion—it's emotional intelligence applied to money.

This three-dimensional model—value, frequency, and emotional impact—also encourages trade-off thinking. Instead of binary categorisation, children begin to ask, "Which item gives me more across these categories?" Perhaps they want two things: a trendy jumper and a new set of paints. The jumper may score high in emotional impact and social signalling, but low in use frequency if it's too warm for everyday wear. The paints, though less socially visible, may offer weeks of creative engagement. Suddenly, the choice is not framed as *right versus wrong*, but as *higher yield versus lower yield*, based on personally meaningful criteria. *This is what it means to cultivate intentional spending.*

Adopting a more nuanced model also prepares children for the moral ambiguity of adult financial life. Needs and wants blur when adults face questions like: "Should I pay for therapy?" "Is it okay to upgrade my phone if the old one still works?" "Do I enrol my child in a costly extracurricular that feeds their passion?" These are not frivolous dilemmas. They are the texture of modern life. And they cannot be resolved by simplistic rules. By equipping children early with a more refined evaluative framework, we give them tools that scale with complexity. *They learn not to obey rules, but to reason with clarity.*

Parents can facilitate this learning without turning every shopping trip into a lecture. Begin by modelling the thought process aloud. "I'm deciding between two water bottles. One is cheaper, but I know I'll use the other one more because it fits better in my bag. That makes it a better buy for me." This verbalisation externalises internal reasoning. Children pick up not just the *conclusion*, but the *process* behind it. This kind of modelling is especially useful when the choice involves spending more—for it teaches children that frugality is not always about picking the lowest price, but about maximising the return on money, time, and satisfaction.

The model can also be visualised for younger children. A simple three-column chart or circle with the three dimensions—value, frequency, emotional impact—lets them score or colour in their options. This gamified approach turns abstract reasoning into concrete play, which aligns with how young minds best absorb complex ideas. As children mature, the framework can evolve with them. Teens might be encouraged to write short justifications for purchases over a certain threshold, reflecting on how the item scores on each dimension. These exercises build the meta-cognitive muscle essential for autonomous adulthood.

Of course, no model is foolproof. Children will still make irrational or impulsive choices. That's not failure—it's curriculum. Sometimes a child needs to buy something they later regret to fully internalise these distinctions. The role of the adult is not to prevent all poor decisions, but to equip the child to *make sense* of those experiences. "How would you rate that purchase now, looking back?" is a powerful question. It encourages reflection without shame and converts error into wisdom.

Ultimately, moving beyond "wants versus needs" is about cultivating a philosophy of discernment. It's about raising children who can make decisions that are not only financially sound but *personally coherent*—aligned with who they are and what they value. That is a far more empowering objective than simply policing consumption. Because when children learn to consider value, frequency, and emotional resonance, they are not merely choosing between items. They are learning to invest in their lives—thoughtfully, proportionally, and with increasing clarity. And that kind of thinking will serve them far beyond the checkout line.

### The Allowance Burn Rate

One of the most revealing financial habits a child can develop is not how much they save or even how wisely they spend—but how quickly they spend. The speed with which a child moves from full allowance to empty wallet is not just a behavioural quirk; it is diagnostic. It tells us something fundamental about their emotional regulation, impulse control, attention span, value discernment, and concept of time. And yet, *burn rate*—a term often reserved for start-ups consuming venture capital—is rarely discussed in the context of childhood finance. That is a missed opportunity. Because when parents begin tracking not just where money goes, but how fast, they illuminate a pattern far more useful than any static ledger of transactions. *The pace of spending is often more telling than the purchase itself.*

Consider two children, each receiving the same weekly allowance. One spends their money within hours—often on sweets, stickers, or fast-disappearing toys—while the other lets their money sit for days or weeks before making a single, deliberate purchase. On paper, they might spend the same amount. But their burn rates are wildly different, and that difference reflects radically divergent internal processes. The first child is responding to immediate stimuli—dopaminergic spikes, peer influence, novelty-seeking. The second is exercising delay, weighing options, considering trade-offs. Neither approach is necessarily pathological. But one suggests an impulsivity bias; the other, a developing sense of financial pacing. Recognising this distinction allows adults to shift their attention from the *symptom* ("They always buy silly things") to the *rhythm* behind the behaviour.

Allowance burn rate is, at heart, about *tempo of decision-making*. Most adults underestimate how crucial this concept is to long-term financial health. High-income earners can go broke when their spending velocity outpaces their intake. Conversely, modest earners who master pacing often build durable wealth. The issue isn't simply what you earn or what you buy—it's how often you activate the cycle of *earn-decide-spend*. Children who deplete their funds too quickly rarely feel the consequences until the absence of funds coincides with a deeper desire. That moment—when they want something meaningful but have nothing left—is not a failure. *It is an ideal learning window.*

Parents can harness this window by helping children reconstruct their spending timeline. "How long did it take you to spend your allowance?" is a more productive question than "What did you spend it on?" Follow-ups like "Did you still want those things a day later?" or "Was there anything you wish you'd waited for?" foster meta-cognition. These questions are not meant to shame or scold, but to develop a reflective loop that slows the child's future burn rate organically—not through imposed restriction, but through experiential insight.

It is also worth considering how the *structure* of allowance affects pacing. A weekly allowance often encourages short-term cycles—spend and refill—whereas fortnightly or monthly distributions stretch the time horizon and introduce natural scarcity. Scarcity, in this context, is not punitive. It is educational. It creates friction between desire and fulfilment, allowing time for priorities to reorder. Parents should calibrate the allowance cycle not only to the child's age but to their emerging behavioural patterns. A child with a lightning-fast burn rate may benefit from a less frequent, slightly larger distribution paired with visual tools that help them monitor the passage of time against the depletion of funds.

One such tool is a simple allowance timeline: a strip of paper marked with the days between allowance payments.

Children can draw when and on what they spent money, visually mapping their consumption across time. When paired with reflection—"What day did your money run out?"—this tool externalises abstract concepts. Time becomes visible; pacing becomes trackable. For older children, digital banking apps or spreadsheets can serve the same function, offering graphs of balance over time. The point is not surveillance. It is *pattern literacy*—learning to see their own behaviours as data they can interpret and influence.

Importantly, burn rate also intersects with emotional and social dimensions. Children with rapid burn rates may be using money to manage boredom, gain attention, or soothe anxiety. A trip to the school vending machine might have less to do with hunger and more to do with social rituals—"spending to belong." In these cases, slowing burn rate is not just a financial skill, but an emotional one. It requires helping the child understand what they're *really* buying. "Did you want the snack, or did you want to be part of the group?" Such questions are not accusatory—they're clarifying. They train children to locate the emotional driver behind the transaction.

Another overlooked factor is the *feedback cycle* of purchases. When children spend quickly, they often don't revisit the outcomes of those decisions. They remember the moment of acquisition but not the arc of experience. Creating structured moments of "spending reviews"—brief conversations where they assess which purchases felt worth it and which did not—builds a culture of accountability without blame. Over time, children begin to self-monitor burn rate with greater sophistication: "I think I rushed that buy," or "Next time I'll wait a bit longer before I decide." This is the inner dialogue of a maturing financial thinker.

Contrary to popular belief, a high burn rate is not necessarily a red flag. In some developmental stages, it is a feature, not a bug. Younger children, whose sense of time is still forming, are naturally prone to rapid consumption. The issue arises when the burn rate doesn't slow with age or experience. Adolescents who continue to spend reflexively often struggle later with budgeting, savings, and delayed gratification. Recognising this, parents can shift focus from enforcing external controls to cultivating internal pacing mechanisms. "You've spent quickly two weeks in a row—what do you want to try differently this week?" empowers the child to intervene in their own pattern.

Burn rate also offers a surprisingly effective way to teach budgeting in reverse. Instead of starting with the traditional model—plan spending in advance—some children may learn better through *retrospective* budgeting: track how you've spent, analyse patterns, then build a forward-looking strategy based on observed rhythms. This bottom-up approach meets the child where they are and transforms reactive spending into proactive planning. Over time, they learn not just to stretch money, but to synchronise spending with value.

Finally, allowance burn rate introduces children to the concept of *priority revelation*. In economics, how someone spends tells you more about their true preferences than what they say. Children often claim to value certain things—saving for a goal, waiting for a bigger item—but their burn rate tells a different story. Helping them reconcile these two domains—aspiration versus action—is a critical step in developing financial integrity. "You said you wanted to save for a larger item, but your money was gone in two days. What happened?" is not an indictment. It's an invitation to align behaviour with intention.

In sum, the speed of spending is one of the most overlooked diagnostic tools in financial parenting. It reveals the tempo of thought, the maturity of impulse control, the depth of planning, and the presence (or absence) of reflection. Teaching children to observe, interpret, and eventually adjust their allowance burn rate is not about enforcing prudence for its own sake. It is about building *internal governors* that allow them to pace their desires in step with their values. That skill—more than any dollar amount—determines whether a child grows into an impulsive consumer or a deliberate steward. And it begins with a deceptively simple question: "How fast does your money disappear?"

### How to Handle Envy and Peer Pressure

Few forces shape a child's spending habits more powerfully—or insidiously—than the opinions and behaviours of their peers. In the world of children and adolescents, purchases are rarely just transactions. They are performances, markers of identity, attempts to belong, declarations of status. A pair of trainers isn't merely footwear; it's a ticket to social inclusion. A trending gadget isn't just functional; it's symbolic capital. And for parents trying to teach financial responsibility, this creates a fraught tension: how does one teach discernment in a culture where value is so often determined by the collective gaze rather than intrinsic utility?

At the core of this problem lies a developmental truth: children and teens are *wired* to care what others think. Social comparison is not a character flaw—it's a fundamental mechanism of adolescent identity formation. But while the impulse is natural, the way it is expressed through spending has been radically amplified by contemporary consumer culture. Social media, influencer branding, and algorithm-driven marketing have transformed peer pressure from a schoolyard phenomenon into a 24/7 psychological drip. Children are no longer just comparing themselves to the handful of classmates in their circle. They are benchmarking against curated avatars from around the world, many of whom are incentivised to provoke desire. The result is a volatile blend of envy, insecurity, and artificial urgency—a dynamic few adults manage with grace, let alone children.

And so the task before parents is not to suppress envy or deny the social currency of goods, but to *equip children to interrogate it.* To name the force at play. To separate the object from the story being told about it. This begins by giving language to the experience. When a child says, "I want that hoodie," the parent's first question should not be, "Can we afford it?" or "Do you need it?" but rather, "What do you think it will say about you if you wear it?" This gentle reframing opens a conversational door: Is the hoodie about warmth, about trendiness, about matching someone admired, about avoiding ridicule? The deeper the inquiry, the more space the child has to surface motivations that are often subconscious. And once they are surfaced, they can be examined—without shame, without sermons, and with growing self-awareness.

Equally important is normalising the experience of envy without catastrophising it. Many adults, uncomfortable with the rawness of their children's desire, default to scolding or dismissiveness. "Don't be jealous," they say, as if jealousy itself were a sin to be eradicated. But envy is instructive. It reveals what we perceive to be missing, what we think matters, what we fear others see in us. Helping children sit with these emotions—rather than immediately resolving them—builds emotional literacy and resilience. "It sounds like you feel left out when you don't have what others do. That's understandable. Let's talk about whether what they have aligns with your values or just their image." This approach treats the child as an emerging thinker, not a passive consumer.

That said, conversation alone is insufficient. Children need frameworks—practical mental models—to evaluate their choices in the face of social pressure. One such model is the distinction between *signal value* and *personal value*. Signal value refers to what others see, perceive, or interpret about a possession. Personal value relates to how the item serves the child's own preferences, interests, or needs. When a child is eyeing an item driven by peer trends—a bag, phone case, or accessory—the parent can ask: "Do you like this because it's useful or because of how others might see you with it?" Framed non-judgementally, this question introduces a dual-lens view of purchasing, one that helps children disentangle influence from intention.

Over time, the goal is not to eliminate performative consumption (an unrealistic expectation in a social species), but to *dilute its dominance* in decision-making. The child should develop the capacity to hold two thoughts at once: "I know this makes me look cool, and I also genuinely enjoy it," or conversely, "I'm aware this is popular, but it doesn't actually matter to me." This metacognitive clarity doesn't arrive automatically. It is cultivated—slowly, incrementally—through many conversations, gentle provocations, and the occasional regretful purchase followed by reflection.

That last piece is crucial. Children learn from their own spending misfires more than from parental warnings. When a child buys something expensive because "everyone has it," only to find it quickly discarded or obsolete, that experience is gold—*if* it is processed well. Rather than rescuing them from disappointment, parents can lean in. "Did it feel as good as you expected? What changed? Would you make the same decision again?" These questions do not shame—they frame the mistake as a learning asset. This method fosters what researchers call *autonomous internalisation*: adopting a value or insight not because it was imposed, but because it was discovered and integrated.

Another underappreciated strategy is to expand the child's peer reference group. If a child is constantly surrounded by peers who measure worth through possessions, the gravitational pull of consumerism becomes almost inescapable. But exposure to role models—older siblings, cousins, family friends—who model different value systems can create contrast. When children see admired individuals choosing not to perform wealth, or expressing style through thrift and creativity rather than brands, their internal compass is recalibrated. This is especially powerful in preteens and early adolescents, who are beginning to shape identity but still crave role congruence.

Parents can also model non-performative decision-making themselves. Children absorb not just what their parents buy, but *why and how*. If a child sees a parent debating the merits of an expensive purchase not in terms of external impression—"What will the neighbours think?"—but internal logic—"Will I actually use this?"—that narrative begins to take root. Similarly, if a parent openly reflects on resisting the pressure to upgrade a car, phone, or outfit for social reasons, it sends a quiet but powerful message: you can choose self-definition over status signalling. These lived examples out-teach lectures every time.

It's also important to remember that peer pressure is not always toxic. Sometimes it catalyses growth. A child might feel inspired by a friend's savings discipline, entrepreneurial venture, or creative DIY fashion. In these moments, the peer becomes not a source of envy, but a model of agency. The question becomes, "What can I learn from them?" rather than "How can I keep up?" Cultivating this discernment—learning to admire without imitating, to be inspired without being hijacked—is a lifelong skill with extraordinary utility beyond childhood.

Still, there will be moments when children feel genuine deprivation or exclusion. Their friends may go on expensive holidays, receive lavish gifts, or flaunt high-end tech. The child, in comparison, feels small. Parents often rush to reassure or compensate, but the more powerful response is empathy coupled with re-anchoring. "Yes, they have that, and it's okay to wish for it. But let's remember what we prioritise as a family." This is not about moralising frugality. It's about reaffirming intentionality—"We make choices with meaning, not for show."

In the end, resisting performative consumption isn't about turning children into stoics or denying them the joy of material things. It's about equipping them with *discernment*. So they can pause when envy whispers, ask themselves whose voice they're really hearing, and decide whether their desire is *borrowed or chosen*. When children learn to trace their longings back to their source—and when they are taught that not all sources are wise—they begin to build a financial identity grounded in clarity, not conformity. And that is a far more enduring form of wealth than any trending item could ever deliver.

# Chapter 7
# Giving That Matters

Few human instincts are more lauded—and yet more easily misunderstood—than generosity. We celebrate it in stories, reward it in children, and link it to moral worth, yet too often we treat it as innate: a trait one either possesses or does not. This idealised view does a disservice to both parents and children. Generosity, like any meaningful human capacity, is learned. It requires modelling, practice, occasional missteps, and refinement over time. And in a culture increasingly shaped by entitlement and digital self-focus, generosity must be deliberately nurtured; the world will not cultivate it on a child's behalf.

Children enter the world with limited capacity for prosocial thought. This is not a flaw but a developmental reality. Early brains prioritise self-preservation over altruism. Acts such as sharing a toy, waiting one's turn, or giving without expectation of return are complex behaviours, demanding emotional regulation, perspective-taking, and patience. They do not emerge spontaneously; they develop through repeated exposure to giving, scaffolded reflection, and reinforced experience. Just as we do not expect children to grasp budgeting without handling money, we cannot expect them to internalise generosity without opportunities to practise it.

Yet most early experiences of "giving" offered to children are hollow. Dropping a coin into a charity box, wrapping a toy for a sibling at an adult's behest, or participating in school fundraisers often emphasise procedure rather than intention. The child becomes a conduit for someone else's values rather than an originator of purpose. For giving to resonate, it must carry authorship: children need to understand not only what they are giving, but why, to whom, and with what anticipated impact.

Allowing children to choose their own causes is not indulgent—it is essential. When a child allocates a portion of their allowance to a wildlife fund, a local food bank, or a classroom project, they step beyond mere participation in a parental ritual. They exercise agency, beginning to grasp that they are not just recipients of wealth but allocators of value. Even a modest donation of £2 becomes a moral choice rather than a transaction.

Choice also cultivates empathy through specificity. Abstract appeals such as "help the poor" or "support animals" rarely inspire children. But seeing that a gift contributes to a named child's education abroad or helps a particular dog find a home activates emotional circuitry. Giving becomes relational rather than rhetorical, a gesture of connection rather than compliance. Such experiences lay the foundation for a prosocial identity: the enduring sense of "I am the kind of person who helps when I can."

Generosity extends beyond money—and it should. One of the most powerful lessons parents can introduce is that giving exists in multiple currencies: time, attention, effort, and advocacy. Helping a sibling with homework, volunteering at a community centre, or including a classmate in a game are all acts of giving. By explicitly naming these behaviours as generous, parents elevate their significance, signalling that generosity is an everyday posture, not merely a seasonal or financial act.

Each form of giving teaches something distinct. Financial giving develops economic awareness and prioritisation; time-based giving cultivates patience and commitment; attention sharpens empathy; advocacy nurtures moral courage and social literacy. To instil a robust sense of generosity, children must encounter all four, with each framed as meaningful and accessible. Parents, as first educators, must model these behaviours transparently, not performatively: "I donated to this fund because it matters to me," or "I'm helping a friend move because relationships require effort." Such commentary provides a window into value systems that children might otherwise never articulate.

Well-meaning parents often falter by framing giving as sacrifice. "Think of those less fortunate," or "You don't need that—others are starving," can instil guilt, leading either to performative charity or suppressed resentment. Children may comply outwardly yet grow cynical inwardly, equating giving with personal loss rather than communal connection.

The antidote is framing giving as impact, not deprivation. Children shift motivation when encouraged to consider outcomes rather than costs: "Because you donated part of your birthday money, this child got school supplies," or "Because we spent time cleaning the park, others can enjoy it too." These reflections cultivate competence as well as compassion, reinforcing that giving is not simply about being "good," but about being effective.

Simple rituals deepen this understanding. Writing letters to recipients, tracking updates from sponsored projects, or visiting local organisations helps children witness the tangible consequences of their generosity. Real-world feedback reinforces that giving is power, not loss, and such experiences tend to be self-reinforcing.

Families can also introduce systemic thinking: moving beyond episodic charity to structural awareness. Discussing housing policy alongside donations to the homeless, or animal welfare legislation alongside shelter support, encourages children to see giving as part of a broader ecosystem. The goal is not to produce miniature activists, but to cultivate an understanding that generosity operates within social, institutional, and cultural frameworks, elevating it from sympathy to strategy.

Economic context matters, too. Families with limited resources may be unable to give financially, but children can still practise generosity through time, effort, and attention. Conversely, affluent children taught only to give money risk cultivating hollow philanthropy without solidarity. Balance and intentionality matter more than sheer monetary value.

Resistance to giving is normal. Some children will be possessive, reluctant, or indifferent. This is not failure—it is an invitation to reflection. Questions such as "What makes this hard to give away?" or "What might happen if you shared this?" invite consideration without demanding generosity. Reflection, more than compliance, is the true soil in which generosity grows.

Generosity, at its best, is not virtue signalling or box-ticking. It is human alignment: recognising that choices ripple outward, that resources carry responsibility, and that our lives are intertwined with others. Teaching children to give thoughtfully is not a peripheral component of financial literacy—it is its moral core. Ultimately, what children choose to give, intentionally and freely, will be the clearest reflection of the values we pass on.

### Why Generosity Needs Practice

The belief that children are naturally generous is a comforting illusion—one that flatters our hopes but does little to prepare us for the work of raising prosocial humans. Altruism, empathy, and giving are not pre-installed virtues; they are cognitive and emotional skills that must be taught, modelled, reinforced, and repeated. A toddler clutching a toy with iron resolve is not demonstrating moral failure; they are demonstrating developmental normalcy. What we call selfishness in early childhood is, more often than not, a lack of *practice*, not a lack of character.

This distinction matters deeply. If generosity is assumed to be innate, then its absence feels like a deficiency. But if generosity is understood as *a learned behaviour*, its absence becomes an opportunity—a signal that more modelling, dialogue, and experimentation are needed. And more than almost any other pro-social skill, generosity requires repetition across varied contexts. It must be experienced not once, but often. Not abstractly, but concretely. And not just directed, but reflected upon.

Why does it require so much scaffolding? Because generosity challenges several core instincts of the developing brain: the desire for ownership, the drive for fairness, the impulse to hoard or hedge against loss. These instincts are adaptive. Evolutionary psychologists argue that human survival depended not on indiscriminate giving, but on strategic reciprocity. From an early age, children are wired to track who gives, who receives, and whether exchanges are fair. They are exquisitely attuned to social dynamics, but not necessarily inclined toward self-sacrifice. This does not make them ungenerous—it makes them *human*. And it makes the work of teaching generosity more about *shaping instincts* than fighting them.

This shaping begins with experience, not exhortation. Telling a child to "be kind" or "share with your sister" often yields compliance without comprehension. The child may act as told but remain emotionally resistant. Instead, practice means building *muscle memory for giving*. It means creating low-stakes, high-frequency opportunities for children to share something they value, whether it's time, a toy, or a treat. The key is not the size of the act, but the *intention* behind it—and the *post-act processing* that follows.

Consider a simple example: a five-year-old offers part of their snack to a classmate. On its own, the act is meaningful but fleeting. But if a parent or teacher later says, "I saw you gave part of your snack—how did that feel?" or "What made you decide to do that?" the moment becomes pedagogical. The adult is signalling: *that was not just an action—it was a choice worth noticing*. Over time, these conversations help children construct a narrative of themselves as someone who gives. And identity, once formed, becomes internal motivation.

Importantly, practice also includes permission *not* to give. Forced charity breeds resentment. When children are routinely pressured to share or donate without consent, generosity becomes performance, not value. This is especially true during holiday seasons, when parents often orchestrate charitable acts as rituals of family virtue. While the intention may be admirable, the child may feel used—as if their actions serve someone else's moral self-image. A more effective approach is to invite giving, not insist on it. To ask: "Would you like to choose something to donate?" rather than command: "You need to give one toy away." This shift may seem minor, but it repositions the child as an *agent*, not a puppet.

Agency matters because true generosity is not about obedience; it's about orientation. It's about learning to see others' needs, and choosing to respond. But seeing those needs takes *exposure*. Children raised in hyper-insulated environments, where poverty, illness, or inequality are kept out of view, struggle to develop meaningful empathy. They may be taught to care abstractly—about "those less fortunate"—but without stories, faces, or names, their care remains vague. Generosity is a response to specificity. When a child understands that their donation helped a real person—a refugee child, a neighbour in need, a local animal shelter—the emotional circuitry lights up. Giving becomes personal, not theoretical.

Still, exposure alone isn't enough. Practice also demands *variation*. Children must encounter multiple forms of giving—not just financial. In fact, for most young children, money is the least emotionally resonant medium of generosity. Time, attention, service, and kindness often teach far more. Helping a friend clean up, writing a thank-you card to a teacher, visiting a lonely neighbour—these acts build the internal repertoire that later translates into more complex expressions of generosity. Each act subtly reinforces a message: *your effort has value; your actions affect others*.

The developmental progression is subtle but real. In early childhood, generosity may be situational—guided by adult cues or simple imitation. By middle childhood, it becomes semi-volitional: the child may give to feel good, gain approval, or reciprocate kindness. Only in adolescence, with the maturation of abstract thought and moral reasoning, does generosity begin to take on philosophical weight. Teens may start to ask, "What kind of person do I want to be?" or "What matters enough for me to act?" These are critical turning points. But they only occur if the groundwork has been laid early—if giving is familiar, not foreign.

Even then, practice must continue. Adolescents, caught between autonomy and peer pressure, often face competing incentives. Generosity can feel socially risky, especially in cultures that prize individualism, competition, or ironic detachment. A teen who chooses to spend time volunteering may be mocked. One who donates a prized item may be questioned. This is where *narrative reinforcement* from adults becomes vital. Parents who say, "That was brave," or "That mattered," are helping teens stabilise a generous identity amid turbulence.

Of course, no child gives perfectly—or consistently. They will hesitate, backtrack, and misjudge. They will sometimes give for the wrong reasons or refuse to give when it counts. This is not failure. It is *practice in motion*. Adults must resist the urge to moralise every choice. Instead, they should remain curious: "What made you decide that?" "How did it feel?" These questions invite reflection without shame. They keep the path open.

The broader cultural context, too, cannot be ignored. Children today are socialised in a marketplace of influence, where success is equated with accumulation and visibility. Acts of giving are often performative—posted, shared, and tracked. While public generosity can inspire, it also distorts. Children may come to believe that giving "counts" only if it's seen. Or that large donations are more important than small, consistent ones. This is why private, quiet acts of giving must be celebrated too. A child who spends their pocket money on a friend's birthday gift, without announcing it—*that* is generosity in its most authentic form.

Ultimately, generosity is not a lesson delivered once. It is a long-form conversation between parent and child, teacher and student, person and community. It is a habit of mind, a way of seeing the world that says: *I have enough to share; I am connected to others; my actions matter.* This mindset is not born—it is built. And like all structures of value, it needs patience, support, and time to rise.

If we want our children to grow into adults who give freely, wisely, and with empathy, we must ensure they've had *enough chances to try*. Not once a year, but often. Not for applause, but for meaning. Generosity doesn't emerge from lectures or rules. It emerges from *practice*. And it flourishes when that practice is made visible, valued, and varied enough to feel real.

## The Four Kinds of Giving

It is a common misconception that generosity begins and ends with money. This notion, while convenient, is also profoundly limiting—especially when shaping a child's understanding of contribution. If a young person learns that generosity is only about writing a cheque or dropping coins in a jar, they internalise a transactional view of value: if you don't have money, you have nothing to give. The consequences of this belief are wide-reaching. It discourages civic participation, suppresses empathy, and subtly trains children to conflate material worth with moral worth. But generosity is broader, richer, and more varied than any wallet could hold. At its most robust, it is a *composite skillset*, expressed across four domains: time, money, attention, and advocacy. Each form of giving teaches a different aspect of empathy—and each matures a different part of character.

Money, of course, is the most visible form. It is also the most misunderstood. When children first encounter monetary giving—perhaps through a charity drive or school fundraiser—they often experience it as extraction: "Give a pound. Empty your piggy bank. Forego a treat for someone else." While the cause may be noble, the framing often lacks nuance. No one explains the architecture of intentional giving: how to evaluate causes, how to balance spontaneity with sustained support, how to assess impact beyond emotional gratification. Without this scaffolding, children are left with the surface ritual of donation but not the reflective depth. More than the act of giving money, what matters is *the thinking behind it*. Who is this for? Why this cause? What do I hope changes? These questions, when asked aloud and answered together, turn a donation into a decision.

But money is not always accessible—nor should it be the default. Many children have limited control over financial resources. Some have none. To teach that generosity only begins when money is present is to exclude a vast population from the moral conversation. That's why *time* must be recognised as an equally legitimate, and often more instructive, medium. When a child spends their Saturday helping a neighbour rake leaves or their afternoon reading to a younger sibling, they are giving something even more finite than money: presence. And unlike money, which can be passively given, *time always costs attention*. It is never thoughtless. In this way, it teaches a different emotional economy: the discipline of showing up, the humility of labour, the intimacy of shared effort. It is often in the act of giving time that children first taste what it means to *feel needed,* and that sensation—of being useful to someone else—is often the first flicker of self-worth not rooted in achievement or approval.

The third form of giving, *attention,* is the most overlooked, and perhaps the most urgent. In an era of divided screens and curated distractions, attention has become a rare commodity. Yet children can be taught early that offering full attention is not just good manners—it is a form of care. Listening to a friend's story without interrupting, noticing a classmate's discomfort and offering comfort, asking thoughtful questions rather than dominating a conversation: these are not small gestures. They are *relational investments,* and they model a generosity that values people not for what they do, but for who they are. Importantly, attention-based giving is accessible to all ages and all abilities. A six-year-old can comfort a crying peer. A teenager can listen to an elderly relative's stories with curiosity. In both cases, the message transmitted is powerful: *you matter enough to be seen.*

And then there is *advocacy*—the form of giving least talked about in family contexts, yet one of the most morally consequential. Advocacy means using your voice, your platform, or your privilege to elevate someone else's experience. For a child, this might begin with standing up for a classmate being bullied or refusing to laugh at a cruel joke. As they mature, advocacy might involve raising awareness for a cause, speaking up in community spaces, or participating in acts of solidarity. What advocacy teaches is that generosity is not always quiet. Sometimes it is loud, public, and risky. It teaches that giving doesn't always mean *giving up* something—it can mean *stepping forward*. Advocacy connects children to the idea of social justice. It positions them not just as helpers, but as *participants in change*.

Importantly, these four forms are not hierarchical. One is not more "real" than the others. In fact, the healthiest understanding of generosity is *intermodal*: money, time, attention, and advocacy co-exist and reinforce one another. A child who gives money to a food drive may also volunteer at the food bank (time), ask questions about hunger (attention), and speak at school about poverty (advocacy). When these forms intersect, they create what developmental psychologists call *prosocial identity integration*—the internalisation of values as part of the self, not just as isolated behaviours. This kind of identity takes years to build, but it begins with exposure, reflection, and reinforcement.

Some families fear that talking too much about giving will make it performative or self-congratulatory. The opposite is true. *What makes giving performative is silence*. When children are never invited to reflect on what they gave, why they gave, and how it felt, they fill in the gaps with guesswork or mimicry. But when adults make these conversations explicit—"Why did you choose that cause?" "What was hard about offering your time?" "How do you think they felt when you listened?"—they create a reflective loop that builds emotional intelligence alongside moral maturity.

Each form of giving also maps onto a different moral lesson. Money teaches resource stewardship. Time teaches availability. Attention teaches presence. Advocacy teaches courage. Together, these capacities form a more complete picture of generosity than any donation receipt ever could. And when children are taught that they have all four currencies at their disposal, regardless of their socioeconomic status, they begin to understand that they are never powerless in the face of need.

There is also a strategic function to this multi-modal model. Not every child will feel equally drawn to every form. One may struggle to part with money, but find joy in volunteering. Another may be shy in public but write passionately for causes they care about. By exposing children to all four types, parents help them find their natural entry points into generosity. Over time, exposure breeds fluency. And fluency allows for adaptability. A child who knows how to give in more than one way can respond flexibly to life's demands. If they are short on funds, they offer time. If they can't volunteer, they offer attention. If they feel unsure, they speak up.

Moreover, the four kinds of giving equip children to resist transactional thinking, which dominates so much of adult economic life. In the adult world, generosity is often filtered through metrics: return on investment, donation matching, tax deductibility. These are not inherently wrong, but they are not moral guides. A child steeped only in monetary giving may grow up to measure compassion by cost. A child who understands generosity in all four dimensions, however, learns to ask better questions: *What does this person need most? What do I have to offer? What kind of help creates dignity rather than dependency?*

In a society that increasingly defines value in terms of visibility and scale, the four-fold framework of generosity reminds us that some of the most meaningful forms of giving are small, unseen, and deeply human. When a child offers their time without reward, listens without interrupting, donates their allowance with intention, or speaks up when it would be easier to stay silent, they are not just being kind. They are practising a complex form of social intelligence—one that will serve them in relationships, work, citizenship, and self-respect.

True generosity is not a single act, but a lifelong fluency. And just as literacy requires more than knowing the alphabet, generosity requires more than knowing how to donate. It is a language spoken across many mediums—money, time, attention, and advocacy—and when taught well, it becomes *a mother tongue for empathy*.

### Let Kids Choose Their Causes

Children are natural observers of fairness, but not natural architects of generosity. The emotional machinery for empathy may be present in early childhood, but the ability to translate that feeling into action—deliberate, sustained, and values-driven action—requires training. This is why giving becomes truly transformative not when children are merely instructed to donate, but when they are invited to *choose* where and how to give. Control over one's giving—however modest the amount—increases both the meaning and memorability of the act. Without choice, giving risks becoming obligation. With choice, it becomes conviction.

To appreciate the significance of child-led giving, one must first confront an uncomfortable reality: most charitable decisions in family settings are adult-centred. Parents determine which causes to support, which organisations to trust, and which moments to participate in. Children may be recruited to carry the envelope or drop coins into the tin, but they're rarely invited into the deliberation. The gesture becomes ceremonial, not intentional. And yet, intention is the very thing that turns charity into character. If we want generosity to take root in a child's identity, we must give them something deeper than instructions—we must give them *agency*.

Agency in giving doesn't mean unbounded freedom. It means guided autonomy: the ability to make real choices within a framework of thoughtful discussion. A child who earns £5 a week and chooses to give £1 to a local animal shelter is learning more than generosity. They are practising discernment. They are aligning resources with values. They are building what behavioural scientists call "identity-congruent behaviour"—actions that reflect and reinforce one's developing sense of self. In other words, they are not just doing good. They are *becoming* someone who does good.

The psychological literature supports this model. When people—children included—feel that their actions arise from internal choice rather than external compulsion, they show greater persistence, engagement, and emotional investment. This is known as self-determination theory, and its relevance to giving is profound. Donations made under pressure may elicit temporary compliance. Donations made through ownership produce *lasting affiliation*. The cause matters more. The impact feels personal. The giver remembers.

Of course, for parents, surrendering control over where donations go can feel risky. What if the child picks a trivial cause? What if they're influenced by a passing fad? What if the donation achieves little beyond novelty? These are valid concerns—but they are also teachable moments. A child who donates to a trendy campaign that quickly disappears might feel momentarily disillusioned, but that experience can become an invaluable prompt for deeper questioning. What made you choose it? What did you hope would happen? How would you decide differently next time? In this sense, misfires are not failures. *They are rehearsals for wisdom.*

Real-world examples abound of families who have structured their giving practices to honour children's agency. In one such household, parents created a "giving circle" at the dinner table once a month. Each family member—regardless of age—nominated a cause they cared about, presented a short explanation, and made the case for a collective or individual contribution. The youngest child, age seven, once argued passionately for a donation to a local bee conservation initiative after learning about pollinators at school. The parents didn't overrule the choice. They honoured it. That moment, minor on the financial ledger, was major on the developmental one. It told the child: *your convictions matter here*.

Such practices cultivate what moral philosophers call *moral imagination*—the capacity to see oneself as part of a moral community, with the power to influence it. When children choose their causes, they are forced to ask big questions: Who is suffering? What is fair? What do I care about? How do I help? These are not abstract questions for later in life. They are the foundations of ethical thinking, and the earlier they are exercised, the stronger the framework becomes.

Critics may worry that allowing children to select their own causes opens the door to triviality or narcissism. But this assumes that children are incapable of meaningful concern. In fact, children often possess a moral clarity that adults lose—an unfiltered sense of justice and an instinctive compassion for vulnerability. What they lack is not feeling, but context. The role of the adult, then, is not to dictate but to *scaffold*: to provide background, help them ask better questions, and expose them to a diversity of needs. A ten-year-old who wants to give to a dog rescue because "dogs are cute" is on a valid path—but that path can be widened. What else do shelters need? What happens when there aren't enough homes? Are there people facing similar problems? With each layer, the understanding deepens, and the giving becomes not just emotional, but *informed*.

This process also confronts an important cultural bias: the elevation of monetary giving above all else. When children choose causes, they may sometimes want to give time, voice, or service rather than money. That's not a failure of the lesson. That's its evolution. A teenager who volunteers at a youth climate march or writes letters to local government officials about refugee policies is engaging in advocacy—a form of giving as critical as any cheque. Letting children choose their cause also means letting them choose *how* to express their commitment. If we force every act of generosity into a financial box, we may inadvertently teach that those without money have no power to contribute. That is a dangerous lesson. And it is untrue.

Parents who are serious about cultivating meaningful giving should also consider how causes are introduced in the first place. If children are only ever exposed to suffering through emotionally loaded media appeals—starving children, natural disasters, sick pets—their giving may be driven more by guilt than values. Instead, parents can help children identify causes that align with their own interests and emerging identities. A child who loves nature may care about reforestation. One who enjoys reading may support literacy programmes. When giving is tied to identity, it becomes not just a charitable act but a form of self-expression—and *self-expression with consequences* is one of the most powerful developmental tools available.

This is not to say that every cause a child picks must be approved or amplified. There is pedagogical value in letting them give to a niche idea, see little visible result, and then reflect on it. The key is the reflection. Adults often underestimate how much children can learn from simply being asked what they thought, what they felt, what they'd do next. It signals respect. And it builds the habit of internal accountability.

There is also a long-term benefit. Children who practise directed giving from a young age are more likely to grow into adults with what behavioural economists call *prosocial agency*—the belief that they can affect the world through intentional action. They give more frequently. They research their giving. They view philanthropy not as a tax write-off or a branding opportunity but as *an act of alignment between inner values and outer needs*. That is the kind of giver every society needs.

None of this requires large sums. In fact, small giving is often better for building the muscles of discernment. A child deciding how to allocate £5 must think critically about trade-offs: How many causes can I support? What does each pound do? Do I want to give it all to one, or split it? These are the same questions a foundation director might ask when managing millions—just scaled down. In that sense, small donations aren't lesser practice. *They are distilled practice.*

Letting kids choose their causes isn't about creating future philanthropists. It's about creating conscious citizens. Citizens who don't just wait for a crisis to care, but who notice, who act, and who do so with a clear sense of why. That clarity begins not in adulthood but in childhood—at the dinner table, in the classroom, during a trip to the animal shelter or a community event. It begins when an adult says, "This is your money. Who do *you* want to help?" and then listens without correcting.

Ultimately, giving isn't something children grow into. It's something they grow *through*. The more opportunities they have to choose, reflect, and revise, the stronger their internal compass becomes. And if that compass is well-developed, it will serve them far beyond donation slips or charity drives. It will shape how they treat people, how they build careers, how they use power—and, most importantly, *how they define a meaningful life*.

## Celebrating Impact, Not Sacrifice

If children grow up believing that generosity is synonymous with self-denial, they will either avoid it or resent it. This is not a minor pedagogical oversight—it is a fundamental miscalibration of what it means to contribute meaningfully to others. When giving is framed as a subtraction, a diminishing, or a noble loss, the implicit message is that virtue is incompatible with joy. Parents who wish to raise generous children must therefore shift the narrative away from sacrifice and towards *impact*—from what is relinquished to what is achieved. Generosity is not a painful discipline but a form of agency. And the earlier children experience it as power rather than penalty, the more enduring and self-directed their giving becomes.

The legacy of sacrificial framing runs deep. In many religious, cultural, and moral traditions, giving is celebrated most when it hurts. The phrase "giving until it hurts" is still used unironically in charitable circles. While the sentiment may intend to underscore commitment, it often warps a child's early impressions. If generosity must be accompanied by hardship to be authentic, then what message do we send when they give easily, joyfully, or playfully? That it doesn't count? That it's performative? That they should feel ashamed for enjoying the act? These are corrosive associations. They confuse moral worth with emotional suffering. And they make giving less sustainable because it becomes something to endure rather than something to *own*.

Instead, we must teach children that the measure of a gift lies not in what it cost the giver, but in what it enabled. This is not semantic indulgence—it is a strategic realignment. Impact-oriented giving asks, "What changed because you gave?" rather than "How much did you give up?" The difference is critical. One builds a sense of purpose; the other builds a ledger of martyrdom. When children see their donation buy school supplies for a refugee child, or their volunteer hours help a local animal shelter find homes for strays, they begin to grasp that generosity is not about proving goodness—it is about *amplifying outcomes*. It is a mechanism of influence, not a badge of pain.

There is also a psychological dividend. Research in developmental psychology and behavioural economics consistently finds that when individuals perceive their contributions as *efficacious*—when they can see a clear line from action to result—they are far more likely to continue giving. This holds true across age groups. In children especially, perceived impact increases self-efficacy: the belief that their actions have tangible effects in the world. Self-efficacy, in turn, reinforces autonomy, motivation, and moral development. Put simply, when kids see that their small actions matter, they internalise a powerful truth: *I can make things better*. That belief is foundational not only to generosity, but to citizenship itself.

Parents play a pivotal role in shaping this belief—not just through what they say, but through what they emphasise. Imagine a scenario where a child donates £5 to a food bank. A sacrifice-centred parent might say, "Wow, that's a lot of your money. You must really care." The tone is one of solemnity, the subtext being that pain equals meaning. An impact-centred parent might instead say, "That £5 helps feed two families tonight. How incredible is that?" The difference is profound. The child in the second example walks away with a sense of *effectiveness*, not deprivation.

This shift is particularly important when it comes to recurring giving. Children who are encouraged to set aside a portion of their allowance for monthly donations may initially comply out of routine. But if they are continually told, explicitly or subtly, that the money they're giving away is a "sacrifice," they are less likely to sustain the habit once external supervision ends. Conversely, if they receive regular feedback on the impact of their giving—photos, stories, letters, or even a simple update from the organisation—they develop what educators call *consequence awareness*. They learn that choices have ripple effects. That they are part of a larger ecosystem. That their resources are levers, not losses.

Critically, this framing also helps inoculate against performative giving—the kind driven more by social image than moral impulse. When children are taught to focus on the result of their giving rather than its optics or perceived moral purity, they are less susceptible to guilt-based appeals or status-driven donations. They give to *solve,* not to be seen. That orientation is vital in a media-saturated world where virtue is often commodified and generosity reduced to hashtags.

Moreover, celebrating impact fosters emotional resilience. Children will not always get the response they expect when they give. A thank-you might be delayed. The results of a fundraiser might fall short. The person they helped may not even know it was them. If their giving is rooted in sacrifice, these outcomes can feel like invalidation: "I gave something up, and it didn't matter." But if their giving is framed as contribution—*as an act of possibility*—then imperfect results are part of the learning, not the undoing. They become curious, not discouraged. Reflective, not bitter.

One practical tool for reinforcing this framing is to build "impact rituals" into family life. These might include short debriefs after charitable activities ("What do you think changed because of what we did?"), impact trackers (a wall chart showing how many people were reached), or periodic story-sharing sessions where each family member presents a cause they supported and what difference it made. These rituals don't require large budgets or dramatic gestures. They require only intentionality. Their power lies in repetition and reflection—not in spectacle.

There is, of course, a balance to be struck. Shielding children entirely from the reality that giving sometimes *does* cost something can lead to a shallow, transactional model of generosity. That, too, is undesirable. Giving may sometimes mean missing out on a toy, skipping a treat, or spending a weekend helping someone else instead of relaxing. The key is not to deny these moments, but to contextualise them. Parents might say, "Yes, you gave up something—and look what it made possible." In this framing, the sacrifice becomes *instrumental*, not *existential*. It is not the essence of generosity, but occasionally its cost. And even then, the cost is purposeful.

Another benefit of focusing on impact over sacrifice is that it democratises giving. If the social story of generosity centres only on those who can afford to give lavishly—or suffer visibly in the process—then we risk teaching children that meaningful giving is the province of the wealthy or the heroic. That's simply false. A child who bakes cookies to raise £10 for a clean water project is not "less generous" than one who donates £100 gifted by a grandparent. What matters is *intention combined with action,* not scale. Celebrating impact ensures that every child sees themselves as capable of making a difference, regardless of age or income.

This lesson is especially salient in moments of collective crisis—natural disasters, pandemics, or humanitarian emergencies—when children may feel overwhelmed or powerless. Teaching them that even small, directed actions can create real change transforms despair into agency. And that agency is not fleeting. It becomes part of how they navigate future challenges. They begin to approach the world not just as witnesses to suffering, but as contributors to solutions.

Ultimately, celebrating impact is not a feel-good rhetorical strategy. It is a developmental imperative. It changes how children experience their role in society. It builds both compassion and confidence. It aligns the act of giving with the emotions of competence, purpose, and connection rather than with shame, scarcity, or obligation.

And perhaps most importantly, it tells children the truth. Generosity is not a subtraction. It is an addition—to someone else's life, and to their own. It is not about the weight of what is given up, but the lift of what is made possible. That is the story worth telling. That is the lesson worth passing on.

# Chapter 8
# Conversations That Stick

No child stumbles into an understanding of money by chance. Just as emotional intelligence or moral reasoning develops through repeated, meaningful engagement, so too does financial literacy. It grows through conversations long before children themselves demand them. Yet all too often, parents wait for a "teachable moment"—the question asked, the mistake made, the allowance spent—before addressing money. In doing so, they forfeit the most crucial advantage: foresight. Families who nurture financially thoughtful children are not merely reactive; they prepare the terrain before the questions arrive.

Money is never a purely technical subject. It entwines identity, security, fairness, and control. Children do not approach it as a ledger; they approach it as a mirror. A question such as "Are we rich?" or "Why can't I have what they have?" is never just fiscal—it probes belonging, worth, and honesty. Yet most parents are unprepared, not due to lack of values, but because they have rarely paused to consider how money and language intersect. This chapter seeks to create that space. It does not provide scripts; it offers a lens—a way of seeing financial conversations as stewardship rather than stress.

Authenticity, rather than perfection, is the aim. Parents need not have all the answers, but they must cultivate a home where questions are welcomed, language is calibrated, and money is neither sacred nor shameful. Generic binaries like "wants versus needs" or evasive replies—"We can't afford that," when the truth is "we're choosing not to buy it"—fall short. Children notice hedging. Clarity, delivered with nuance, is essential. It does not require adult-level spreadsheets, but it does demand respect for a child's cognitive stage, alongside honest insight: "Here's how our family thinks about spending," rather than "Because I said so." Over time, such nuanced communication builds a vocabulary—emotional and practical—through which children navigate not only financial decisions, but ethical and social ones too.

Every transaction offers a potential lesson—not because money itself is profound, but because our choices reveal priorities. Comparing the cost-per-use of items at the shop is not merely maths; it models discernment. Discussing birthday party budgets or the ethics of fast fashion is not excessive seriousness; it shows that spending rarely concerns price alone. Grocery aisles, donation jars, delayed purchases, shared bills—all serve as unfolding scripts, constructing a working model of intentional living. When approached thoughtfully, these moments transcend compliance; they become architecture for independent judgment.

Yet not every moment should be instructive. Over-explaining is a common error. Sometimes the most potent parental response is to listen—not correct, justify, or redirect. Children's financial curiosity is often a test of trust, a probe of whether their uncertainty can be safely held. Questions like "Why do some kids have more?" "Is money fair?" or "What happens if someone runs out?" are rarely requests for economic theory. They are emotional disclosures. Responses that offer empathy, rather than immediate instruction, deepen connection and sustain inquiry.

Conversations that resonate are never singular events; they are iterative and cumulative. Memorable lessons emerge in car rides, folding laundry, after a loss or mistake, or when a relative sends a cheque. The parent's role is not to orchestrate, but to notice, to respond with presence rather than pre-programmed lines. Curiosity opens a doorway—into money management, certainly, but also into the values and assumptions money illuminates.

This chapter examines how to cultivate such openings with skill and sincerity. It challenges the assumption that money talk should wait until a child is "ready." Readiness is not chronological; it is contextual. When parents speak openly—without fear, defensiveness, or dogma—they create that context. The chapter addresses common and complex questions, unpacking not only what can be said, but why certain approaches resonate more than others. It guides parents in transforming everyday spending into practical and meaningful dialogue, and it emphasises the often-overlooked art of listening: sometimes, the most potent contribution a parent can make is to bear witness.

Perfection in financial upbringing does not exist. Intentional conversations do. Conversations that transmit agency as much as information. Conversations that help children understand not merely how money works, but how they wish to work with it themselves. Conversations that endure not through polish, but through authenticity. The task is not merely to inform—it is to invite. Not simply to answer—but to awaken. To open doors to lifelong reflection. And once that door is opened, everything changes.

### Start Before the Questions Come

By the time a child asks, "Are we rich?", the groundwork for how they interpret money has already been laid. The tone of a family's financial dialogue is established not when a child first poses a question, but in the thousand small cues, reactions, and overheard conversations leading up to it. In many households, money remains an implicit topic—hinted at, joked about, sometimes argued over, but rarely discussed in a structured or intentional way. Children don't need formal education to absorb meaning; they're expert anthropologists of adult behaviour. They notice tension at the checkout, reluctance around debt, discomfort with tipping, or resentment when something feels unaffordable. When there's no language to make sense of those patterns, the child supplies their own. Often incorrectly.

Waiting for the "right time" to talk about money assumes children will signal their readiness with explicit curiosity. In reality, many children are forming mental models long before they ask. A child watching a parent refuse to buy a branded cereal may register it as unfairness, scarcity, or moral discipline—depending on what context they've previously been offered. The lack of a conversation doesn't mean there's a lack of meaning-making. It simply means that the meaning is being constructed invisibly. *The cost of silence is that children form assumptions without calibration.*

Starting early matters, not because toddlers need to understand compound interest, but because financial literacy begins in the soil of emotional literacy. If a child never hears parents narrate values like saving, restraint, sharing, or prioritisation, they're left to associate money primarily with denial or indulgence. The first financial conversations should not be lectures but observations. "We're bringing lunch today instead of buying it because that helps us save for our holiday." "We chose not to buy that toy because it doesn't get used much." "That treat costs more than it's worth to us." These comments plant the idea that money is not about what you *can* buy, but about what you *choose* to value. No shame. No over-explanation. Just fluency.

Parents often worry that early conversations will overburden children with adult concerns. But age-appropriate discussion isn't about revealing your mortgage stress—it's about narrating decisions with clarity and compassion. A four-year-old can grasp trade-offs. A six-year-old can begin to link effort to reward. An eight-year-old can learn about planning for future wants. These are not adult topics shrunk to child-size; they are child-relevant ideas presented with intellectual honesty. *Starting early doesn't mean saying everything—it means saying something, consistently and coherently.*

One of the most underused entry points for financial conversation is the moment of routine spending. Children are rarely interested in abstract discussions about budgeting, but they are deeply alert to the fairness of who gets what and when. Supermarket trips, shared restaurant bills, new shoes, birthday gifts, streaming subscriptions—

these are all silent curriculum. When a parent explains not just the "no" but the *why,* they turn the moment from rejection into education. "That's not in our budget this week" is informative. "We're choosing to spend on something else we value more" is formative. It tells the child that money is about deliberate choice, not arbitrary withholding.

Starting before the questions come also allows parents to define their values on their own terms, rather than reacting defensively when confronted. A child asking "Why don't we have a nicer car?" puts a parent in a reactive posture. But if the child has previously heard their parent speak with pride about saving for education or choosing not to finance luxury items, they're less likely to interpret "no" as lack or failure. They begin to understand that *spending is a reflection of identity, not income alone.* Proactive conversation inoculates against the shame and confusion that often accompanies peer comparison.

The most powerful early conversations are those that feel embedded in life, not bolted onto it. When children help count coins in a donation box, they're not just doing arithmetic—they're linking values to action. When they observe how parents respond to a sale, they learn how scarcity or urgency affects decision-making. When they are invited to choose between two treats instead of receiving both, they confront trade-offs in a tangible, manageable way. *The goal is not to transfer knowledge in one sitting—it's to normalise curiosity and equip discernment.*

It's also worth recognising that many parents struggle to begin these conversations because they themselves have never had them. They may still be navigating inherited beliefs about money—associating it with control, fear, guilt, or even silence. The act of initiating early conversations with children becomes, then, not just an educational gesture but a generational correction. It says: "In this family, we talk about things that matter, even when they're complicated." That in itself is a profound gift. It communicates that *money is not taboo—it's a tool.* And tools are meant to be learned, shared, and respected.

Crucially, the point of starting early isn't to accelerate a child's economic maturity. It's to build a framework of interpretation so that when questions do arise—about wealth, inequality, fairness, earning—they land on prepared ground. Children raised in financially fluent households are not necessarily savvier spenders at age seven. But they are more likely to approach money with openness, context, and a working vocabulary. They are less likely to collapse into shame when they can't afford something, or entitlement when they can. *Early dialogue builds both confidence and humility—the two traits most predictive of wise financial behaviour later in life.*

It's also important to understand that waiting too long doesn't just delay knowledge—it changes its nature. When a child first learns about family finances in adolescence, often prompted by conflict or comparison, the conversation tends to be charged. Teenagers are acutely aware of fairness and status. A delayed conversation is more likely to be interpreted as secrecy, distrust, or inequality. Proactive conversation, by contrast, creates a sense of shared ownership. It says, "You're growing into someone who can think about these things with us." That's a powerful developmental message—one that supports autonomy without overwhelming it.

None of this requires perfection. What it requires is *presence*. The willingness to begin before you feel fully prepared. The humility to narrate values as they evolve. The steadiness to speak when silence would be easier. The patience to listen when the child's understanding is limited. Starting early doesn't guarantee smooth outcomes. But it creates a foundation of trust—and trust is the one currency that compounds faster than any financial asset. When children grow up in households where money is discussed with clarity, curiosity, and care, they carry those patterns into every financial decision that follows.

The choice is not whether financial conversations will shape your child—it's *whether you will shape them intentionally, or let them be shaped by guesswork, advertising, and peers*. To start early is not to be overbearing—it is to be responsible. It is to say: before the world tells you what money is, *let me show you what we believe it means*. That belief, articulated early and lived consistently, is the seed from which all lasting financial wisdom grows.

## Answering the Hard Ones

There are few parenting moments more disarming than a child's direct financial curiosity. "Are we rich?" "Why don't we have a house like theirs?" "How much do you make?" These questions often land like pebbles dropped into the middle of a calm pond—producing ripples of discomfort, introspection, and the temptation to deflect. For parents who may still be sorting out their own financial narratives, these conversations can feel prematurely complex. But when a child asks a difficult money question, they are not demanding spreadsheets or philosophical manifestos. They are reaching for orientation in a world they're beginning to decode—and they're hoping to do it with you.

Children do not ask these questions in a vacuum. They are often triggered by contrast: a classmate's lavish birthday party, a neighbour's new car, a television advert full of smiling families on tropical holidays. At a surprisingly young age, children begin to register patterns of material difference, even if they cannot yet articulate inequality, status, or scarcity. The mistake many adults make is to interpret such questions as precocious or impolite, when in fact they are cognitively normal. *What matters is not just what we say, but how we respond to the asking itself.*

Dismissiveness—"That's not something you need to worry about"—may seem like protection, but it can backfire. It teaches children that money is a topic shrouded in secrecy or shame. Overexposure, however—detailing income, debts, or financial stress in ways that overwhelm—is equally unproductive. The skill is in the middle path: offering honest, developmentally appropriate responses that frame money as a navigable, values-driven subject.

Consider the question "Are we rich?" On the surface, it appears to be about net worth. But more often, it's about belonging. A child asking this isn't calculating your assets; they're trying to locate your family in a social hierarchy they've only just begun to perceive. A productive response avoids yes-or-no binaries. One approach is to situate the family within a spectrum of global and local realities: "Compared to many people around the world, yes, we're very fortunate. We have a safe home, enough to eat, and choices about how we live. But there are also families with more than us. What matters most to us isn't being rich, but being thoughtful with what we have." This reframes the question away from absolutes and toward perspective, responsibility, and gratitude.

When children ask, "Why don't we buy what they have?", the emotional content often eclipses the factual. This is less about the object and more about visibility, difference, or perceived exclusion. Parents can use this as a moment to reflect aloud on priorities: "That's not something we choose to spend money on, because we value other things more." Or, "We could buy it, but we're choosing not to, because it doesn't feel worth it to us." This subtly introduces the idea that money is not just for satisfying desires—it's an extension of values, timing, and judgement. *The point isn't to moralise against others' spending—it's to clarify your own family's logic in a way that builds agency, not deprivation.*

Not all questions come from envy or confusion. Some emerge from sincere curiosity. "How much do you make?" is a test of transparency, but also of emotional tone. An appropriate answer depends on the child's age and your comfort, but the principle is this: respond without panic. One strategy is to focus less on the number and more on its function. For instance: "I earn enough for us to live comfortably and to plan for things like your education, holidays, and some savings. Part of being a grown-up is managing that money carefully so it supports the things we care about." This creates a frame in which money is not a measure of identity but a mechanism for stewardship.

Financial questions that touch on inequality—"Why do some people sleep outside?" or "Why can't they just get a job?"—require special care. These are formative moments where a child's moral and economic worldview begins to take shape. The temptation to simplify must be resisted. Rather than offering reductive answers, it is more powerful to model complexity and empathy: "That's a really good question, and there's not one simple answer. Some people don't have the same chances or support. Sometimes people face problems that are hard to fix without help. That's one reason why we believe in helping where we can." *It's not about solving the social problem in a single reply—it's about widening the lens through which your child sees it.*

What's common to all these difficult conversations is the underlying need for security. Children want to know not just how much is enough, but *whether they are enough* within their family's economic landscape. Parents who express confidence—not in having everything, but in knowing what matters—offer a sense of stability that transcends material comparisons. This doesn't require rehearsed speeches or perfect phrasing. It requires presence, emotional regulation, and a willingness to engage the question beneath the question.

There is also a developmental case for repeated conversations. The first time a child asks about wealth or possessions, the answer should match their level of abstraction. But as they grow, revisit the topic with deeper nuance. A nine-year-old can understand opportunity cost. A twelve-year-old can grapple with the idea of invisible labour or unequal starting points. A teenager may be ready to discuss privilege, taxation, or ethical spending. *The currency of credibility is not a one-time explanation—it's the pattern of returning to difficult subjects with respect and clarity.*

When children sense discomfort in their parents, they often interpret it as danger. A brief pause is fine. But if your response is laced with anxiety or judgment, the child learns to tiptoe around money topics in future. This undermines trust. Instead, if a question catches you off guard, it's entirely fair to say: "That's a thoughtful question—I'd like to take a moment and give it the answer it deserves." Then circle back. *The act of revisiting a hard question signals to the child that you take them seriously—and that complexity is not something to be feared, but worked through.*

There's a common misconception that children need to be protected from financial reality. In truth, they need to be protected from *financial confusion*. Honesty builds resilience—not brutal honesty, but measured, wise, attuned honesty. The kind that names trade-offs without inducing shame. That contextualises affluence without breeding guilt. That models compassion without performative pity. And most of all, that treats the child not as a passive recipient of parental resources, but as an emerging participant in the ethical use of money.

In responding to hard questions, we are not just imparting information—we are shaping how our children will one day speak to others about these same issues. We are showing them how to navigate power, fairness, inequality, and identity through the lens of resource distribution. Whether we answer with fear or fluency becomes their internal script. Whether we deflect or explain becomes their future posture.

Ultimately, the most powerful answer is not one that closes the question, but one that invites the child to keep asking, thinking, and wrestling. The parent who says, "That's complicated, and we can keep talking about it," communicates not only financial insight, but relational trust. And in the landscape of money and meaning, that trust is worth more than any figure on a payslip.

## Turn Transactions into Teachables

Children are rarely taught money in classrooms, but they are watching it taught every day—in supermarkets, in restaurants, in gift shops, and in birthday aisles. The irony is that the most effective financial education doesn't require a curriculum or an app. It requires presence. The ordinary moments when adults spend, hesitate, compare, or defer are a live theatre of values. Children notice what gets bought, what doesn't, and—perhaps most critically—why. The grocery checkout becomes a seminar on trade-offs; the birthday gift bag becomes a referendum on social norms and self-worth. *When parents frame transactions as decision points, not just logistics, they raise children who think critically rather than consume reflexively.*

Children form monetary beliefs not from what we say, but from how we act. A parent who lectures about frugality but casually adds a £3.99 chocolate bar at checkout models indulgence, not restraint. The adult who negotiates a better price or walks away from a non-essential item teaches discernment by example. This gap between stated principles and lived behaviour is precisely where most financial literacy efforts collapse. *If you want your child to become a mindful spender, start by narrating your own decision-making out loud.* There is enormous developmental power in hearing phrases like: "I really want this, but I've already spent my fun money for the week," or, "Let's compare this with another brand to see if it's better value."

Consider the weekly grocery shop. For children under ten, this setting offers dozens of micro-lessons: unit pricing, budgeting, brand marketing, impulsivity, delayed gratification, needs versus wants. A child who sees a parent pause before buying berries out of season learns that scarcity has cost. A brief aside about "this cereal is on special, but only if we buy two" introduces the subtle economics of bundling. Even choices such as bulk versus single-use items offer a chance to discuss environmental and long-term cost considerations. None of this requires a whiteboard or worksheet—only that the adult voices the choices already being made in their head.

Birthday parties, often loaded with emotion and expectation, are equally ripe for teachable moments. When a child receives money as a gift, the way that money is framed—windfall, entitlement, or opportunity—has lasting psychological effects. Does it go straight into the till of a toy store? Is part of it saved? Are charitable options discussed? The framing is everything. More powerful still is involving the child in planning gifts for others. When children are given a fixed budget to choose a friend's present, they begin to grapple with balancing generosity, taste, and cost. They learn that money has relational weight—it speaks not only about value, but about care, attention, and respect.

What's often underestimated is how receptive even very young children are to complex economic ideas, provided those ideas are anchored in tangible contexts. A four-year-old may not understand inflation, but they can grasp that a bottle of juice now costs more than it did a few months ago, and that this influences what the family can afford. An eight-year-old may not grasp the mechanics of compound interest, but can understand the difference between spending all one's pocket money today and having enough for a movie ticket next week. *By contextualising economic concepts inside familiar rituals—shopping, gifting, choosing—we transform abstraction into comprehension.*

One of the most effective techniques parents can employ is the "think aloud" method. This doesn't mean explaining every financial move, which would be exhausting and counterproductive. It means selectively voicing thoughts that model deliberation. For instance: "I like this jumper, but I already have two that work just fine. It's not a need, and I'd rather use that money for something more lasting." When children consistently hear this kind of reasoning, they begin to internalise that spending is an act of agency, not automation.

However, there's a danger in overdoing it. Turning every errand into a sermon will quickly backfire. Children learn best when they're invited to think, not told what to think. The tone matters—curiosity over control, questions over directives. A parent might say, "What would you pick if you had £5 to spend in this shop? Why that?" and listen without correcting. These conversational probes create psychological space for reflection, rather than compliance.

This balance between guiding and overmanaging is especially delicate when money enters the child's direct control. Suppose a child wants to spend all of their weekly allowance on a novelty item. The parental impulse might be to intervene—to caution against waste or suggest a more 'responsible' use. But there's wisdom in restraint. *A child who never experiences buyer's remorse will never learn its cost.* Watching a toy lose its appeal within hours is a more effective lesson than any lecture. The key is to remain available for debriefing: "How do you feel about what you bought? Would you choose the same next time?" The goal is not to avoid poor decisions, but to mine them for insight.

Equally valuable is seizing spontaneous, unplanned moments. A queue at the corner shop. A decision about a takeaway meal. A choice between two snacks. These are not interruptions to learning—they are the learning. One family kept a shared "money question jar" on the kitchen counter. Anyone—parent or child—could write a spending dilemma or observation on a scrap of paper and toss it in. Once a week, the jar was opened and discussed over dinner. No preaching, no right answers—just shared reflection. It normalised uncertainty and opened the floor to ideas from all age levels.

Technology complicates this picture. Digital spending, contactless transactions, and in-app purchases often eliminate the tactile cues that help children calibrate money's significance. It is vital that parents do not let convenience erase consciousness. If a child never sees physical currency leave a wallet, they may struggle to appreciate money as a finite resource. This is why some educators still recommend using real coins and notes in early years, even if the family's real-world spending is digital. The visual and kinaesthetic elements encode lessons in a way screens cannot replicate.

Yet the goal isn't to resist technology, but to harness it. Budgeting apps for kids, digital piggy banks, or visual savings trackers can add structure to everyday decisions. The key is that the app supplements, not replaces, the conversation. No app can transmit your values unless you articulate them alongside. *The screen is a tool. The adult is the teacher.*

Finally, it's essential to treat these learning moments with emotional depth, not just economic analysis. Money is never just arithmetic—it is identity, status, freedom, security, and love, all wrapped into one volatile symbol. A child who is told "We can't afford that" hears not just a denial of a purchase but potentially a limitation of worth. A better phrase might be, "That's not how we choose to spend our money," or, "We're saving for something else more meaningful." It shifts the conversation from scarcity to values. From denial to intention.

What makes a transaction teachable is not the money, but the meaning we wrap around it. *Every receipt carries a story. Every purchase is a small vote for the kind of life we're living or hoping to build.* If we let children into that story—not by sermon but by inclusion—we empower them not only to manage money, but to think through it. That, ultimately, is the lesson that sticks.

### When to Talk, When to Listen

The temptation to fill silence with wisdom is one of the most persistent instincts of well-meaning parents. Especially when it comes to money—a topic layered with personal history, ethical tension, and economic consequence—adults often believe that speaking first, explaining often, and clarifying quickly is the best path to a financially literate child. But in reality, the moments that leave the deepest imprint are not always those that are packed with guidance. Often, *it is our restraint, not our instruction, that builds trust and influence*. Knowing when to talk and when to listen is not merely a social skill—it is a moral stance, one that determines whether children see money as something to be managed thoughtfully or feared quietly.

Children's questions about money rarely arrive with neat framing or convenient timing. They come out of nowhere, loaded with curiosity and sometimes with subtext: "Why can't we go on holiday this year?" "Why does Max get a new phone, and I don't?" "Are we poor?" "Why don't you buy that nice coffee anymore?" These aren't just inquiries about financial logistics—they are invitations into a child's sense-making process. To answer them reflexively, or dismiss them altogether, is to miss a deeper opportunity: *to understand what the question is really about*.

This is where listening becomes both an interpretive act and a relational investment. Before rushing to correct or inform, the adult must pause long enough to ask themselves: What is my child trying to learn about the world—and about us—

in this moment? Is this a question about money, or about status, fairness, belonging, or identity? A parent who reflexively replies, "We're not poor, don't be silly," may think they are reassuring the child, but in fact they are closing off a conversation that the child was brave enough to start. *The cost of shutting down curiosity is far greater than the discomfort of sitting with it.*

Non-judgmental presence means more than just silence. It means responding with a posture of genuine curiosity. "That's an interesting question—what made you think about that?" or, "Tell me more about what you mean," signals to the child that their thoughts are taken seriously. The goal is not to reward questions with lectures, but with *attention*. Many children stop asking about money not because they lose interest, but because they've learned that questions are either met with shame, stonewalling, or overwhelm.

Even well-intended enthusiasm can derail an emerging conversation. A child who expresses interest in starting a lemonade stand might be met with a barrage of adult-level business advice: budgeting, signage, return on investment. But the original idea may have been more about play than enterprise, about social interaction rather than profit. When parents leap too quickly into teaching mode, they risk *colonising the child's curiosity* rather than stewarding it. A better initial response might be: "That sounds like a fun idea—what are you imagining it might look like?" Only once the child begins to articulate goals should the adult consider offering practical scaffolding.

In financial conversations, timing is rarely neutral. Children absorb tone and context as much as content. A casual remark about someone's expensive shoes can plant the seeds of value judgement. An offhand comment like "We can't afford anything fun anymore" can calcify into a belief about scarcity or powerlessness. Likewise, well-meaning corrections—"That's not how saving works" or "Don't say things like that in front of other people"—can subtly teach children that money is a taboo subject, best kept quiet unless one is sure of the 'right' answer. *If money is treated as emotionally charged or intellectually gated, children will either overcompensate with performance or disengage altogether.*

The alternative is to treat money conversations as a kind of open-source dialogue, where questions evolve, insights are co-created, and silence is not treated as a void to be filled but as *space for thinking*. This becomes especially important during adolescence, when the parent-child dynamic shifts from instructor-pupil to something closer to advisory partnership. A teenager who sees a parent always rushing to conclusions may learn that their own intuitions are irrelevant. A teenager who sees their thoughts held and explored—"That's an interesting way to see it; what else do you think?"—is more likely to return with deeper questions later.

But restraint is not the same as abdication. There are moments when silence is unhelpful—when a child makes a value judgment about a homeless person, for example, or mimics classist language picked up from peers. In these moments, speaking with clarity is essential—but not with condemnation. "Let's talk about what that means," or "Where did you hear that idea?" allows for correction *through context,* not punishment. The aim is to raise children who think ethically, not just correctly.

Listening also helps reveal what a child already believes about money, much of which they've inferred long before any direct conversation. A six-year-old who says, "That person's poor because they don't work hard," is not announcing an original philosophy—they are echoing signals received from media, overheard conversations, and subtle adult cues. Responding with surprise or reprimand—"That's not nice!"—shuts the door. Responding with engagement—"What makes you think that?"—opens a discussion about luck, systems, dignity, and justice. *Every assumption is a gateway to a teachable moment, but only if the adult is willing to listen without flinching.*

One of the least discussed dynamics in financial education is the emotional landscape of the adult. Parents carry their own money stories—shaped by trauma, pride, secrecy, or lack. When a child's question touches on those nerves—"Why don't we have a bigger house?" or "Did you ever get into debt?"—the adult's internal reaction often eclipses the content of the conversation. It takes emotional maturity to resist projecting guilt, anxiety, or defensiveness onto the child. *To listen well, the adult must first make peace with their own financial past.* This doesn't mean perfection—it means transparency with boundaries: "That's something I'm still figuring out myself," or "It's a complicated story, but I'll share what I can."

Indeed, some of the most powerful moments occur when the adult allows themselves to be a learner alongside the child. "I don't know, but let's find out," models intellectual humility. It shows that knowledge isn't a fixed asset handed down from parent to child—it's a shared currency of exploration. This stance transforms money conversations from didactic exchanges into relational rituals. Not just how we teach, but *how we are together in the face of the unknown.*

This relational framing also means acknowledging when a child isn't ready to talk—and honouring that. A parent may want to unpack a child's impulsive purchase or lack of saving strategy, only to be met with shrugs or avoidance. Rather than force the conversation, it's often wiser to *signal availability and wait*: "You don't have to talk about it now, but I'd love to hear what you think when you're ready." Silence, in this context, is not resistance—it is often the soil in which reflection germinates.

Ultimately, teaching children about money is not a monologue but a dialogue—and not every line of dialogue requires an answer. Sometimes, the best response is presence. The child asks, and the adult listens—not just to the words, but to what lies beneath them. And sometimes, when the child is silent, it is the adult who must pause long enough to ask themselves: *What is being said in the quiet?* To raise children who are thoughtful, ethical, and empowered with money, we must be willing to offer them not just our knowledge, but our attention. In a world full of noise, the adult who listens well teaches best.

# Chapter 9
# Digital Dollars, Real Risks

A generation is growing up without ever feeling the heft of coins or the crumpled texture of notes between their fingers. For today's children, money often exists as nothing more than a string of digits on a screen. Tap, swipe, click—spending has become so frictionless that the tangible anchors of value have all but disappeared. There is no wallet to empty, no counter to approach, no moment of separation from the money they once held. While this abstraction offers speed and convenience to adults, it introduces subtle developmental challenges for the young. When money is invisible, its meaning must be deliberately conveyed.

The loss is more than sensory; it is cognitive. Behavioural research across decades demonstrates that physical interaction strengthens understanding. A child counting three coins and placing them into a till engages in a multisensory lesson in arithmetic, prioritisation, and sacrifice. Contrast that with tapping a screen to "buy" an upgrade in a game using a parent's card—the link between cost, effort, and consequence is broken. Without careful guidance, digital transactions become weightless, invisible inputs producing instant, dopamine-fuelled rewards.

Even more insidious are the small, incremental purchases within apps, games, and subscriptions—the so-called microtransactions. Loot boxes, energy boosts, battle passes, or cosmetic skins often masquerade as progress, status, or access. To adults, these may seem trivial; to children, they function as currencies of social belonging and peer approval. Designed by behavioural economists and gamification specialists, these purchases are intentionally impulsive, exploiting cognitive immaturity and fostering patterns that resemble addiction more than agency.

Yet banning digital spending entirely is neither realistic nor productive. The economy is now digital by default. Children require tools—language, reflection, boundaries—that allow them to navigate this environment with discernment. This begins with observation, not lectures: Which games do they play? How does money function within those ecosystems? What social status is conferred by premium features, and how do peers or influencers shape these norms? Parents who ignore these questions often enforce rules that feel arbitrary to children and are easily dismissed.

Boundary-setting in the digital space requires a different approach. Punitive language—"You wasted all your allowance on that?"—erodes trust and encourages secrecy. Limits framed as empowerment are more effective: "Learning to make your money last is part of becoming independent." Concrete structures—weekly spending caps, time-limited sessions, cooling-off periods before significant in-app purchases—support this framework. Above all, parent-child dialogue must be ongoing, honest, and reciprocal, evolving alongside both platforms and the child's maturity.

Children must also grasp not just what they spend, but how they are being spent. In the digital economy, attention is currency, and personal data is the new commodity. Clicking "accept all" on terms-of-service pop-ups may unknowingly consent to surveillance, manipulation, and targeted persuasion. Financial literacy today cannot be disentangled from digital literacy. Children should ask: What am I trading for access? This entails understanding free-to-play models, the psychology of notifications, and subscription fatigue.

Consider a teenager enrolling in multiple music streaming trials, only to end the month with £30 of recurring charges they never intended. Companies rely on inertia, making cancellations inconvenient. Teaching children to track recurring costs, read statements, and evaluate opting out is as vital as budgeting for lunch or clothing. Similarly, scams, phishing, and impersonation exploit inexperience. Children should not be shamed for mistakes; instead, they should internalise simple heuristics: pause if something feels urgent, emotional, or too good to be true.

Digital environments are neither inherently harmful nor inherently benign—they are unregulated classrooms. Some lessons reinforce scarcity thinking, peer comparison, and mindless consumption; others cultivate autonomy, goal-setting, and entrepreneurship. A teen running a small business on Instagram or a Discord server may learn more about finance, marketing, and risk than through formal schooling. The critical factor is intentionality. Guided reflection allows even complex digital experiences to become fertile ground for learning.

To nurture financially literate children in this landscape, adults must first acknowledge its differences: faster, noisier, and less anchored in the tangible. Children need language for what they encounter and tools for what remains unseen. This includes narratives of resistance—choosing not to upgrade, delaying a purchase, or deleting an app is quiet heroism in a culture that rewards immediacy. It also includes clarifying values: "What does this purchase say about what you care about?" and "Will it matter next week?" Adult modelling of vulnerability—"I forgot about subscriptions I had to cancel last month"—further reinforces learning.

This chapter does not demonise screens or lament the disappearance of piggy banks. It re-imagines financial education in a world where money no longer jingles, transactions are gamified, and children carry potential marketplaces in their pockets. The risks are real, but so too are the opportunities. To raise thoughtful digital citizens rather than passive consumers, children must be taught to read between transactions, pause before they click, and recognise that even invisible money leaves tangible traces.

## The Vanishing Wallet

A child born today may never touch cash in any meaningful way. Their early encounters with money are less likely to involve counting coins or folding notes than tapping screens and watching numbers shift on a digital interface. Gone is the familiar drama of handing over a tenner and receiving change in clinking metal. In its place: biometric scans, stored passwords, invisible balances. For adults, the transition to a cashless world has been largely practical. For children, it is developmental—and the implications are profound. *When money becomes invisible, so too does its weight.*

To understand what has been lost with the vanishing wallet, one must first recall what it did. The wallet was not just a storage device; it was a theatre of decision-making. Physical money demanded presence. Children could feel the diminishing heft of a coin purse after buying sweets or sense the effort of saving for a toy through visible accumulation. Every transaction was tactile, spatial, and often communal. There was deliberation, ritual, even friction—a minor but crucial pause between wanting and spending. That pause, however small, reinforced the idea that money was finite, and choices mattered.

Contrast this with today's child navigating digital payments, where those frictions have largely disappeared. A purchase might require nothing more than a fingerprint or a glance at a face-recognition sensor. Transactions are seamless by design, and while seamlessness may be desirable for adults with complex schedules, it is *developmentally unearned* for children. Without tangible cues, there is no intuitive sense of loss, trade-off, or consequence. What remains is a kind of magical thinking: money goes away, things arrive, and the connection between the two is opaque at best.

This disconnect isn't just anecdotal—it's observable. Studies in developmental psychology and behavioural economics consistently show that children (and adults) are more cautious and discerning when handling cash compared to digital equivalents. A five-pound note carries more psychological gravity than a tap on a contactless card, even when the amounts are identical. The phenomenon, often referred to as "payment decoupling," diminishes the salience of cost and undermines self-regulation. In effect, the further removed we are from the mechanics of payment, the less conscious we become of our decisions.

Children raised in this environment are not inherently careless—they are simply *untethered*. The mechanisms that once rooted money in time, effort, and limitation have been abstracted away. Parents, meanwhile, are often unprepared for the consequences. They find themselves reacting to spending behaviours they don't fully understand—why did my child blow their entire allowance on digital skins?—without recognising that the child may not have had a clear sense that they were spending at all. The architecture of value has been stripped of its scaffolding.

Some argue that this is simply the new normal—that children will adapt to a cashless economy as fluently as they've adapted to touchscreens and streaming. But adaptation is not the same as understanding. A child may learn to navigate digital interfaces with speed and fluency, but this does not guarantee a corresponding development in financial judgement. In fact, the illusion of mastery may mask critical gaps in comprehension. *Being digitally native is not the same as being financially literate.*

What's needed, then, is not a nostalgic return to cash, but a reimagining of how value is taught in a world without it. This begins by reinstating the concept of *friction* in otherwise frictionless systems. For instance, some families use prepaid debit cards for children that require manual top-ups, creating intentional pauses that mimic the deliberation of cash-based spending. Others tie digital spending privileges to completed chores, saved goals, or reflective conversations. The goal is to restore a sense of effort, threshold, and intentionality—even if the medium is screen-based.

Visual cues also matter. Physical jars have long served as effective savings tools for young children, and digital analogues can replicate this. Apps that show animated coins filling virtual piggy banks or graphs tracking savings growth can help bridge the sensory gap. But it's not just about seeing—it's about *feeling*. If a child cannot feel the consequences of a poor spending decision, they are unlikely to learn from it. Allowing them to exhaust a weekly balance early, and then sit with that limitation, is often more instructive than a parental bailout. These moments create the internal calibration that digital systems erase.

There's also a deeper philosophical challenge at play: in the absence of physical money, children must be taught not just to *manage* value, but to *construct* it. This requires deliberate conversation about what money is and what it isn't. That it is not infinite. That it represents choices foregone. That it carries responsibilities beyond the self. These were once implicit in the mechanics of cash—they must now be made explicit through guided dialogue. When a child receives a digital allowance, do they know where it comes from? Do they understand what had to be earned or sacrificed to fund it? The answers to these questions are not self-evident. They must be taught.

Some parents worry that introducing complexity too early may burden or confuse. But simplicity is not always a gift. Shielding children from the realities of money delays the formation of critical reasoning. Instead, we should offer clarity without condescension: "This money came from work I did," or "We budgeted for this, which means we didn't spend on something else." These statements build a scaffold for abstraction—a scaffold now missing from the architecture of childhood.

Even so, we must resist the urge to over-engineer the solution. Not every moment needs to become a lesson. But *enough moments must be intentionally constructed* that the child begins to internalise the rhythms of value. When they pay for a snack with a QR code, the parent might ask, "How much did that cost in real money?" When they want a game upgrade, one might pose, "Is this worth what you've saved?" These are not tests; they are invitations to think.

The vanishing wallet is not just a metaphor—it is a developmental fault line. It divides the world children inherit from the world their parents remember. Bridging that divide requires vigilance, creativity, and above all, presence. We must meet our children where they are—not in lecture halls, but in checkout lines, game menus, and app subscriptions—and guide them not just to *use* money, but to *understand* it. Because in a world where money no longer weighs anything in the hand, we must teach it to weigh something in the mind.

## Games, Tokens, and Microtransactions

Children today are not simply playing games—they are entering economies. Whether navigating elaborate fantasy worlds or swiping through mobile puzzles, they encounter systems of currency, trade, reward, and upgrade. But unlike traditional games with clear boundaries—board games with fixed rules, card games with finite stakes—modern digital games blur the line between entertainment and economic participation. *What begins as play often becomes consumption,* with real financial consequences camouflaged behind virtual currency and behavioural design.

The introduction of microtransactions into children's gaming environments has transformed the nature of how young people experience money. Tokens, gems, skins, energy boosts, and "battle passes" are often purchased using real currency, but rarely with direct transparency. Instead of seeing "£5," children are shown "500 coins," obscuring the value exchange. Many games employ multiple layers of currency conversion—real money buys credits, which buy gems, which unlock treasure boxes—which *may* contain the desired item. This intentionally convoluted design is not an accident. It mirrors techniques used in casinos, loyalty programmes, and even speculative markets: *the more abstract the currency, the weaker the psychological brakes on spending.*

To a developing brain, especially one primed for reward-seeking, this environment is irresistible. Neuroscientific research confirms what any parent has observed: children and adolescents have heightened dopamine sensitivity in response to novelty, anticipation, and perceived gain. Game designers exploit this with variable reward schedules, scarcity tactics, countdown timers, and social comparison—all calibrated to encourage repeated spending. The result is not merely a risk of overspending; it is the *training of habits and impulses* that can be difficult to unlearn.

Consider the case of "loot boxes"—randomised reward mechanisms that mimic gambling. These are now so ubiquitous in games popular with children that regulators in several countries have issued formal warnings or outright bans. But even beyond the overtly controversial mechanisms, the quieter issue is behavioural drift: children being conditioned to see spending as a reflexive action in response to frustration or social pressure. Ran out of energy in a game? Pay to play again instantly. See a friend's character with a rarer skin? Spend to match or surpass. The feedback loop is swift, seamless, and emotionally loaded.

Yet it would be both naive and ineffective to attempt to eliminate these games from children's lives entirely. Digital play is part of the cultural fabric they inhabit. Blanket bans and prohibitionist approaches often backfire, driving behaviour underground or creating resentment. *The more effective strategy is to intervene—not by controlling every transaction—but by shaping the child's understanding of what the transactions represent*. The goal is not to eliminate digital economies from their experience, but to cultivate agency within them.

This begins with transparency. Children must be taught, in plain and precise terms, how virtual currencies translate into real money. If 1,200 V-Bucks cost £7.99, they need to learn to calculate what each cosmetic upgrade *actually* costs—not just in tokens, but in effort, trade-off, and opportunity. A parent might say, "That's the same as a cinema ticket," or "You could get a paperback book for that." These are not criticisms, but cognitive anchors. They provide reference points in an otherwise abstract system.

Equally essential is the introduction of *purchase pause rituals*—practices that interrupt the impulse to buy and allow time for reflection. Some families institute a 24-hour wait rule before any in-game purchase above a modest amount. Others require the child to verbalise why the purchase matters to them and what they might be giving up. These rituals do not suppress desire; they *strengthen discernment*. They give the child the internal space to separate transient want from genuine value.

Crucially, interventions must also engage the child's sense of autonomy. The most successful families tend not to dictate every spending decision, but to scaffold it—offering guidance, modelling thoughtfulness, and trusting the child with gradually increasing discretion. A parent might co-review monthly spending logs on gaming platforms—not to shame, but to *reflect*. "Where do you think your money went this month? Did any purchases feel especially worth it—or not worth it?" The aim is to shift the focus from enforcement to metacognition.

Peer dynamics further complicate matters. Children do not spend in isolation; they spend *in relation to others*. In many games, appearance and performance are social currencies. A child may not care intrinsically about a limited-edition skin, but they care deeply about being excluded from a peer group who all have it. The language around this must be gentle but clear: "You don't need to buy status to belong," or "People worth being close to won't base friendship on what your character looks like." These statements, when repeated over time, plant seeds of resistance to performative consumption.

Still, acknowledging the child's desire to participate in social rituals is important. Parents can create bounded zones of indulgence—setting specific times (e.g., birthdays, holidays) or budgets for such purchases, rather than allowing endless drip transactions. The key is not to moralise spending, but to *contextualise* it. A digital skin is not inherently bad—it may even be a form of creative expression—but it should be understood and chosen with clarity, not compulsion.

There is also pedagogical value in encouraging children to *earn* digital spending power. Tying in-game purchases to household contributions or saving targets reframes the act: spending becomes not just consumption, but culmination. The psychological experience of spending £5 that one has earned through chore systems or micro-jobs is fundamentally different from tapping a preloaded card.

One is passive, the other participatory. And participation builds ownership.

The conversation, of course, is ongoing. As games evolve, so too do monetisation strategies. New forms of digital value—NFTs, in-game marketplaces, creator economies—are already reshaping the landscape. But the underlying educational need remains constant: *children must be equipped not just to navigate these systems, but to see through them*. To ask, "What is this game trying to make me do?" "How is it designing my attention?" "What are the real costs of this decision?" These are questions that empower, not restrict.

Ultimately, the role of the parent is not to shadow every click or veto every spend, but to build the intellectual and emotional muscles that let the child stand tall in a digital marketplace. By focusing on reflection over reaction, transparency over control, and participation over prohibition, we can teach children to inhabit virtual economies with real-world wisdom. Because while the tokens may be fake, *the habits they teach are very real.*

## Setting Boundaries Without Shame

It is a paradox of modern parenting that in an era of unprecedented convenience, setting limits has become more psychologically complex than ever. Nowhere is this more evident than in the digital economy—where children are not merely consumers, but participants in platforms intentionally engineered to bypass restraint. The challenge is no longer simply saying "no," but saying it in a way that builds competence rather than resistance, confidence rather than secrecy, and above all, *agency without shame.*

The traditional script for setting spending limits often draws on two extremes: restriction or indulgence. On one side, parents impose tight rules—prepaid cards, blocked purchases, revoked access—out of a protective instinct to prevent loss. On the other, they give in, usually in the name of "not wanting a fight" or "treating them once in a while," which soon becomes every weekend. Neither model develops the child's internal framework for managing money. One suppresses growth; the other encourages dependency. *What's missing in both is a collaborative approach to limits: limits that are understood, accepted, and integrated, not merely enforced.*

To build that kind of culture, it is necessary first to separate two often conflated ideas: *limits* and *punishment*. A limit is a boundary of expectation—designed to protect and teach. A punishment is a response to wrongdoing—designed to correct or deter. When children perceive a financial boundary as a punishment, they may associate it with guilt, shame, or secrecy. "Why can't I just get the upgrade like everyone else?" quickly becomes "I must be bad, or less, or deprived." Shame then drives concealment. The next time they want something, they may not ask.

That spiral can be interrupted early with a simple shift in posture: *from rule-setting to co-creation*. Imagine a parent sitting with their 10-year-old and saying, "You'll be using digital money more and more, so let's figure out a spending plan that works for you—not just for this week, but for the habits you'll carry into your teenage years." The tone here is not adversarial. It invites the child into a process of shared problem-solving. The result is more likely to stick, because the child has contributed to its creation.

Scripts matter, especially in emotionally loaded conversations. Consider the difference between "You don't need that, it's a waste of money" versus "I hear that it feels important to you—tell me what you think it's worth, and let's look at your budget together." The former shuts down dialogue; the latter builds it. Similarly, when declining a request, avoid personalising the refusal. "We're not spending money on extra game tokens this month" is healthier than "You've already spent too much." One refers to a policy; the other to the child's character. *Boundaries must be firm, but never moralised.*

Transparency about family values also strengthens boundary conversations. If you're limiting subscriptions, in-app purchases, or game add-ons, explain *why*. Say, "In our family, we try not to spend on things that disappear in a day," or "We believe your money should give you lasting value." This reinforces the idea that boundaries aren't random—they're ethical. Children may not always agree, but *they will remember that your decisions had coherence*. That memory builds trust, even if it temporarily sparks frustration.

Timing matters too. The best conversations about limits happen *before* the desire is acute. If your child is already mid-game and requesting £3.99 to unlock the next level, it's too late for philosophy. Their emotional state—dopaminergic, impatient, tunnel-visioned—won't support negotiation. That's why proactive financial rituals are more effective than reactive discipline. Weekly money check-ins, allowance reviews, or goal-setting sessions are opportunities to establish default expectations in moments of calm. Those habits allow you to say, later, "Remember what we agreed on Thursday?" rather than improvising rules in the heat of conflict.

There is also merit in creating *bounded freedoms*—spaces where children can make their own choices within a preset container. For example, a monthly digital wallet with a fixed limit: "This is your £10 for apps or games. You can choose how to use it, but once it's gone, it's gone." This gives the child both control and consequence. They may overspend in the first week, but they'll learn from that pinch—*without the parent having to step in or scold*. The pain is intrinsic to the choice, not imposed externally.

Still, boundaries will be tested. That is not failure—it is the curriculum. Every "But why not just this once?" is an opening to reinforce decision-making. One helpful script in these moments: "It's hard to wait for things you want—I've been there too. What would help you feel better about not buying it right now?" This acknowledges the feeling, shows empathy, and redirects attention to coping skills rather than control battles. It models emotional regulation, not just fiscal restraint.

Technology can also assist when used thoughtfully. Many digital platforms offer parental controls, spend alerts, and usage caps. These are not about spying or catching children out—they are about creating structure and clarity. When used transparently ("We'll both get a notification if spending goes over this amount"), these tools reinforce accountability. But they must be framed as scaffolding, not surveillance. Otherwise, children may internalise the message that trust is conditional and precarious.

Perhaps most important is that limits be coupled with *recognition of autonomy*. When children make wise spending choices, acknowledge it—not with inflated praise, but with specific feedback. "I noticed you waited a few days before deciding to buy that download. That kind of patience takes maturity." Over time, these recognitions build a new self-concept: "I am someone who makes smart decisions with money." That identity becomes its own boundary, stronger than any imposed rule.

There is a deeper cultural undercurrent at play here, too. We live in a society that often conflates generosity with indulgence and boundaries with coldness. Parents are subtly shamed—by other parents, by media, by marketing—for not giving their children "everything." But everything is not what children need. *They need experiences of decision, of friction, of restraint,* because these are what allow them to grow. A parent who says "Not this time" with calm, grounded confidence offers more love than one who says "Yes" out of guilt or fatigue.

Indeed, the emotional tone of a financial conversation may be the most enduring thing a child takes from it. Not the decision itself, but the atmosphere in which it occurred. Was there mutual respect? Did the parent listen as well as instruct? Was the child allowed to feel disappointed without being shamed for it? These affective cues shape not only financial beliefs but relational ones: about authority, fairness, and dialogue.

Setting digital spending boundaries, then, is not a technical challenge—it is a philosophical one. It requires parents to resist both the tyranny of indulgence and the reflex of restriction. To move instead toward a practice of deliberate, collaborative constraint. To speak not from fear or control, but from care and clarity. And to remember that every boundary, wisely placed, is not a wall but a scaffold: *a structure that supports growth from the inside out.*

## Digital Literacy as Financial Literacy

One of the quietest shifts in modern childhood is that the first experience many children have with money is not coins in a piggy bank or notes exchanged at a shop, but digital transactions—silent, abstract, often invisible. A tap on a screen, a click on a prompt, a one-time password. No jingling change, no folded banknotes, no physical wallet to remind them that money is finite. And yet, behind every frictionless purchase and every glowing interface lies a system of value, cost, and consequence. To understand digital money is to understand money. Which means that *digital literacy is no longer adjacent to financial literacy—it is financial literacy.*

Consider subscriptions. Once limited to magazines and newspapers, they are now embedded in nearly every digital product: streaming platforms, mobile games, cloud storage, learning apps. For children, especially those using family-linked accounts, the default model of payment has shifted from one-time purchase to automatic renewal. This isn't merely a technical change—it's a behavioural one. A subscription, by design, requires *passive spending*. The money leaves without a moment of decision. Unless actively cancelled, it recurs. This introduces a crucial concept: not all spending feels like spending.

Children need to be taught this distinction. The psychological effect of subscriptions is precisely that they do not trigger the same internal brake that a purchase does. There is no checkout, no tally, no dramatic moment of commitment. Which is why they must learn to *check what doesn't ask to be checked*. Parents and educators can build this awareness by reviewing app store settings, reading the fine print of "free trials," and setting calendar reminders for renewal dates. Even better: have the child themselves track the start and end date of a subscription they've requested, and check whether the benefit matches the cost. *The lesson here is not that subscriptions are bad—but that they demand vigilance.*

Then there is the question of data: the invisible currency of the digital world. Children are often told to "be careful online" in abstract, moralising terms—but rarely are they shown how their personal information functions as a form of payment. Every time they sign up for a game using a social media login, every time they click "accept" without reading terms, every time they enter an email address to access a discount, they are trading *privacy for convenience*. And while that trade-off may seem trivial, the long-term accumulation of personal data can be monetised in ways few young users fully grasp.

Here, digital literacy must include *data literacy*. That means helping children ask new kinds of questions: "What does this site know about me?" "Why is this ad following me?" "What am I giving away when I sign up?" Framing these inquiries in the language of economics—cost, value, exchange—makes them more accessible. When a child sees that their email address has economic worth, that their click-through behaviour informs algorithms, that their online attention fuels a marketplace, they begin to understand that *not all currency is monetary*. A password is a key, but also a liability. An identity is a profile, but also a product.

Equally vital is understanding the architecture of scams. Gone are the days of crude phishing emails riddled with spelling errors. Today's scams—especially those targeting children and teens—are increasingly sophisticated. Fake brand accounts on social media offering giveaways, influencers pushing dubious products, clone websites mimicking legitimate services, and even friend impersonations via messaging apps. The psychology behind these scams is simple: *create urgency, reduce friction, evoke trust*. They prey on a sense of reward, speed, and fear of missing out. Exactly the impulses children are still learning to regulate.

To counter this, teaching must go beyond "Don't talk to strangers online." It must equip children to detect *patterns of manipulation*. For example: if a message includes a countdown timer, promises a prize, or discourages them from asking adults—pause. If a site demands immediate action without allowing inspection—pause. Parents and schools can even use "mock scam spotting" as a family or classroom activity: show screenshots of fake emails, dubious pop-ups, or counterfeit e-commerce pages and discuss the red flags. *The aim isn't fear—it's discernment*.

Digital financial education must also address the culture of *microtransactions*, especially within games and apps. These aren't merely minor purchases—they are psychological experiments. Designed with precision to exploit intermittent reward systems, they blur the line between play and payment. A new skin, an extra life, a surprise box—available for £1.99. But that £1.99, multiplied across time, desire, and dopamine, becomes something far more costly. Children need to learn the language of accumulation: not just "How much is this item?" but "How often do I buy it?" "What pattern is emerging?" "Is this spending intentional or impulsive?"

Framing microtransactions as *habit-forming mechanisms* rather than mere entertainment allows young users to see them with greater clarity. Encourage children to ask: "What's this game trying to sell me?" "How does it make me feel when I don't buy something?" "Why do I want this right now?" These are not questions of deprivation—they are questions of agency. And agency is the cornerstone of responsible financial behaviour.

Another key layer is the growing prevalence of *digital peer influence*. Influencers and online personalities now shape purchasing behaviour as strongly—sometimes more so—than traditional advertising. A favourite YouTuber uses a particular product, a gamer streams with a premium membership, a TikTok trend features a specific outfit or item. Children aren't just seeing content; they're witnessing a curated lifestyle, *interwoven with monetised choices*. Understanding that these decisions are rarely organic—that they are often sponsored, staged, or incentivised—is critical.

Here, digital literacy requires media literacy. Teach children to ask: "Is this a genuine recommendation, or is someone being paid to say it?" "What's the motivation behind this post?" "How does seeing this make me feel about what I have?" Again, these aren't negative or cynical questions—they are financial questions. Because the modern economy is not just in shops or banks—it's in scrolls, swipes, and stories.

As children grow, they will eventually encounter *financial tools masquerading as toys*: cryptocurrency apps with slick design, investment platforms gamified with bright colours and leaderboards, budgeting apps that resemble social media feeds. These tools aren't necessarily dangerous—but they are not neutral either. They teach particular habits and assumptions about money. If children are to use them wisely, they must be shown how to analyse their design: "What does this app encourage me to do more of?" "What kind of behaviour is it rewarding?" "Is it helping me make better decisions, or just faster ones?"

Finally, the most important lesson may be the simplest: *digital financial responsibility starts with noticing*. Noticing what you're paying for. Noticing what you're giving away. Noticing when a product is too easy to get. Noticing when spending becomes a habit, not a choice. That kind of noticing isn't instinctive—it's cultivated. Through dialogue, practice, and example.

Parents and educators don't need to be digital experts to teach this. They need to model curiosity. To say, "I wonder what this site does with our data," or "Let's check how many subscriptions we've signed up for this month," or "This influencer is pushing a product—do you think they really use it?" These comments invite children to think critically. They make financial learning a shared exploration, not a set of lectures.

In the 20th century, financial literacy meant balancing a chequebook and avoiding debt. In the 21st, it means understanding that *value flows invisibly as much as visibly*. That your digital choices have monetary implications. That money is no longer just what you earn or spend, but what you reveal, click, and subscribe to. Teaching children this is not a luxury—it is a necessity. Not just to protect them from loss, but to prepare them for participation in a digital economy where *literacy is leverage, and ignorance is a liability.*

# Chapter 10
# When Kids Earn More Than You Expect

It is a conversation that takes many parents by surprise—not because they lack the desire to guide their children financially, but because their children often arrive ahead of them. A teenager triumphs in a national gaming tournament and suddenly finds five figures in their account. A twelve-year-old's YouTube clip goes viral, generating ad revenue that eclipses a parent's monthly income. A child receives a windfall in cryptocurrency via an airdropped token or experiences an unexpected surge in commissions from handmade crafts sold online. These scenarios are no longer edge cases; they are increasingly common, highlighting the modern paradox: children are earning real money in unprecedented ways—fast, digital, and often without the emotional or structural preparation to manage it.

The contemporary economy has lowered barriers to earning dramatically. Platforms like Etsy, Twitch, Roblox, TikTok, Substack, and YouTube allow anyone to access markets that were once tightly gatekept. Yet access does not equate to maturity. Just because a child can monetise content or sell a product does not mean they have the scaffolding to navigate income responsibly, nor do they necessarily grasp its fragility, its effect on identity, or the subtle ways it can reshape family dynamics.

When children begin to out-earn adults in the household, even temporarily, difficult questions arise: how should these earnings be handled? Who should oversee them? How can autonomy be balanced with protection, especially when the income itself is a source of pride? And crucially, how can parents prevent a child's self-worth from being tethered entirely to transaction histories or online applause?

Panic is unhelpful, and ignoring the money is worse. A steadier response is to normalise financial exception without mythologising it. Sudden earnings often tempt families to celebrate, elevate, or overcorrect—but such reactions can backfire, inflating expectations, fostering anxiety about loss, or linking self-esteem to performance. A wiser approach is to treat the income as capital, not character: something to respect, steward, and gradually render ordinary.

This chapter is not a warning against children earning money. It is a guide to creating systems that support young earners in an attention economy designed for rapid burnout. Families are shown how to structure windfalls not only logistically, but psychologically. When a child receives a substantial sum—whether through viral success, digital royalties, creator income, or entrepreneurial effort—the immediate priority is not what to spend, but how to frame it. Is it a jackpot? A business? A seed? Each perspective opens different paths.

We explore practical structures: dual-account models, graduated access systems, and rules for liquidity that protect against impulsivity while preserving dignity. Fast fame and sudden cash often trigger identity confusion, peer tension, or shame, particularly when adult financial competence is still forming. The chapter examines how parents can de-glamourise income without diminishing effort—maintaining values even as numbers grow.

Equally important is the emotional landscape of early financial success. Children who earn unexpectedly may feel disoriented rather than elated. They may hesitate to discuss their income, struggle to relate to peers, or feel awkward about parental reactions—whether celebratory or sceptical. In such vacuums, money becomes secretive, and secret money is rarely well-managed.

Creating an environment where money—however large or rapid—is discussed with neutrality and clarity is essential. This means distinguishing between funds for immediate use and resources meant to serve the future self. It involves clarifying the difference between a sustainable income stream and a one-time windfall, and embedding reflection, restraint, and recalibration as regular practices.

The chapter also considers the broader implications of youthful wealth in a precarious economy. What does it mean when a child earns more than a teacher? When a teenager's cryptocurrency holdings exceed a parent's savings? When household dynamics invert around income? These are not trivial questions—they can become relational flashpoints that, if left unexamined, breed entitlement, resentment, or alienation.

Strategies offered here address both money and identity. How can a child who earns unusually avoid an unusual burden? How can safeguards coexist with autonomy? How can young earners contextualise success economically, socially, and developmentally without exaggerating or dismissing its significance?

Legal and tax considerations, as well as long-term planning, are briefly addressed, with the caveat that structure alone is insufficient. Custodial accounts and financial advisers help only if the child understands the system. Inclusion fosters literacy and prevents confusion; ownership without comprehension is fragile.

Finally, the chapter reframes windfalls as a learning opportunity for the whole family. Earnings ripple across siblings, shape household conversations, and surface latent assumptions about fairness, work, and value. When handled with care, these moments deepen trust; handled poorly, they cement divisions. Transparency tempered with sensitivity, structure balanced with flexibility, and dialogue guided by humility—these become the true currencies.

Financial growth should never outpace understanding. This chapter invites families to slow down, step back, and help young earners grow into their income with wisdom rather than wonder. Not every child will strike it rich early—but all will face financial change. How we guide them through it, particularly when it comes sooner than expected, shapes not only their finances, but their emotional resilience, too.

## Managing Windfalls

A child who suddenly earns a large sum of money—through a viral video, a coding prize, or a lucky bet on cryptocurrency—enters territory few parents are prepared to navigate. The very term "windfall" implies surprise and imbalance: a financial event out of proportion to typical expectations. And when that windfall lands in the hands of someone whose prefrontal cortex is still under construction, the implications stretch far beyond spreadsheets and savings accounts. They reach into identity, values, power dynamics, and emotional regulation. Managing windfalls isn't just about structuring money—it's about structuring meaning.

Children who come into money before they've built up the internal scaffolding to contextualise it are particularly vulnerable to emotional distortion. In developmental psychology, we know that children, especially adolescents, anchor their sense of control and competence through concrete experiences. Sudden wealth, without earned effort or clear guardrails, can short-circuit that process. A £10,000 prize might feel like unlimited purchasing power to a 12-year-old, but what it actually triggers is an intense need for grounding—often disguised as compulsive generosity, status-spending, or impulsive experimentation. If unmoderated, these behaviours risk becoming scripts.

The first step in managing a child's windfall is reframing the situation—not as a gift or opportunity in the traditional sense, but as an inflection point. The goal is not to prevent spending altogether, nor to impose rigid control. It is to absorb the emotional shock of sudden gain, and use structure to teach stewardship. This begins by separating the windfall into conceptual buckets: one for access, one for protection, and one for discussion. A small accessible portion (often no more than 5–10%) can be allocated for short-term wants. The protected portion—held in custodial investment or savings vehicles—should be explicitly identified as long-term. And the discussion bucket, which may be metaphorical, is where you cultivate reflection: what this money could represent, how it aligns with values, and what it could fund beyond consumption.

Wealth—even in small doses—magnifies character. For children, it magnifies identity formation. The family's response to a child's earnings sends lasting signals. If the response is anxious restriction, the child learns to view money as dangerous. If it's unqualified celebration, they may equate earnings with self-worth. The more effective posture is balanced mentorship: acknowledging the legitimacy of the child's agency while offering financial structure as a gift, not a penalty. "You're now in a situation most people don't encounter at your age. That's exciting—and it means we get to learn some grown-up financial strategies together."

Parents can look to legal and financial instruments to support these strategies. Junior ISAs, custodial brokerage accounts, and family foundations can all provide buffers against premature access. But these instruments mean little without narrative. A savings account does not teach discipline unless it's paired with conversation about why the money is being set aside, what it will eventually make possible, and how waiting strengthens decision-making muscles. Windfalls provide a unique opportunity to model principles like capital preservation, compounding, and opportunity cost in real, personal terms.

Crucially, the family must address the emotional subtext of sudden wealth. In many cases, children who receive unexpected income feel an obligation to share, perform, or spend as a form of justification. They may fear peer resentment, or feel alienated from friends whose economic realities haven't changed. Some become secretive. Others broadcast. The task is not to pathologise these responses but to surface them. Open-ended questions can help: "How do you feel when people ask about your earnings?" "What would you do with this money if no one else knew about it?" "What part of this feels exciting? What part feels heavy?"

Windfalls also provide the perfect proving ground for the practice of *deliberate delay*. With young earners, it can be powerful to institute a 'waiting period' for any purchase over a given threshold—say, £100. This is not a punishment; it's a reflective pause. As with any habit of financial maturity, the goal is not restriction, but intentionality. You might say: "The money is still yours. We're just creating a window to let you think fully about what you want most." Over time, this cultivates a sense of agency rooted not in consumption, but in discernment.

Some families choose to build a governance structure around a child's windfall. This might take the form of a "Family Financial Panel," in which the child participates in a quarterly review with parents and perhaps a trusted adviser to discuss spending, saving, and investing decisions. This elevates financial choices into a realm of responsibility without stripping autonomy. It also frames wealth management as an ongoing conversation, not a one-time intervention.

Culturally, we need to shed the assumption that financial maturity is age-dependent. A 15-year-old can learn about tax implications, dollar-cost averaging, or ethical investing if the material is framed correctly. Likewise, an adult can remain financially immature if they've never been taught to think long-term. Windfalls don't have to derail a child's development. But they must be integrated with care, narrative, and sustained coaching.

There is also the temptation to tie money management to moral worth: to use phrases like "you need to be responsible" or "don't let this go to your head." These statements often mask adult discomfort. A more effective approach is value-based anchoring: "What kind of person do you want to be with this money?" "How do you want others to experience your generosity or discretion?" When children define their own money ethos—with guidance—they internalise it. When they feel coerced or judged, they often rebel.

Finally, we must talk about permanence. Most windfalls are not recurring. A viral sponsorship, a lucrative NFT sale, or a startup jackpot can vanish as quickly as it arrived. Helping a child understand the difference between a windfall and a reliable income stream is essential. That means introducing concepts like sustainability, cash flow, and the difference between asset growth and income dependence. The child's first experience with disproportionate earnings shouldn't teach them that money is infinite. It should teach them that it is powerful—and that such power, to be enduring, must be earned again and again through stewardship, reflection, and choice.

To manage a windfall well is to give a child more than financial tools. It is to give them a sense of pace in a world obsessed with velocity. It is to teach them that just because money arrives quickly doesn't mean decisions should. And most importantly, it is to affirm that their worth was never measured by the windfall itself—but by what they chose to build with it.

## The Problem of Fast Fame and Fast Cash

A sudden surge in money or public attention can be psychologically disorienting for anyone. But for children—whose identities are still forming and whose sense of self-worth is easily entangled with external validation—rapid financial success or online visibility can act as a destabilising accelerant. What begins as an exciting breakthrough—a viral video, an NFT sale, a prize cheque, a game stream gone big—often leaves behind not empowerment but confusion, anxiety, or an inflated sense of self divorced from substance. *Fast success often skips the developmental steps that give earnings meaning.*

In developmental terms, adolescence is a period marked by increased sensitivity to reward, particularly social reward. The prefrontal cortex, which governs judgement and impulse control, is still catching up to the dopamine-rich circuits that drive attention-seeking and novelty pursuit. Overlay this with a culture that monetises visibility and celebrates spectacle, and the danger is clear: when a young person's face goes viral, or their content starts generating real income, the psychological scaffolding needed to carry that experience with steadiness is often missing.

One of the least discussed consequences of fast fame is disassociation. A child may struggle to understand how their "normal" identity—student, friend, sibling—sits alongside their "public" self as an influencer or high earner. This split can be subtly reinforced by adult reactions: teachers who treat them differently, parents who share their content widely, strangers who comment on their worth. When fame or money become the lens through which a child is perceived, it's difficult for them not to internalise that valuation. In the absence of grounding, they may come to see their worth as transactional—tied to metrics, followers, or earnings.

Money that arrives suddenly also collapses the traditional arc of skill development. A child who stumbles into a viral revenue stream hasn't necessarily built the financial muscles of patience, budgeting, or long-term planning. Nor have they absorbed the social cues and emotional maturity that typically accompany earning over time. In that vacuum, distorted lessons fill the gap: that money comes easily; that more is always better; that earning validates personality. *Without intervention, fast cash teaches kids that accumulation is achievement, and attention is currency.*

Parents may feel torn between pride and panic. On one hand, their child has done something creative, entrepreneurial, or opportunistic. On the other, they sense the imbalance—the developmental lag between the financial power now available and the maturity required to wield it wisely. One of the most helpful things a parent can offer in this moment is *non-reactivity*. This doesn't mean ignoring the windfall, nor does it mean minimising its significance. It means refusing to get swept up in the emotional froth. Modelling calm, steady reflection sends a deeper message than any lecture could.

A parent might say, "This is a big moment. Let's treat it with the respect it deserves. Not by rushing, but by thinking together about what matters most." Language matters. Avoid praising the money itself—"That's so much!"—and focus on the process: "What do you think worked well here? What do you want to keep learning about?" This reorients attention away from the reward and toward the effort, judgement, or creativity that made it possible.

Another pitfall of fast success is the illusion of permanence. Kids often assume that this level of income or visibility will continue. Few understand the volatility of internet attention or the tax implications of irregular income. It is tempting for them to upsize their expectations accordingly: buying expensive tech, giving extravagant gifts, or making promises they can't sustain. Parents need to introduce the idea of financial seasonality. You can say: "Some money comes regularly, like a drip. Other money arrives all at once, like rain. The trick is learning how to store some of that rain for the dry times." Metaphors grounded in real-world rhythms—weather, farming, energy use—can make abstract financial concepts stick.

The emotional side of sudden wealth is just as complex. Fast earnings often trigger guilt, isolation, or imposter syndrome. The child might feel unworthy, or worry that their success will make others envious. They might also feel a need to maintain their earnings or visibility, even at the cost of their mental health. These are adult-sized burdens being shouldered by someone still developing a sense of self. They need emotional permission to feel ambivalent about their success—and to know that their value doesn't hinge on sustaining it.

At the same time, it is essential not to romanticise hardship. Some well-meaning adults suggest that "kids need to struggle to build character," and therefore downplay or dismiss financial windfalls. This is misguided. The issue isn't that the child avoided struggle—it's that they haven't yet been supported in extracting meaning from their experience. Rather than manufacturing artificial difficulty, the task is to *deepen reflection* and introduce structure. What does this money mean to you? What kind of person do you want to be with it? What would it look like to honour this moment with wisdom?

The problem of fast fame is not just internal. It often changes how others treat the child—peers, teachers, extended family. They may become the target of jealousy, undue flattery, or subtle resentment. The child may lose trust, not knowing if people like them for who they are or what they've earned. Help them name this dynamic explicitly. You might say: "When money shows up, it sometimes messes with relationships. You may notice people treating you differently—not always in ways that feel good. If that happens, you can talk to me about it. You're not alone." Giving a child a safe place to process these shifts helps them preserve their authenticity.

There's also the question of *exit ramps*. What happens when the earnings slow down, or the fame fades? If a child's identity has become tethered to their financial success, its absence can feel like personal failure. This is where *reframing* is critical. Help them understand that their early success was a chapter, not a verdict. That the skills they developed—editing videos, solving problems, negotiating rates—are portable. That wealth comes and goes, but capability endures. Frame the experience not as a peak they'll never reach again, but as an early exposure to real-world dynamics they'll now be better equipped to navigate.

One practical approach is to *channel some of the windfall into learning*. This might mean taking a financial literacy course, funding a mentorship relationship, or investing in a passion project with clear parameters. The idea is to *transform passive reward into active growth*. This not only stretches the benefit of the money but also reinforces the idea that wealth is a tool, not an endpoint.

Above all, what children need in the face of fast cash or fame is *relational steadiness*. They don't need micromanagement. They need presence. Adults who neither panic nor over-celebrate. Adults who stay curious, who listen without rushing to correct, who offer structure without shame. They need people who will hold space for their excitement and their confusion, and who will help them write a narrative more enduring than the balance in their account.

Because fast money is not the problem. It's the lack of emotional infrastructure around it that creates risk. With thoughtful support, a child who earns early can become not arrogant or anxious, but anchored. Anchored in values, perspective, and the kind of inner stability that no amount of attention can counterfeit. That is the real return on investment—and it compounds for a lifetime.

## Making Big Money Boring

Wealth, when framed as spectacle, can quietly distort a child's sense of what is meaningful. This distortion is rarely sudden. It creeps in through the social praise that trails visible success, the amplified reactions to earnings milestones, and the implicit belief—broadcast through adult behaviour—that money is inherently exciting. When a child earns more than expected, especially in a digital-first world where rapid monetisation is increasingly possible, adults often unintentionally reinforce a narrative that equates money with status, attention, and exceptionalism. Left unchecked, this narrative fosters financial performativity rather than stewardship. *Normalising wealth is not about diminishing ambition—it is about anchoring identity in values that outlast income.*

Making big money boring is a protective strategy. It counters the psychological inflation that comes when children start believing their worth is tethered to the scale of their earnings. It helps preserve intrinsic motivation, cultivates emotional equilibrium, and repositions money as a tool—not a trophy. The aim is not to suppress a child's pride or momentum, but to reroute the meaning they assign to their success. In a culture where headlines glorify the overnight millionaire or teen crypto prodigy, this quiet reframing becomes an act of resistance—and clarity.

A child who earns early is at risk of building their identity around exceptionalism. The compliments shift: no longer for effort, thoughtfulness, or growth, but for outcomes. Comments like "You're so ahead of your peers!" or "You're going to be a billionaire!" land with seductive power. Even when meant as praise, they subtly reinforce a hierarchy of value: your earnings make you more interesting, more important. Adults must remain vigilant to avoid projecting their own awe or anxiety onto the child's experience. *The goal is not to pretend success doesn't matter. It's to help the child locate it within a broader framework of life, contribution, and meaning.*

One of the simplest ways to de-glamorise big money is to treat it procedurally. When a child receives a large sum—through business income, gifts, contests, or royalties—anchor the response in structure, not celebration. "Let's decide how we want to handle this" is more constructive than "Wow, that's amazing!" The language of stewardship matters. Terms like "allocation," "distribution," "future use," and "buffer" subtly signal that wealth requires thought, not just enjoyment. Create categories for use—spending, saving, learning, giving—and make the process visible but undramatic. When money becomes a routine part of family conversations rather than a source of surprise or spectacle, it loses its performative edge.

Another strategy is to *integrate wealth into long-term systems* rather than short-term decisions. Children who experience their money as immediately spendable are more likely to associate earnings with consumption. But when that same money is channelled into a diversified framework—savings accounts, charitable funds, learning investments—it becomes part of a life infrastructure. Consider this framing: "Some of this money is for now. Some is for later. Some is to grow. Some is to give." The language is plain. The distribution is deliberate. And the result is a quiet internal message: money does not rule you; you manage it.

Parents and mentors must also examine their own cues. Are you over-praising success, checking account balances too frequently, or talking about the child's earnings with extended family in ways that feel performative? These behaviours may be unintentional, but they teach children that money is a spectacle to be watched and broadcast. One antidote is to *emphasise craft over cash*. Instead of asking, "How much did you make?" ask, "What are you learning?" or "What are you building next?" Redirect focus to the work, the improvement, the process. This shift reclaims autonomy from external metrics and nurtures sustainable motivation.

A useful parallel can be drawn from families with inherited wealth who successfully raise grounded children. In many of those households, money is not hidden—but it is not dramatised either. Financial capacity is framed as a platform for contribution, education, or responsibility. Daily life is intentionally structured to avoid dependency on wealth for identity or fulfilment. Young people are expected to engage in service, take on responsibility, and live within clear financial boundaries—regardless of what is technically affordable. *This is not austerity for show. It's values in practice.*

Children who earn early are uniquely vulnerable to what psychologists call "affluenza": a condition marked by entitlement, anxiety, and distorted relationships due to early and unmanaged exposure to wealth. But the problem is not the money itself—it is the emotional isolation that often accompanies it. When money is made boring, it becomes integrated into the child's narrative, not the central plot twist. They are more likely to maintain friendships based on shared values, make spending decisions grounded in reflection, and resist the temptation to seek constant external validation.

There is also pedagogical value in demystifying financial management. Let children sit in on budgeting sessions, attend meetings with financial advisers, or review quarterly statements. Involve them in tax planning, donation allocation, and the selection of investment vehicles. Not to burden them, but to normalise complexity. Children who understand that even large sums require thought, planning, and trade-offs are less likely to view money as magic. They begin to see that wealth is not a destination but an ongoing series of responsibilities, decisions, and recalibrations.

*Silence, too, plays a role in normalisation.* Avoid over-discussing big earnings, especially in front of others. When every family dinner includes a reference to how much the child made last month or what they're earning from their latest project, the currency of attention shifts. Instead, keep financial conversations private, purposeful, and rare. Let other dimensions of the child's life—relationships, learning, service—take up more conversational space. *When money is just one thread among many, it no longer dominates the fabric of identity.*

Importantly, this reframing doesn't mean discouraging ambition or ignoring success. Children should feel proud of what they've achieved. But pride must be metabolised in the context of broader life values. Ask: "What kind of person do you want to be with this money?" or "How can this support what you care about?" These questions prompt self-reflection and reinforce the idea that wealth is a means, not an end. They also create space for the child to articulate their evolving values—and for adults to affirm them.

When wealth is glamorised, it demands constant attention. But when it is normalised, it quietly enables freedom. The freedom to say no. The freedom to delay gratification. The freedom to walk away from opportunities that don't align with one's deeper goals. And perhaps most crucially, the freedom to define success on one's own terms.

The child who learns to make big money boring is not underestimating its power. They are placing it in proportion. They are building the emotional and cognitive infrastructure required to be both financially capable and psychologically resilient. They are rehearsing the most mature form of wealth management: stewardship without spectacle, discipline without detachment, gratitude without glorification.

And in that quiet, understated clarity lies something far rarer than early riches: wisdom that lasts.

## Build the Buffer

The idea of "building a buffer" is not simply about saving money—it's about installing psychological architecture that enables restraint, resilience, and responsibility. For young earners, especially those encountering income before adulthood, the buffer serves as both a boundary and a permission structure. It limits the risk of impulsive depletion, but it also legitimises agency by offering controlled access. It's the financial equivalent of training wheels—not to prevent motion, but to teach balance through containment. And in a culture that equates freedom with unfettered access, that containment is radical, and necessary.

Children who earn early—whether through side gigs, gifts, royalties, or digital ventures—face a structural problem: their earnings outpace their cognitive and emotional readiness. Money arrives before frameworks are built. Without scaffolding, they are more likely to conflate liquidity with liberty. The result is often one of two extremes: a precocious spender who burns through funds without pause, or a nervous saver who hoards out of vague anxiety. Neither response is mature. *What's needed is a deliberately designed system that segments access in ways that grow both confidence and competence.*

The most effective method is a two-tiered account structure: one for spending, and another for protected savings. This distinction must be more than nominal—it must be functional. The spending account should be liquid, visible, and low-friction. It's the sandbox for decision-making, where mistakes are educational rather than catastrophic. In contrast, the buffer—sometimes called a protected or delayed-access account—should involve some psychological distance. That could mean it's stored in a different institution, managed by a parent or third party, or simply governed by a shared agreement that withdrawals require discussion. The point is not to create secrecy or control, but to create space. *Distance reduces impulse. It forces deliberation.*

One of the overlooked benefits of a buffer is the calibration of emotion. When every pound is instantly accessible, money becomes a trigger: excitement when the balance is high, stress when it drops. But with a structured buffer in place, day-to-day fluctuations matter less. The young earner learns to operate within finite means, knowing that security exists in the background. It's akin to teaching a child to swim while knowing there's a lifeguard present. They feel free to try, to fail, to learn—without the paralyzing fear of drowning.

To be effective, the buffer must be defined with clarity and consistency. A simple model might allocate earnings along the lines of 50% to spend, 30% to buffer, and 20% to long-term or charitable goals. But the percentages matter less than the permanence. The buffer is not for next week. It is for the unplanned, the significant, or the strategic. A first laptop? Yes. A third hoodie because it's on sale? No. A delayed summer trip that rewards sustained effort? Perhaps. An impulse microtransaction in a game? Absolutely not. These are not just fiscal decisions—they are value signals. And the consistency of enforcement matters more than the size of the fund.

Of course, transparency is crucial. Children should know what's in their buffer. Hiding numbers creates mystery, and mystery breeds fixation. Instead, show them the numbers but pair them with context. "This is what you've put aside for your future. It's not locked, but it's not casual." Let them see their decisions as part of a larger arc, not a string of disconnected purchases. Involve them in reviewing balances quarterly, setting rules for access, or brainstorming what's worth saving for. These conversations create financial dialogue rather than parental diktat. They build financial literacy through collaboration rather than restriction.

For children navigating larger-than-usual earnings—say, digital creators, tech-savvy coders, or enterprising teens who monetise early—the buffer becomes more than a personal safety net. It becomes a system for managing scale. As income increases, temptation does too. Without segmentation, it becomes easy for spending to inflate alongside earnings, normalising a lifestyle that quickly outruns maturity. The buffer disrupts this inflation. It installs lag. It builds intentionality. *The presence of money does not justify its use. The buffer teaches that earnings deserve not just celebration, but structure.*

There's also a social dimension to the buffer that's rarely acknowledged. When children control large sums, they can become accidental outliers among their peers. Friends may not understand why one child can buy freely while others can't. This can lead to performative generosity ("I'll cover it for everyone"), peer envy, or distorted dynamics. A well-articulated buffer system offers an elegant explanation: "I can only use part of what I earn. The rest is set aside." It reduces awkwardness by converting wealth into structure. It shifts the narrative from freedom to framework.

This idea is not new. In fact, it echoes principles long embedded in institutional finance. Endowments separate spendable income from protected capital. Governments set aside reserves. Entrepreneurs divide revenue from profit. The buffer is the child's version of capital discipline. It teaches that liquidity and availability are not the same thing—that just because you can, doesn't mean you should. And more importantly, that waiting, planning, and separating are not signs of limitation, but of leadership.

Some will argue that children should have free reign over their money in order to learn through error. That's not wrong, but it's incomplete. Learning requires safety. A buffer creates a zone in which failure is instructive but not ruinous. It allows children to experiment with autonomy without endangering stability. This balance—between freedom and friction—is where the richest learning happens. Not when they're told what to do. Not when they're left entirely alone. But when they're equipped to manage complexity in graduated stages.

Even the language around buffers should be chosen carefully. Avoid calling it a "locked account" or a "no-touch fund." These imply constraint and punishment. Instead, describe it as *a runway, a foundation, a support layer*. Let the child internalise that the buffer is something they build—not something imposed. Ownership of that language leads to ownership of the behaviour. A child who believes, "I've built a strong buffer" thinks differently than one who says, "Mum won't let me spend it."

As children grow, the nature of the buffer evolves. For a ten-year-old, it might mean a piggy bank that's stored on a high shelf, opened only for major goals. For a fourteen-year-old, it might be a youth savings account with a monthly cap on transfers. For a sixteen-year-old, it might involve multiple sub-accounts for tuition, travel, or investments, monitored through a digital dashboard. The point is not to fix a static rule, but to adapt structure to stage. *The sophistication of the buffer should grow alongside the child's sense of purpose.*

Ultimately, building the buffer is an exercise in delayed gratification, but it's more than that. It's about creating habits that align with character. It's about offering young people a system that reflects the reality of the adult financial world—not an oversimplified sandbox of either/no control. It's about showing that discipline doesn't limit freedom; it multiplies it. The child who can differentiate between what they can spend and what they choose not to is already wealthier in wisdom than many adults with full access and no internal guardrails.

The buffer, then, is not a constraint—it's a signal. It tells the child: *You are a steward, not a consumer. You are building, not just buying. You are trusted to hold complexity.* And in that quiet structure lies one of the most enduring financial gifts a parent or mentor can offer.

# Chapter 11
# Building a Family Financial Culture

Family culture is never simply declared; it is lived. It does not exist in a list of aspirational values on a wall, nor in a single dinner-table conversation—it is the accumulated rhythm of daily behaviour, the subtle cues, repeated rituals, and recurring language that shape how members think, decide, and act. When it comes to money, families either construct this culture deliberately or inherit it by default. Most households—irrespective of wealth—default to silence, avoidance, or reactive decision-making. But what if we approached family financial culture as something intentional, something alive?

Money is never merely technical; it carries psychological, emotional, moral, and relational weight. It intertwines with identity, upbringing, ambition, fear, fairness, and power. These tensions are most vivid within the household, where generations, personalities, and priorities collide. A family's financial culture is therefore not simply about what is spent or saved—it is about how choices are made, how trade-offs are navigated, and how values are embodied over time. Crucially, children absorb these lessons long before they can articulate them.

Research in behavioural economics and developmental psychology consistently highlights an overlooked truth: children internalise their earliest financial beliefs by observing the tone, consistency, and emotional temperature of decisions around them. Stress, disagreements, giving, and reward—all carry meaning. A household that hides tension, masks disagreement, or frames generosity as obligation teaches children far more than the explicit words ever could. If what parents say diverges from what they do, the result is confusion, not neutrality.

The premise of this chapter is simple yet potentially disruptive: your family already has a financial culture. The question is whether it serves your values, and whether it is visible enough for children to participate meaningfully. To cultivate a deliberate culture, families must shift from reactive decisions to proactive rituals, from secrecy to structured transparency, and from focusing solely on outcomes to recognising the formative power of the decision-making process itself. Money ceases to be a private concern and becomes a shared literacy.

Rituals are central to this approach. Unlike rules, which constrain, rituals encode meaning. Weekly "money check-ins" that include every member, regardless of age, signal that money is not solely an adult concern. Save-spend-give jars, positioned centrally rather than hidden away, transform into visual reminders of priority. Family giving days, where each person nominates a cause and explains its importance, convert abstract charity into concrete empathy. These are not gimmicks; they are deliberate acts of cultural architecture. Over time, they convey that financial decisions are opportunities for reflection, alignment, and connection rather than burdens.

Culture also demands voice, particularly the child's. Inviting children into conversations about budgeting, goal setting, or major trade-offs does not mean relinquishing authority. It recognises that learning to think financially requires the freedom to question, challenge, and contribute. Too often, parents shield children under the guise of protection, leaving them to infer meaning with no context. A child who witnesses a declined holiday without explanation may conclude: "we can't afford it." With context, however, they understand: "we are choosing to spend less now to invest in something more meaningful later." The action is identical; the financial identity it fosters is profoundly different.

Transparency, handled thoughtfully, cultivates trust without creating burden. Begin modestly: explain why a grocery bill is higher this week, why utility costs matter, or how a family goal necessitates short-term sacrifice. Expand to shared planning: reviewing a child's spending habits, co-setting savings targets, or even including them in discussions about larger family expenses. These seemingly casual, unscripted moments are foundational—they tell children their voice matters, their participation is real, and their learning is valued.

Yet, even with rituals and inclusion, the linchpin of culture is emotional tone. One of the most effective shifts a family can make is to celebrate thoughtful decision-making, even when outcomes are imperfect. A child who compares prices but chooses poorly should be recognised for their analytical effort. A teen who saves consistently yet splurges impulsively still deserves acknowledgment for building the habit. These moments are not merely teachable—they are cultural. They signal that financial skill is not about perfection but about progress, weighing options, tolerating delay, and aligning actions with values.

This requires a subtle reframing: praise the discipline, not the result; acknowledge intention, not just payoff. When families adopt this approach, children develop what psychologists call a growth mindset around money—the understanding that financial capability is learned, not innate. They become more willing to experiment, reflect, and adapt, seeing themselves as active stewards rather than passive consumers of wealth.

Finally, perhaps the least visible but most critical component of family financial culture is recognising the household as a financial ecosystem. Money is often treated transactionally: each person has needs, parents provide, and the cycle repeats. In a healthier system, choices are interdependent. One sibling's delayed gratification can create space for another; a parent taking on extra work represents not only income but emotional labour; a child contributing part of their birthday money to a family goal participates in a shared economy.

This ecosystem perspective fosters empathy and mutuality. Children learn that money does not flow in isolation—it circulates, affects others, and carries consequences. They begin to ask not just "what do I get?" but "how does my choice affect us?" Over time, this instils resilience and teaches that the family is a unit of co-decision-makers, co-planners, and co-investors rather than simply cohabitants.

Building a family financial culture is not about adopting techniques alone. It is about weaving meaning into every interaction, every transaction, and even the silences. It transforms money from a source of stress or secrecy into a medium for shared values. It helps children become not just numerically literate but fluent in decision-making. It creates a household where money is managed, understood, honoured, and used to build trust rather than tension.

This chapter will offer concrete strategies and evidence-based guidance, but it begins with an invitation: see your family as the financial culture it already is—and imagine what it might become with a few thoughtful rituals, greater inclusion, and deliberate intentionality.

## Rituals That Reinforce Values

Children do not absorb financial values through lectures. They absorb them through repetition, tone, and participation. What's remembered in family culture is rarely the content of a lesson; it's the rhythm of a ritual. Long before a child grasps the abstract principles of budgeting or compound interest, they understand something far more formative: *what money means here*. And what it means is shaped not by what adults say, but by what families do—consistently, visibly, and together.

Rituals offer more than structure. They offer narrative. They encode the family's beliefs in action. Weekly money meetings are not just logistical check-ins; they're reminders that money decisions are collaborative, not secretive. Save-spend-give jars are not simply containers; they are physical manifestations of priorities. Shared giving days are not just acts of charity; they are social proof that generosity is a responsibility shared by all, not reserved for the wealthy. These practices create a living curriculum, one that teaches children not only how to handle money, but how to locate their values within it.

One reason rituals work so effectively is that they reduce ambiguity. In families where financial decisions happen behind closed doors—or worse, only in crisis—children are left to guess at the rules. They may internalise that money is taboo, volatile, or shameful. Or they may develop distorted expectations, assuming that resources are limitless or that asking questions is inappropriate. *Rituals replace ambiguity with rhythm*. When there is a time and place for money conversations, the emotional charge surrounding them diminishes. Clarity replaces secrecy. Patterns emerge, and from patterns, habits are born.

Weekly money meetings are an especially powerful example. Held not in response to problems but as a proactive habit, they normalise conversation and model deliberation. For younger children, these might last just ten minutes—discussing allowance balances, naming savings goals, reflecting on recent purchases. For adolescents, the meetings can evolve into more sophisticated discussions about budgeting, debt, value-for-money analysis, or even ethical spending. What matters most is consistency. The meeting is not a performance, nor is it a lecture. It is a shared space—structured but welcoming—where thinking out loud is encouraged and where reflection is as valued as accuracy.

Over time, children who participate in these meetings develop a particular form of internal speech: *they begin to narrate their own spending choices in the language of priorities, trade-offs, and opportunity cost*. And crucially, they begin to see money as a shared tool, not a personal entitlement. This shared sense of stewardship is difficult to teach through isolated lessons—but it emerges naturally through regular, respectful engagement.

Save-spend-give jars function on a different, but complementary level. Their power lies in their tangibility. In a world of contactless payments and digital wallets, children rarely see money move. The jars reintroduce visibility—and with it, intentionality. When a child sees coins accumulate in a "save" jar, they understand that delayed gratification is not abstract; it is physical and trackable. When they move money from "spend" to a wallet for an upcoming purchase, they see the connection between decision and consequence. And when they place coins in the "give" jar—especially if accompanied by discussion about where it will go—they learn that generosity is not incidental. It is planned. It is expected. And it is theirs to own.

These jars work best not as stand-alone artefacts, but as part of a weekly ritual—perhaps reviewed during money meetings, or as part of a weekend routine. The point is not perfection. Sometimes a child will put all their money in "spend." Sometimes they will resent having to "give." These moments are not failures; they are teaching opportunities. They reveal emotional associations, unconscious beliefs, and habitual patterns that can be gently named and shaped. Over time, the jars become more than a budgeting tool. They become mirrors.

Shared giving days take this learning further. They elevate generosity from a private act to a public ritual, one that links money with moral imagination. When families designate time—monthly, quarterly, or annually—to give as a unit, they communicate a radical message: *we are not just consumers or savers; we are contributors*. In these sessions, children can nominate causes, research charities, and decide together how to allocate funds. They learn to compare not just products, but values. They practise empathy, perspective-taking, and civic responsibility—all through the lens of real, consequential choices.

Just as importantly, these giving rituals reframe what it means to "have enough." In affluent households, generosity can be a form of deflection—something done out of surplus, with minimal involvement. But when giving becomes a family ritual, it is no longer optional or performative. It is relational. It says: our abundance carries obligations. Our money is not just for us. And our values must be more than stated—they must be enacted.

Notably, the success of these rituals depends not on wealth, but on intention. A family of modest means can hold weekly meetings, use jars, and give communally with just as much (if not more) meaning than a wealthy household. In fact, the impact is often greater. Children from lower-income households who are included in structured financial rituals often report higher financial confidence and a stronger sense of agency. They learn that money is not something that simply "happens to them," but something they can plan for, talk about, and influence.

Still, rituals must evolve with age. What works for a six-year-old may feel patronising to a sixteen-year-old. The jars might give way to budgeting apps. The meetings might shift toward shared goal setting. The giving days might expand into hands-on service or advocacy. What matters is not the format, but the continuity. *Children must be able to trace the through-line: money is connected to values, and values are enacted in rhythm.*

This brings us to a deeper insight: rituals shape not just financial behaviour, but moral memory. The child who remembers Friday evenings sorting coins with a parent, or the sibling debates over which local cause to support, is not just learning arithmetic. They are forming identity. They are building associations between money and meaning—between autonomy and responsibility, between self-interest and collective good.

Such memory becomes particularly important in adolescence, when peer pressure, digital marketplaces, and shifting identities collide. In those moments of tension—whether at a shopping mall, a donation drive, or a checkout screen—rituals act as anchors. They remind the teen: you've done this before. You know how to weigh options. You've practised aligning actions with values. These aren't just rules; they are *your* tools. And that kind of resilience, that kind of fluency, cannot be summoned in the heat of a moral dilemma. It must be built—slowly, ritually, repeatedly.

To reinforce values through rituals, families must also practise a kind of humility. No ritual is a guarantee. No meeting will be perfect. Children will roll their eyes. Parents will forget. Life will interrupt. But that, too, is part of the message. *We keep showing up*. Not because it's glamorous or easy, but because money deserves our attention. Because values require reinforcement. And because children learn less from what we say than from what we return to, again and again, with presence and care.

Ultimately, rituals are not about control. They are about coherence. They link intention with action. They make the invisible visible. And in a world of distraction, volatility, and financial complexity, they offer children something increasingly rare: a sense of rhythm, a sense of belonging, and a sense of clarity about what really matters—and how to live it, one habit at a time.

### Letting Kids Into the Conversation

Children are not oblivious to money. Even before they can articulate numbers or understand compound interest, they are acutely aware that money exists, that it matters, and that it shapes what is possible or denied. They see the tension in checkout queues, the hesitation before big purchases, the quiet stress when bills arrive, or the celebratory tone when bonuses are mentioned. What they lack is not observation, but *context*. Without context, they guess. And when children are left to guess about money, they almost always get it wrong—overestimating, misinterpreting, or blaming themselves for dynamics they barely understand.

This is why age-appropriate transparency is not a luxury. It's a necessity. It creates emotional safety, fosters intellectual clarity, and—most importantly—grounds abstract money decisions in shared values and real-world reasoning. Letting children into financial conversations does not mean burdening them with adult worries or exposing them to every line of the household spreadsheet. It means treating them as people who will one day need to navigate complex trade-offs with competence and care—and beginning that journey with insight, not mystery.

The common objection—"children aren't ready for these conversations"—misunderstands the task. The point is not to explain tax brackets to a six-year-old. The point is to invite children into a culture where questions are welcome, trade-offs are discussed, and decisions are made visible. Even very young children can grasp the idea that money must be managed—that we don't always get what we want, and that saying yes to one thing often means saying no to another. They already encounter this reality when choosing between toys, treats, or time. What they need is language to make sense of it, and models that show how such decisions are made with thoughtfulness, not secrecy.

Transparency is not a binary state; it is a spectrum. What a five-year-old needs to know is not what a fifteen-year-old needs to know. But at every stage, the principle is the same: *honest framing builds resilience*. For example, when a younger child asks, "Why don't we buy a new car like our neighbours?" a productive response might be, "We choose to keep our old car because it still works well, and that way we can save for other things we care about." There's no shame, no panic—just a calm explanation that values shape decisions. Later, that same child may ask, "How much money do we have?" or "Are we rich?" Instead of retreating into vague reassurances, families can use these questions to introduce ideas like budgeting, saving, earning, and giving—all tailored to developmental readiness.

This practice becomes especially critical in families with visible wealth or visible scarcity. Children notice disparity—between classmates, between neighbourhoods, between their own experience and that of characters in media. If parents do not address these observations directly, children will fill the gap with assumptions, often laced with guilt, entitlement, anxiety, or misplaced judgment. Transparency is the antidote. It lets children know: *you are not alone in wondering about this, and you are not wrong for asking.*

In affluent households, withholding financial information often stems from a desire to preserve humility or protect innocence. But silence can have the opposite effect. When children see material abundance—trips, homes, electronics—but are never given the reasoning behind financial choices, they may assume wealth is automatic, infinite, or somehow unrelated to effort or values. Over time, this breeds entitlement, detachment, or insecurity. Conversely, when parents say, "We can afford this, but we choose not to spend on it because we value other things more," they plant seeds of discernment. They show that wealth is not just what you can afford—it's how you choose to use what you have.

For families with limited means, the stakes of silence are even higher. Children sense financial strain, even if no one speaks it aloud. If they are excluded from the conversation, they may assume they are the cause of stress, or that asking for small things is inappropriate. But when parents invite them into basic budgeting—"We're planning this week's groceries together so we can make sure we have what we need"—children feel trusted, not sidelined. They develop practical skills, yes, but more importantly, they feel part of the solution. *This builds agency rather than anxiety.*

There is a middle ground between overexposure and secrecy. It lies in *scaffolding*—adjusting the level of transparency based on maturity and curiosity. Younger children might benefit from simple visuals: pie charts showing where family money goes, jars that represent different expense categories, or stories about trade-offs (e.g., choosing to rent a smaller home so there's room for travel). Older children can be invited to co-create a budget for a family outing, manage part of their clothing allowance, or research mobile phone plans with guidance. Teenagers—especially those nearing financial independence—should be introduced to income statements, utility costs, insurance, and the reasoning behind savings goals or investments. The point is not to treat them as peers, but to help them see that financial decisions are made intentionally, not reactively.

One powerful practice is to involve children in real-time decision-making with limited stakes. For instance, a parent might say, "We have £50 to spend on entertainment this month—what do you think would be the best use of it?" or "We're thinking of switching internet providers—can you help compare options?" These exercises are not performative; they are practical rehearsals for adulthood. They also model *deliberation,* showing that money is not about impulse or image, but about values, needs, and long-term thinking.

Equally important is how adults model emotional regulation around money. If financial discussions are always tense, panicked, or avoidant, children internalise that money is a threat—or worse, a taboo. But when they see parents approach budgeting with composure, evaluate trade-offs calmly, and acknowledge limits without shame, they learn that financial discomfort is not a crisis. It's just a challenge to be met with clarity and confidence.

Letting children into the conversation also deepens trust. When a child hears, "We'd love to go on holiday this summer, but we're saving for a home repair instead," they don't just learn about budgeting. They learn that their parents are honest, even when the answer is disappointing. They learn that information is not withheld arbitrarily. Over time, this strengthens the family's emotional fabric. Children who feel included tend to be more forthcoming with their own questions, struggles, and decisions. They also tend to develop a healthier relationship with money—

less driven by shame or secrecy, more anchored in understanding.

There is a cultural resistance to this kind of openness, particularly in societies where money is tightly bound to identity, pride, or status. But normalising financial conversation in the home is one of the most effective forms of long-term resilience building. Children who grow up discussing money with nuance are far more likely to seek guidance when they face financial dilemmas later. They are less likely to be seduced by image-driven consumption, and more likely to view money as a tool—one that serves a purpose, rather than defines a person.

Ultimately, the aim is not to prepare children to mimic adult decisions, but to prepare them to make their own. Letting them into the conversation signals that money is not something done to them, but something they can learn to understand, question, and navigate. It says: your voice matters here. Your curiosity is welcome. And your future will be stronger because we began these conversations early—before the stakes were high, before the habits were set, and while the lines between learning and living were still porous enough to shape something lasting.

## Celebrate the Process, Not Just the Outcome

Most parents can recall praising a child for getting a good grade, scoring a goal, or saving enough for a toy. But when the outcome is poor—when the money is misspent, the plan miscalculated, or the budget abandoned—there's often silence, or worse, criticism. Yet if we want children to develop sound financial judgement, the metric must shift. The outcome matters, yes, but the thinking behind it matters more. *Good money thinking—planning, reflecting, evaluating trade-offs—deserves recognition even when the end result is imperfect.* Failing to acknowledge this not only discourages effort but reinforces the false belief that financial competence is about perfection rather than process.

Children do not arrive at financial wisdom by divine spark. They get there through dozens of imperfect choices—some impulsive, some misguided, many entirely age-appropriate. The task is not to prevent error, but to cultivate judgement. That cultivation requires *practice,* and practice, by definition, includes mistakes. If we only celebrate the moments where the numbers line up neatly—when a child saves precisely what they intended, or resists an impulse flawlessly—we reward luck, not learning. Worse, we signal that money is a test you either pass or fail, rather than a landscape to navigate with growing discernment.

The deeper problem lies in the broader cultural script around money, which tends to elevate outcomes: profit, savings totals, ROI. Children absorb this quickly. They begin to equate financial success with fixed results—"I'm good at money if I saved X," or "I made a bad choice because the toy broke." But adult money management rarely functions this way. Decisions are made under uncertainty, goals shift, prices fluctuate, and trade-offs evolve. The outcome is not always an accurate reflection of the thought process. *Learning to reflect on the quality of a decision independently from the result is a rare but crucial skill*—and one best taught early.

Consider a child who spends their allowance on a trendy gadget that breaks within a week. A natural adult instinct is to say, "Well, that was a waste—you should've waited." But a more constructive response might be: "What did you think about before buying it?" or "Would you make the same choice again?" If the child says, "I wanted it badly and didn't think about durability," that's an opportunity. Not to scold, but to unpack. What made it feel urgent? Did they consider alternatives? Would they set different criteria next time? Even if the outcome was poor, the analysis of *how* the decision was made can lead to insight. That insight is infinitely more valuable than the temporary sting of a lost toy.

On the other hand, imagine a child who saves up carefully, compares options, and purchases a well-reviewed product—only to find it disappointing. Here, the impulse might be to offer a pitying "That's too bad," or to dismiss the experience. But that child made a sequence of thoughtful, deliberate choices. That deserves recognition. "You did everything right: you budgeted, you researched, you made a patient decision. Sometimes the result isn't great, but the way you got there was solid." Such reinforcement tells the child that their effort and reasoning *matter*, and that outcomes, while important, are not the only yardstick of financial maturity.

In fact, many adults would benefit from this same reframing. Investor behaviour studies consistently show that those who chase high returns based on headlines or emotions fare worse than those who follow steady, process-driven strategies—even if the latter sometimes underperform in the short term. The same principle applies to children. Teaching them to anchor their sense of success in the quality of their decision-making, not just the result, builds resilience, reduces shame, and fosters a mindset that is both curious and reflective.

Importantly, celebrating the process does not mean abandoning standards or indulging recklessness. It means *engaging with the thinking behind the choice.* If a child impulsively blows all their birthday money on candy, the response isn't to shrug and say, "Nice try." It's to reflect together: "What made that seem like a good idea at the time? Did it feel worth it after?" This creates space for awareness and accountability—without punishment. The goal is to help children build an internal compass, not to micromanage their transactions.

This is particularly relevant in a world where digital payments, rapid transactions, and gamified spending environments (from online games to streaming platforms) can distort a child's sense of time, cost, and consequence. If the only feedback they receive is after the dust settles—when the money's gone—they learn to associate financial education with correction rather than guidance. But when the adult response is rooted in dialogue—before, during, and after decisions—they begin to see money as a space for growth, not just risk.

One of the most effective tools for fostering this mindset is a simple habit: narrate and acknowledge *good thinking*, even when the spending choice doesn't align with the adult's preferences. A child might say, "I thought about buying that game, but I remembered how quickly I stopped playing the last one." That thought process deserves praise, regardless of whether the purchase happens. Similarly, "I wanted to get the expensive version, but I chose the cheaper one so I could still have enough for next week's outing," reflects mature prioritisation. Even if the cheaper product is subpar, the reasoning was sound. And sound reasoning, when reinforced, tends to replicate itself.

This approach also helps prevent a common trap: *raising money-smart children who are risk-averse to a fault.* When children feel that only perfect outcomes earn approval, they may begin to fear experimentation. They might avoid new decisions altogether, or defer endlessly to adult preferences to avoid error. But real financial literacy requires courage—the courage to try, to fail, to adapt. By celebrating the process, we encourage that courage. We teach children that missteps are part of mastery, not signs of deficiency.

There is also a psychological dimension at play here. Children are in the early stages of forming identity. When they try to make "smart" financial decisions and fail, the emotional blow can be disproportionate. "I'm bad at this," they might think. "I shouldn't try again." That spiral is preventable. But it requires adults to separate *judgement* from *learning*, and to model that money, like any discipline, rewards consistency over perfection.

Practical strategies to reinforce process over outcome include shared debriefs ("Tell me what you considered before you made the choice"), reflective journals ("What would I do differently next time?"), and small planning exercises ("Let's brainstorm three ways you could use your allowance this week"). These are not bureaucratic burdens. They are conversational rituals that normalise thinking aloud, evaluating, and refining over time.

Celebrating process also rebalances the emotional stakes. When the only feedback children receive is applause for a good deal or criticism for a misstep, their financial confidence becomes brittle. But when adults say, "That was a thoughtful decision," or "I liked how you weighed the options," or even, "You noticed something you didn't before—that's progress," children begin to internalise a healthier message: *I am learning. And learning counts.*

What emerges from this approach is a more durable kind of competence—not just the ability to manage money, but the capacity to reflect on how money decisions are made, with all their complexity, uncertainty, and nuance. That skill will serve children not just as consumers or savers, but as future partners, parents, entrepreneurs, citizens.

Money thinking is rarely binary. There is often no single "right" choice. There are trade-offs, patterns, habits, and mindsets that accumulate over time. When we honour the quality of that thinking—especially when the results don't dazzle—we teach children that financial wisdom isn't about winning the moment. It's about showing up again, more thoughtful each time.

## The Family as a Financial Ecosystem

In every household—whether consciously cultivated or not—a financial ecosystem exists. It is composed of visible elements like income, expenses, savings, and debts, but also of subtler forces: attitudes, assumptions, habits, permissions, and tensions. It is shaped not only by what is earned or spent but by how decisions are made, who participates in them, and how ripple effects are handled when they reach beyond the origin point. This is not simply an accounting model; it is a social and moral structure. And within it, the smallest action—an impulsive purchase, a generous gift, a withheld conversation—can influence the health and direction of the whole.

The notion of a family as a financial ecosystem is not just a metaphor—it's a practical framework. It challenges the outdated idea that financial decisions live in silos. In many homes, adults handle "grown-up" money matters, while children are given a sliver of autonomy—perhaps an allowance, a savings jar, or a supervised debit card. The message, often unintended, is that money decisions exist in parallel lanes: one for the adults, one for the kids. But children are constantly participating in, observing, and shaping the family's financial culture, even when not invited explicitly. And the impact of their choices—or more accurately, of how their choices are responded to—can shape both family dynamics and future capabilities in lasting ways.

Take the example of a teenager who orders takeaway food multiple times a week using a shared household account. The transaction may seem minor, especially if the family can afford it. But over time, the pattern changes the emotional and financial atmosphere of the home: it might increase tension, lead to unspoken resentment, or create a sense of entitlement. If left unaddressed, the behaviour becomes normalised. If challenged harshly, it can cause shame or secrecy. In neither case is the issue merely "a kid buying too much food." It's a sign that the family's financial system is absorbing imbalance without conscious reflection.

Or consider a parent who quietly absorbs a child's recurring expenses—sports equipment, broken electronics, lost items—without setting boundaries or opening discussion. The intention may be generous, even loving, but the result can be corrosive. Children interpret unspoken patterns quickly: if there are no limits, they assume there are no costs. And if costs appear without explanation, they may experience guilt, confusion, or indifference. The financial system becomes opaque, and with it, accountability weakens.

In contrast, families that operate with a systems mindset recognise that *every member is a participant in the ecosystem, regardless of age or earning power*. A six-year-old who forgets their lunch and needs a replacement meal is not just making a minor mistake—they are contributing to a pattern that may require time, money, and energy from others. This does not mean children should be burdened with guilt, but rather, that they should be gradually invited into *awareness*. Not to control, but to contribute with consciousness.

The key shift is from financial independence to *financial interdependence*. Independence has long been the ideal in Western economic culture—"earn your own money," "pay your own way." But within families, this ideal often obscures reality. Parents may preach independence while covering every shortfall. Children may demand autonomy without understanding costs. The ecosystem model suggests something more dynamic and honest: that within a family, financial choices are never purely individual. *They are relational, and their effects are shared.*

This model can be illuminated further by examining systems theory. In ecosystems, resilience depends on feedback loops. When one part of the system changes, other parts must adapt to maintain balance. Similarly, in family finance, feedback is essential. If a child overspends on games or social outings and nothing is said, the system absorbs the shock—but at a cost: perhaps a delayed bill, a silent judgment, or a missed opportunity to teach. But if the feedback is constructive—"We noticed this pattern; let's talk about how it affects the whole picture"—the system rebalances through dialogue, not coercion.

This does not mean families must hold weekly budget summits or put spreadsheets on the dinner table. It means cultivating *a tone of transparency and responsiveness*. When parents say, "We're planning a holiday, and here's how everyone's choices can help make it possible," they are modelling interconnectedness. When a child is invited to consider whether an extra purchase is worth the trade-off—"That item means we might skip this later in the month"—they begin to internalise a core truth of all ecosystems: *resources are finite, but responsibility is shared.*

It is also worth noting that individual choices often become cultural defaults. If one child routinely saves their money and another routinely spends impulsively, the difference can generate not just behavioural contrast, but emotional politics—resentment, pride, rivalry. Left unacknowledged, this can calcify into identity: "I'm bad with money," or "I'm the responsible one." A healthy financial ecosystem creates space for evolution. It says, "We all have patterns, and we all affect each other—but we can learn, adjust, and support each other's growth."

The same principle applies when parents make decisions that affect the whole household. If one parent takes on debt to fund a business or career shift, the repercussions will often be felt across the family: fewer luxuries, increased stress, changes in schedule. When children are left out of these shifts entirely, they may misinterpret the changes as arbitrary or unfair. But when given a developmentally appropriate explanation—"We're investing in something that might take time to grow"—they are more likely to engage with the process and contribute constructively, even emotionally.

This leads to an even more nuanced insight: *Financial choices are not just economic—they are emotional, symbolic, and moral.* They carry meanings about fairness, trust, effort, worth. When one sibling receives a large birthday gift and another doesn't, the issue isn't only about money—it's about perceived value. When a parent splurges on themselves after months of frugality, it may signal permission, relief, or inconsistency. Children notice, and they draw conclusions. Not all such differences are bad—but they must be contextualised. Otherwise, the family ecosystem is shaped by implication rather than intention.

To build a more balanced ecosystem, some families create visible rituals: shared savings goals, donation discussions, monthly spending reviews. These are not about surveillance or control, but about cultivating *shared understanding*. Just as ecosystems thrive on biodiversity and cooperation, family financial health depends on participation across ages, temperaments, and roles. A child may not yet understand compound interest, but they can understand fairness. They can appreciate sacrifice. They can begin to grasp that their choices—however small—carry weight.

Indeed, one of the most empowering shifts for a child is to recognise that they are not simply recipients of family resources, but contributors to family wellbeing. This realisation can take many forms: offering to cover part of a shared expense, delaying a personal purchase for the sake of a group goal, or asking thoughtful questions about trade-offs. These gestures, though modest, signal a maturing relationship with money—one anchored not in entitlement or detachment, but in *relational intelligence.*

A robust family financial ecosystem also includes recovery protocols. Mistakes will happen—impulsive purchases, forgotten commitments, unexpected costs. The question is not how to prevent them entirely, but how to respond in ways that reinforce learning and maintain trust. In ecosystems, resilience is not the absence of disruption but the capacity to absorb and adapt. Families function the same way. A broken agreement can become a teachable moment; a financial strain can invite collective problem-solving. The difference lies in tone, timing, and trust.

Ultimately, to frame the family as a financial ecosystem is to shift the centre of gravity from control to collaboration. It is to say: *We are in this together. Our choices affect each other. And our responsibility is not only to manage our money wisely, but to care for the system we share.* That shift may be subtle, but its effects are profound. Children raised in such environments are not merely better at budgeting—they are better at discerning, empathising, and engaging with the real complexities of shared life.

And in a world where financial choices increasingly intersect with identity, ethics, and global systems, that kind of literacy is not just valuable—it's vital.

# Chapter 12
# Let Them Take the Wheel

There comes a moment in every parent-child relationship that is both inevitable and quietly tense: the handover of responsibility. Sometimes it is literal—the first set of car keys, a personal bank card. Sometimes it is more symbolic—the allowance for a school trip, the authority to make small household purchases. In every case, the principle is the same: children must become decision-makers, not in theory, but in practice. How well they handle that responsibility depends largely on how they were allowed to practise when the stakes were lower.

Financial independence is not a single leap but a series of incremental steps, each carefully calibrated. Parents who treat money like a set of cones—useful only for directing or blocking—may shield their children in the short term but risk delaying readiness for the real world. Conversely, treating it like a busy motorway—dangerous and unpredictable unless navigated alone—can overwhelm or provoke rebellion. What is required is graduated autonomy: a learning curve built on lived experience rather than lectures.

Money, particularly for teenagers, is paradoxical. Abstract in theory, yet profoundly tangible in consequence. It is one of the few arenas where power and vulnerability intersect in everyday life: the teen skipping lunch to save for concert tickets, the young adult overspending to impress friends, the student absorbing the consequences of mistakes out of embarrassment. These are not moral failures; they are developmental inevitabilities. Left unexamined, however, they can accumulate into unhelpful patterns.

This chapter focuses on a pivotal stage in financial upbringing: the shift from parental manager to parental mentor. It is not about withdrawing guidance, nor about cloaking control in rules. It is about constructing frameworks that allow freedom while preserving feedback loops. Think of it as a driving instructor holding the brake lightly: the learner steers, but the instructor intervenes only when absolutely necessary.

"Practice before independence" is a concept familiar in many domains—exams, sports, interviews—but remarkably underapplied to money. Children are often expected to instinctively understand budgeting, trade-offs, peer pressure, and delayed gratification. Yet these are learned behaviours, cultivated through repetition, reflection, and the occasional misstep.

Begin small. Pocket money, birthday budgets, class fundraising duties—these are not trivial exercises; they are dress rehearsals for the more complex financial decisions that await: credit cards, rent, employment contracts. By inviting children to manage low-stakes money early, parents teach not just arithmetic, but discernment, associating money with thoughtfulness rather than mere reward or restriction.

Perhaps the hardest lesson for adults is knowing when to step back. A teen who overspends their mobile data learns far more than from any lecture. A miscalculated weekend budget teaches scarcity more effectively than a conversation ever could. Yet stepping back is not disappearance. It is attentive distance: present without intrusive oversight, available without overbearing control.

This stage often overlaps with what might be called the "college test run": teens simulating adult life within the safety of home. Whether managing a monthly stipend, allocating summer-job earnings, or contributing to shared expenses, financial values can no longer be absorbed passively; they must be interpreted, questioned, and internalised.

Money at this stage is intimately tied to identity. Choices signal emerging self-conception: Am I a saver or a spender? One who shares or hoards? One who indulges or delays gratification? These are not fixed categories but evolving scripts. Reducing money talk to "yes" or "no," "can afford" or "can't," strips these decisions of depth, denying children the far richer conversation: what does your money reveal about who you aspire to be?

Mistakes must be reframed as information, not moral failings. Overspending is often a lack of strategy, forgetting to repay a friend an opportunity to explore reliability, buying status symbols a signal of insecurity rather than vanity. Each incident deserves reflection rather than punishment; the goal is pattern recognition, not perfection.

Autonomy cannot remain purely philosophical; it must be procedural. Teens need real-world tools: functional bank accounts, budgeting apps under their control, conversations in which their voice carries weight. Parents can signal this shift through language: "How would you approach this?" rather than "Here's what to do." Sharing their own missteps and evolving perspectives models that financial judgment is a lifelong process.

Financial independence is often misrepresented as a threshold: one day dependent, the next fully autonomous. In truth, it is a gradient—a gradual slope of increasing responsibility and decreasing oversight. Done well, the transition is marked not by abrupt withdrawal but by progressive delegation. Parents move into the passenger seat, allowing silence after decisions to linger, trusting instincts, accepting that some lessons must be paid for with experience rather than instruction.

The outcome is competence infused with integrity. A young adult who has practised making choices, who has been trusted to fail and encouraged to reflect, sees money not as a minefield or a fantasy but as a medium of agency. Financial capability becomes less about answers and more about judgement, honed by space to discover what works and what does not.

By the time real independence arrives—a job, university, relocation—the teen who has taken the wheel is prepared for the terrain. They may still veer off course, but they understand the mechanics, navigate deliberately, and are neither paralysed by choice nor reckless with freedom.

This chapter provides scaffolding, not control. The objective of financial parenting is not to shield from every error but to cultivate thinkers who can navigate uncertainty, act with intention, recover from setbacks, and regard money as a tool, not a trap. Handing over the wheel is not the end of teaching—it is the commencement of wisdom.

## Practice Before Independence

Children are not transformed into responsible financial actors on the day they become legal adults. Nor does maturity arrive automatically with a part-time job or university admission. Financial competence—like any other form of real-world literacy—requires practice, error, correction, and iteration. And for most young people, the absence of meaningful responsibility before independence is not a gift; it is a risk. *The earlier they are trusted with real decisions, the more capable they will be when the stakes rise.*

A growing body of behavioural research supports what seasoned parents often suspect instinctively: capability is a function of experience, not age. Children who are given small, bounded financial autonomy from an early age are measurably more confident, more adaptive, and more thoughtful with money as teenagers. The path from snack money to travel budgeting is not a casual stroll—it is a critical scaffolding for decision-making, trade-off analysis, and identity development.

But this journey requires intention. A few ad hoc allowances or a one-off lesson on "saving for what you want" do not constitute financial training. The goal is not to lecture kids about responsibility, but to *structure opportunities in which they must demonstrate it.* For instance, a seven-year-old might be asked to manage a weekly snack budget from a set allowance. They may run out early in the week. They may blow it all on Monday and learn what it means to wait. That discomfort is the point. The memory of a missed treat lingers longer than a parent's advice.

As they grow, the complexity of the task should scale. A nine-year-old might be given a fixed budget for selecting a friend's birthday gift. A twelve-year-old could manage their own lunch account. A fifteen-year-old might be asked to oversee the budget for a weekend trip with friends, including transport, food, and entrance fees. None of these should be treated as isolated events; they are part of a deliberate sequence. *What matters is not the outcome, but the process of reasoning, deciding, and adapting.* Even if the result is imperfect—especially if it is—growth is occurring.

This process also has a vital emotional dimension. Children are often shielded from decision-making under the mistaken assumption that exposure breeds stress. In fact, it's often the reverse. *What breeds stress is powerlessness.* Being constantly told what one can or cannot afford, without participating in the rationale, fosters confusion, resentment, or disengagement. By contrast, being entrusted with decisions—even limited ones—fosters clarity, pride, and investment in outcomes.

Parents may worry that this early independence will be misused, and they're right. It will be. Children will overspend, undersave, miscalculate, forget, and sometimes be manipulated by peers. These moments are not evidence of failure; they are *the curriculum.* The real mistake is believing that such errors can be postponed until adulthood. Postponed errors are not avoided errors—they are magnified ones. A teenager who has never misjudged £20 is poorly equipped to manage their first student loan or rental deposit.

Moreover, early practice facilitates a shift in how children perceive money. Rather than seeing it solely as an instrument of permission or denial—something adults use to control outcomes—they begin to see it as *a medium of choice and consequence.* This reframing is essential. It enables them to think of money not merely as a resource to acquire things, but as a language through which values, priorities, and self-regulation are expressed.

Consider the subtle but significant difference between a child who asks, "Can I buy this?" and one who asks, "Is it worth it to me?" The first frames the parent as gatekeeper. The second suggests internalised discernment. That shift doesn't happen from explanation—it comes from *ownership*. And ownership begins when the stakes are low enough to fail safely.

One of the most underutilised tools in this domain is *budgeting for real events*. Instead of surprising a child with spending money for a school trip or party, families can involve them in the planning. Present the total amount available. Ask them how they'd allocate it between meals, souvenirs, gifts, or transit. Let them sit with the trade-offs. Will they forgo a second dessert to buy a small keepsake? Will they opt for a simpler meal to share a treat with a friend? These decisions are more than logistical—they are exercises in self-definition.

That process also fosters appreciation. Children who have played a role in creating a budget are less likely to take the result for granted. They are more aware of costs, more deliberate in their choices, and more likely to notice the work that goes into financial preparation. They move from recipients of generosity to co-stewards of resources. And that transformation often leads to unexpected maturity—not just in money, but in empathy.

However, the efficacy of this approach rests heavily on *how adults respond to mistakes*. If every financial misstep is met with scolding, restriction, or I-told-you-so, the child learns not to be careful but to be secretive. They may still overspend—just without telling anyone. By contrast, if missteps are treated as a learning opportunity—"What happened? What would you try differently next time?"—then the child learns not just to calculate, but to *think*.

This reflective stance is particularly powerful during adolescence, when abstract thinking sharpens and peer influence intensifies. A teenager who is used to running small budgets and reviewing outcomes is better positioned to resist impulsive purchases, performative spending, or brand-driven status plays. They have a history of making money decisions, and perhaps more importantly, they have *language* for those decisions. They know how to talk about value, opportunity cost, and purpose.

That language also creates a bridge between generations. Instead of polarised battles—parents saying no, children insisting yes—there is room for negotiation. A teenager who wants an expensive item might be told, "That's outside our family's budget, but if you want to reallocate some of your own savings, we can look at it together." The conversation shifts from denial to agency.

Over time, this shift builds a platform for deeper conversations—about ethics, priorities, and long-term planning. It's not uncommon for a teenager with sufficient practice to start asking surprisingly adult questions: *Should I spend this now, or save it for university? What if I donated part of my birthday money this year? Is this brand really worth the markup?* These are not anomalies—they are indicators of maturity developed through sustained exposure to choice.

Ultimately, practice before independence is not just about dollars and pounds—it is about *judgement*. Financial literacy is not the memorisation of facts about compound interest or inflation rates; it is the ability to make decisions under constraints, align spending with values, adapt to new contexts, and recover from misjudgement. Those abilities do not spring forth fully formed in adulthood. They are cultivated—quietly, steadily—through years of meaningful practice.

And so the charge for parents, educators, and mentors is not to delay responsibility until it is safe, but to *design for it while it is still safe*. Create boundaries. Offer frameworks. Stay involved. But above all, *let them try*. Give children the space to experiment with being resourceful, with being accountable, with being wrong and recalibrating. The goal is not to prevent all missteps, but to create a track record of agency. Because when independence finally arrives—and it always does—it should feel not like a cliff, but like the next step in a path they already know how to walk.

## When to Step Back

There is a moment in nearly every well-meaning parent's journey when they see a mistake coming and feel the reflex to intervene—to correct, advise, redirect. Often, the impulse is protective: we want our children spared from disappointment, embarrassment, or the sting of a bad decision. But good parenting is not the absence of failure; it is the presence of calibrated freedom. *Knowing when not to interfere is not a sign of indifference—it is a mark of maturity.* In the realm of financial education, it is also one of the hardest and most vital skills to master.

Stepping back does not mean abandoning responsibility or resigning to chaos. It means creating space—space in which a child can learn not just from instruction but from experience. And this is where the real transfer of wisdom happens. *Experience is how theory becomes belief.*

Consider a teenager who has saved up for months and chooses to buy a high-end fashion item. The parent sees the impracticality, the marketing manipulation, the certainty that this item will be forgotten in weeks. They are tempted to step in, to steer their child toward something "smarter." But to do so robs the teen of the very insight the parent hopes to instil. *Without the freedom to choose poorly, there is no path to choosing wisely.*

The tension here is not abstract. It plays out in everyday family life—at the till, on mobile apps, during allowance conversations, or in the digital checkout queue. Children, especially older ones, are watching closely not only how money is used but how authority is exercised. Constant correction or micromanagement teaches them to comply, not to reason. They may follow directions but fail to internalise judgement. What feels like good guidance can quickly become *dependence in disguise*.

Stepping back becomes even more essential as children approach financial semi-independence. During the teenage years, the stakes of experimentation increase, but so does the need for self-regulation. Parents who over-function in this phase unintentionally short-circuit their child's developmental arc. They substitute their own judgement in moments where what's most needed is *scaffolding*—temporary support that allows for balance, not control.

The key lies in shifting from *manager* to *mentor*. A manager oversees inputs and outcomes. A mentor creates frameworks, asks questions, and lets the learner wrestle with uncertainty. For example, instead of vetoing a questionable purchase, a parent might ask: "What makes this worth it to you?" or "What will you be giving up to afford it?" These are not traps—they are prompts. Their purpose is not to enforce but to *surface* values. And values, once articulated, have a surprising power to govern behaviour.

However, to mentor effectively, one must resist the urge to rescue. This can be emotionally taxing. Watching a child run out of money before the end of the month, regret a rushed purchase, or miscalculate costs on a trip is uncomfortable. But the learning that emerges from that discomfort is precisely what builds future resilience. *There is no long-term confidence without short-term consequence.*

In families with high achievement cultures or perfectionist norms, this principle is especially difficult. Parents in such settings often conflate their child's decisions with their own credibility. A financial mistake by a teenager can feel like a reflection on the family's values, intelligence, or status. But this is an illusion. A well-structured mistake—made in a context of support and dialogue—is not a reputational threat. It is a developmental necessity. *Control protects the parent's ego; trust protects the child's growth.*

There is also a gendered layer worth naming. Studies consistently show that girls are more likely to be micromanaged in financial matters than boys, often under the banner of "being practical" or "avoiding frivolity." The result is not greater frugality but *lower risk tolerance and reduced financial confidence*. Parents must be vigilant against the subtle inequities that arise when stepping back is offered more freely to sons than daughters.

Technology complicates the terrain. Today's financial missteps may involve one-click purchases, in-app transactions, or social media-driven trends that escalate quickly. These risks are real, and some boundaries are indeed non-negotiable. But parents must distinguish between *boundaries and override*. A boundary might be a pre-set monthly cap on spending. An override is cancelling a transaction after the fact because it seems unwise. Boundaries teach responsibility. Overrides teach helplessness.

The discomfort of stepping back is not just parental—it extends to educators, mentors, and caregivers. Many well-intentioned adults believe that "teachable moments" require direct intervention. But sometimes, the most effective pedagogy is simply *not interrupting the process*. The teachable moment may be the moment *after* the mistake, not the moment before it. This demands a deep trust in the learner, and in the process of iterative self-correction.

It also demands clarity about the goals. If the aim is to raise a compliant child who follows rules, then micromanagement may work. But if the aim is to raise a discerning adult who can navigate complexity, then the path must include *guided autonomy*. Not unlimited freedom, not blind trust—but carefully expanding zones of discretion, paired with structured reflection.

There are also cultural dynamics at play. In some family systems—particularly those shaped by financial scarcity, migration, or trauma—money decisions are emotionally charged. Parents who have laboured to provide stability may feel intense anxiety watching their children experiment with spending. Their urge to step in is often rooted in past deprivation. But this is where generational progress risks being frozen. *To protect your child from every mistake is to make them reliant on your past, rather than free to build their own future.*

What helps is shared language and shared review. Families that debrief money decisions together—not as blame sessions, but as curious explorations—build a culture of reflection. A parent might say, "When I was your age, I bought something just like that, and I regretted it. What did you think when you clicked purchase?" Or, "I noticed you didn't spend your money this month—what helped you decide that?" These moments require presence, not control. They are acts of co-thinking, not correcting.

Stepping back also builds credibility. When children know that their autonomy will be respected, they are more likely to seek advice voluntarily. They may come to their parent not for permission but for perspective: "What would you do in this case?" This is the holy grail of financial mentoring—not obedience, but inquiry.

Ultimately, the goal is not to raise perfect decision-makers, but to raise thoughtful ones. Children who grow up being trusted with choices—even messy, suboptimal ones—develop the inner tools of discernment. They do not merely inherit financial habits; they *construct financial identities*. And that process cannot be outsourced, micromanaged, or rushed.

Parents must learn to tolerate temporary disorder in service of long-term capability. They must become comfortable with their child's imperfect judgment, confident that the scaffolding they have built—the modelling, the frameworks, the discussions—will hold. And they must understand that their most profound influence often emerges not when they speak, but when they stay silent long enough for their child to think.

Because ultimately, wisdom does not come from instruction. It comes from doing—and from knowing that someone believes you're capable of doing it. Even when you get it wrong. Especially when you get it wrong.

## The College Test Run

One of the most significant shifts in a young person's development is the transition from dependent to self-directed money management. By the time a teenager approaches college, they may have internalised years of conversations about budgeting, saving, or earning—but knowledge without practice is theory in costume. The only way to ensure they are ready for financial independence is to allow them to *rehearse* it. A "college test run"—in which adolescents begin managing real budgets under semi-independent conditions—bridges the gap between conceptual understanding and lived experience. It is not a simulation of adulthood; it is its earliest chapter, deliberately structured to promote reflection, mistakes, and maturing judgement.

The problem is that many families wait too long. Parents may hold off on financial delegation until the moment university begins, and with it, a flurry of new freedoms: new city, new friends, new schedules, and—suddenly—unmonitored access to money. This convergence of novelty creates a perfect storm for poor decision-making. *Money management is not a switch that flips at 18. It's a skill that accumulates with time, autonomy, and consequence.* Without those, even the most intelligent students find themselves surprised by overdrafts, late fees, and impulsive spending that doesn't align with their values.

What the college test run does is bring financial independence *home,* before geography and adult pressures complicate the learning curve. It creates space for experimentation while the consequences remain modest and the safety net remains near. Think of it as a calibrated transfer of power: intentional, responsive, and bound by clear structure. Rather than dictating rules, parents and caregivers become coaches—still involved, but increasingly in the background. The objective is not perfection. It's *pattern formation under pressure-light conditions*.

To begin meaningfully, this shift requires actual responsibility. A teenager cannot build financial judgement if their only choices involve discretionary spending from a parent-managed account. Instead, they need access to a recurring budget—monthly, quarterly, or seasonal—that they control. This budget should include more than treats and outings; it should cover essentials like school supplies, personal care, clothing, transportation, and social events. Where possible, even food outside the home should be factored in. *The goal is to mimic the structure of a college life—not just its temptations, but its logistical demands.*

Predictably, some mistakes will emerge. A teen may spend too much early in the month and find themselves negotiating trade-offs later. They might skip budgeting altogether, lulled by the illusion of abundant funds. These errors are not flaws in the model; they *are* the model. A test run without missteps is either too controlled or too short. What matters is that these missteps lead to reflection, not punishment. A budget meeting at the end of each month can help teens look back: What went well? What surprised you? What would you do differently? These are the questions that build insight—and *insight is what makes future independence feel earned, not imposed.*

It's important that the exercise doesn't feel like a parent's game. Teenagers can spot condescension quickly. They are more engaged when their role is real and their judgement respected. A useful practice is co-creating the budget, rather than handing down a number. Together, parent and teen can outline categories, agree on non-negotiables (such as savings minimums), and identify potential pressure points. This collaborative approach transforms budgeting from a control mechanism into a values conversation. *You are not just teaching your teen how to spend—you're learning together how money reflects intention.*

Many families are understandably cautious about handing over large sums. But independence does not require extravagance. In fact, modest resources can be an asset.

With limited funds, teens are forced to clarify priorities, resist impulsive habits, and plan across time. In contrast, unrestricted access—common among affluent households—can produce a distorted sense of cost, entitlement, or even detachment from financial decision-making. *A small, self-managed allowance often produces deeper learning than a large, parent-curated one.*

Technology can help or hinder. Many banks now offer teen accounts with built-in tracking, category tagging, and spending alerts. These tools are valuable, *not because they prevent mistakes but because they visualise behaviour*. Seeing where the money actually goes is more powerful than any warning a parent might offer. That said, oversight should be calibrated. Excessive monitoring turns autonomy into performance. It signals to teens that their choices are being judged, not developed. A more productive model is mutual review, initiated by the teen when they're ready to reflect—not surveillance under the guise of support.

Crucially, the college test run is not just about logistics. It's also about identity. Teens need space to explore how they want to *be* with money—whether that means discovering they're more frugal than their peers, realising they enjoy gift-giving, or deciding that experiences matter more than possessions. This emerging identity should be met with curiosity, not correction. Parents must resist the temptation to steer their children toward their own values. Financial adulthood means defining what matters *personally*, not just adhering to inherited scripts.

There is an additional benefit that often goes unspoken. When parents involve teens in structured financial autonomy, the conversations shift from instruction to partnership. Discussions about cost, value, and trade-offs begin to resemble the conversations adults have with one another—not lectures, but mutual sense-making. This shift can be deeply affirming for teenagers. *It tells them they are capable of reasoning, not just following.* And that is one of the most powerful messages a parent can send.

Some families may worry that their teen "isn't ready" for this level of responsibility. But readiness is not a precondition—it is the result. Expecting maturity before offering responsibility is circular logic. Instead, it's responsibility, combined with support and reflection, that produces maturity. The college test run makes this process visible, manageable, and iterative. It gives teens the confidence of knowing that they've not only learned financial principles but *used* them—in real time, with real consequences, and growing capacity.

There are, of course, variations. Some families may run the test during a gap year, a summer job, or a school holiday. Others may use study abroad programmes or residential camps as mini-rehearsals. What matters is that the exercise is framed explicitly: *this is a test of financial independence.* That framing invites intention. It tells the teen that this is not busywork or arbitrary—it is a meaningful opportunity to build the muscles they'll soon need to use alone.

Ultimately, the purpose of the college test run is not to inoculate teens against failure. It is to *normalise learning through action*. Financial capability is not a final exam. It is a posture—a way of thinking, prioritising, and recalibrating. By allowing teenagers to practice these skills in a structured but flexible way, families help them build not only competence but confidence. And that confidence—the sense that "I've handled this before, and I can do it again"—is what will carry them through the real transitions ahead, long after the test run ends.

## Money as Identity Formation

For teenagers standing at the cusp of adulthood, money is no longer just a medium of exchange—it is a mirror. It reflects choices, aspirations, assumptions, insecurities, and values in ways that are rarely linear but always revealing. To treat money education as purely technical—how to budget, how to invest, how to avoid debt—is to ignore its deeper psychological and sociological role: *money becomes part of how young people see themselves and how they wish to be seen*. Identity and money are not separate developmental tracks. They are entwined. And it is in adolescence that this relationship begins to crystallise.

The conventional assumption is that teenagers will "figure out money" by trial and error once they are earning or managing their own finances. But delaying this inquiry misses a crucial window: adolescence is not only a period of increasing autonomy, it is also a time of intense narrative-building. Teens are actively constructing answers to questions like *What kind of person am I? What matters to me? How do I want to move through the world?* The way they handle money is not just influenced by these reflections—it becomes one of the languages through which they speak them.

Some teens will gravitate toward generosity, viewing money as a tool for care or justice. Others may prize independence, using money as a shield against dependency or vulnerability. Some will adopt habits that mirror their parents' behaviours—meticulously saving, impulsively spending, or treating money with anxiety-laced caution. Still others will use money to rebel, to differentiate, to perform. These postures are not random. They are identity statements. *And helping teenagers become aware of those postures—not as immutable truths but as expressions they can examine, adjust, or discard—is one of the most powerful financial lessons we can offer.*

To support this process, adults must go beyond instruction and enter into dialogue. Rather than telling teens what they should value, we must ask: *What does money represent to you right now? How does it feel to spend? To save? To give?* These questions do not require perfect answers. What they require is curiosity. If a teen says they like spending on clothes because it boosts their confidence, we do not correct them—we ask what kind of confidence that is. If another says they hate saving because it feels like denying themselves, we probe that feeling gently. These are entry points, not red flags. *The goal is not to police values but to surface them.* Once surfaced, they can be shaped.

This process of exploration must also acknowledge the powerful cultural and peer forces at play. For many teenagers, money becomes a proxy for social identity. What they wear, what they own, how they spend—all of it feeds a quiet economy of status and belonging. A teen might insist on brand-name trainers not out of vanity, but because they fear invisibility or exclusion. They may want to pick up the bill at lunch because generosity signals maturity. Or they may reject consumer norms entirely, embracing minimalism as a form of moral clarity. Each of these choices is loaded. *To understand them properly, we must teach teens that financial decisions are never purely economic. They are social, emotional, and symbolic.*

The digital landscape intensifies this complexity. On social media, wealth is often aestheticised—curated into images of success, style, or self-worth. The line between authentic expression and performance blurs. Teen creators may monetise their identities in ways that simultaneously empower and entangle them. A popular TikTok user earning sponsorship deals may feel proud, but also trapped by a persona they can no longer afford to abandon. A teenager who sees viral content about luxury lifestyles may internalise warped expectations of success. These aren't superficial pressures—they are formative scripts. *We must help teens decode them before they unconsciously adopt them.*

One effective practice is reflective journaling or guided discussions where teens are invited to map their money memories. When did they first feel in control of money? When did they feel ashamed about it? When did it cause tension at home? These recollections often reveal more than any quiz or lesson. A teen who remembers being scolded for asking about prices might internalise silence as the safest posture. Another who was praised for being "good with money" may feel anxious when they make a mistake. These stories carry emotional weight. *By making them explicit, teens begin to reclaim authorship over their own financial narratives.*

We must also introduce the idea that money choices are not fixed identities. A teen who overspends this month is not "bad with money"—they are learning under real conditions. A young person who saves obsessively is not necessarily prudent—they may be anxious or inflexible. Identity is not a label; it's a trajectory. What matters is the ability to reflect, revise, and realign. Financial educators and parents alike must avoid reducing teens to their behaviours. *Instead, we affirm that financial identity is something they are building—consciously, with agency and support.*

This process benefits from modelling. Adults who speak openly about their own financial values—not just their decisions—create space for richer conversations. Saying "we don't buy that because it's expensive" is less illuminating than saying "we choose to spend on travel instead of gadgets because shared experiences matter to us." The former shuts down inquiry. The latter invites dialogue. Even better is inviting the teen into the decision-making: *"We have £200 we could use toward a weekend trip or put toward the family emergency fund. What feels more important to you right now, and why?"* This not only respects their input—it encourages them to see money as a tool for expressing values in real time.

Some teens will resist these conversations, not because they don't care, but because they feel scrutinised. For them, financial autonomy can be a site of tension—one of the last bastions of privacy. Pushing too hard risks alienating them. In these cases, indirect routes work best. Let the teen overhear adults grappling with trade-offs, questioning priorities, or naming regrets. These ambient signals often resonate more than structured talks. And when the teen is ready, they may volunteer their perspective, seeking alignment or contrast.

Ultimately, helping teens shape a healthy financial identity is not about imposing virtues. It is about creating an environment in which reflection, experimentation, and revision are normalised. It is about treating money as more than a tool or threat—it is a language of self-understanding. When teens learn to see it this way, they begin to ask better questions: *What kind of life do I want to build? What role should money play in that? What do I want to be known for—not just earn?*

These questions don't yield quick answers. But that's precisely the point. *We are not trying to equip teens with a static view of money—we are helping them construct a lifelong relationship with it.* One that is conscious, intentional, and evolving. In a world that constantly tells them what to want, giving teens the space to define their own financial identity may be one of the most radical, respectful acts we can offer.

# Chapter 13
# Beyond the Bank Account

It is a curious and disquieting paradox of our era that, despite unprecedented material abundance, the narrative we offer about success remains astonishingly narrow. The prevailing story is both seductive and unspoken: amass wealth, and all else—respect, stability, fulfilment—will follow. Children absorb this script before they have the tools to critique it. They encounter it in the accolades we celebrate, the lifestyles we elevate, the anxieties we normalise. Yet what if this version of success is not only incomplete, but subtly corrosive? What if the most consequential financial lesson we can impart has little to do with net worth and everything to do with net impact?

This chapter takes a deliberate step back from the mechanics and metrics of money to pose a more fundamental question: what kind of financial legacy are we cultivating in our children? Not simply in terms of inheritance, but in worldview. Are we equipping them to define success on their own terms—or merely training them to chase the most visible, socially sanctioned version? Are we modelling stewardship, or simply consumption? In essence, are we raising future investors or future custodians?

To confront this, we must scrutinise the deeper cultural scaffolding around money. The pervasive belief that wealth equates to virtue—so thoroughly embedded in capitalist societies—is intellectually flawed and emotionally limiting. It conflates visibility with value, productivity with worthiness, accumulation with wisdom. Children growing up under this framework often internalise the idea that their identity is inseparable from what they earn or own. When reality inevitably deviates from that script—through loss, failure, or doubt—they have few tools for navigating these experiences with perspective or grace.

The antidote is not rejecting financial ambition but redefining its meaning. True wealth is measured not by what one controls, but by what one can contribute without diminishing oneself. It is less about freedom alone and more about responsibility. Stewardship, then, becomes a mindset in which money is not an end, but a dynamic instrument—capable of building, protecting, healing, or harming. To raise children with such a mindset, we must first examine our own.

This work often begins with repair. Many parents today engage in a quiet, intergenerational mending: correcting secrecy, fear, or financial volatility inherited from their own upbringing. Some are the first in their families to achieve stability, now tasked with translating that achievement into something enduring. Others confront cycles of overwork, scarcity-thinking, or an emotional attachment to status. These parents are not merely budgeting differently; they are choosing a different story. This chapter honours that effort and seeks to carry it forward.

It is not sufficient to say, "We want our children to do better." One must define what "better" truly means. More money? Greater freedom? Heightened discernment? Broader contribution? These are not rhetorical queries but structuring questions, shaping the culture within a household. In many families, financial culture emerges by accident, from unspoken habits: how money is discussed—or avoided—how decisions are justified, how generosity is modelled, how failure is handled. In households that treat money as part of their ethical and relational fabric, however, financial culture is intentional—a space where values are practised, not preached.

Consider budgeting. In a transactional mindset, it is about limits. In a stewardship mindset, it is about clarity: clarity regarding priorities and the discipline to align resources accordingly. The question shifts from "How much can we afford?" to "What are we choosing to prioritise?" Similarly, conversations about spending move from guilt or justification toward curiosity: what does this choice reveal about us? Does it align with who we aspire to be? Over time, these questions form a narrative spine—a shared language that children internalise not as rules, but as reflections of identity.

Crucially, parental success should not be measured solely by a child's financial fluency. The ultimate aim is not a 22-year-old capable of reading a bank statement, but an adult who understands that money is a powerful, morally complex tool—one to be wielded with humility, foresight, and integrity. This standard is higher, but liberating. It allows for imperfection, growth, and individuality. Children's relationships with money are shaped not only by lessons taught but by the models provided under pressure, in moments of uncertainty, change, and trade-off.

Perhaps most radically, this perspective invites us to view children as stewards of a longer story, not merely as future earners or savers. That story may encompass generational wealth, or generational wisdom—ideally both. Money does not exist outside of human context; it is embedded in relationships, systems, and time. Teaching children to think in terms of legacy encourages them to look beyond themselves—not in self-denial, but in self-extension. It says: your financial life is not solely about what you extract, but what you sustain. Not only what you gain, but what you shape.

This chapter calls for sharper vision, not diminished ambition. It asks parents, educators, and mentors to elevate the conversation—from tactics to philosophy, from competency to character. Financial education becomes civic education. The adults we raise will influence not just the economy they inherit, but the society they construct. In the end, success is measured not by accumulation, but by how wisely the next generation deploys what they inherit, earn, or create.

Raising stewards is quieter than raising prodigies, slower than teaching hacks, yet more enduring than teaching rules. It is, fundamentally, an investment in the long view. It deserves to be taken seriously.

## Redefining Financial Success

It is telling that in most societies, asking someone whether they are "successful" is functionally identical to asking whether they are wealthy. This slippage between money and meaning is rarely questioned—yet it colours how children learn to evaluate others, and more critically, how they learn to evaluate themselves. The equation is implied in media portrayals, reinforced in schoolyard comparisons, and echoed in well-meaning adult conversations: the big house, the flashy car, the early retirement, the exponential income. These are the icons of "making it." But when success is measured in financial terms alone, other equally vital dimensions—integrity, balance, contribution—are eclipsed. And the result is not just cultural distortion. It is moral anaemia.

What we reward, we replicate. And if children see that society rewards wealth over wisdom, visibility over virtue, and growth over stewardship, they will orient their aspirations accordingly. The goal, then, is not to demonise financial ambition—it is to *expand the definition of success so that it includes, but is not limited to, money*. To teach children that financial success is not a badge of personal worth, but one lens—among many—through which impact, discipline, and alignment can be measured. That shift is neither sentimental nor semantic. It is structural. Because it changes what young people strive toward, and what they feel entitled—or ashamed—to pursue.

A more intelligent definition of financial success would include four dimensions: sustainability, agency, ethics, and contribution. Sustainability means that wealth supports life, rather than consuming it. Agency means the individual maintains choice, not merely options. Ethics ensures that the means do not betray the ends. And contribution ensures that success is not self-sealing. Together, these elements form a model that is both broader and more durable than conventional wealth metrics.

Take the case of a parent who has chosen a lower-paying but deeply mission-aligned career—say, teaching in a public school or working in environmental justice. Their financial story might not feature six figures or stock options, but it may reflect something equally valuable: a stable relationship with money, transparent priorities, and a daily integration of values and livelihood. To a child, this signals that money is not the only form of capital worth accumulating. Time, purpose, relationships, and self-respect count too. This is not abstract. It is legible in how parents speak about their work, how they treat others, how they spend and give.

Contrast that with the household where money is abundant, but shrouded in anxiety, secrecy, or status anxiety. Here, success becomes a performance: one maintained through appearance, comparison, and insulation from discomfort. Children raised in such environments often absorb conflicting messages—on one hand, they are told to be grateful and grounded; on the other, they are rewarded for accumulation, not discernment. This contradiction erodes clarity. And without clarity, integrity is hard to practise.

Redefining financial success also means addressing the cultural myth of the self-made individual. It is not just inaccurate—it is damaging. Every financial outcome is shaped by variables far beyond individual effort: timing, health, race, geography, social networks, and systemic policies. Teaching children to ignore these forces in favour of a bootstraps narrative fosters arrogance in those who succeed and shame in those who struggle. But recognising structural advantage does not mean abandoning personal agency. It means contextualising it. It means replacing the question "How much did you earn?" with "How did you earn it, and what did you do with it?"

This recalibration has profound implications for how we talk about success with young people. Rather than praising outcomes—"She bought a house at 25"—we can praise process: the patience, planning, or creativity that allowed it. Instead of applauding financial luck without scrutiny—"He made a killing on crypto"—we can ask what's being built, not just banked. These shifts may seem subtle, but they establish powerful mental models. They show that what matters is not just *that* money is earned, but *how* it is used and *what* it reflects.

Models of success that include balance also deserve elevation. Consider the adult who earns enough, works sustainably, contributes to their community, and maintains presence in their family life. This is not a diluted success. It is a considered one. But such models are often invisible to children because they do not come with glossy public metrics. Our task is to make them visible—to narrate them, honour them, and show children that real success often looks like a quiet competence, not a noisy display.

At a deeper level, redefining financial success means helping children connect money to identity—not in the consumerist sense of buying one's image, but in the deeper sense of understanding what one's money choices signal about their values, commitments, and self-concept. A child who saves diligently for a cause, declines peer pressure to overspend, or resists exploitative shortcuts is *already practising success*—because they are aligning their actions with their principles. Financial maturity, then, is not just about metrics. It is about coherence.

To support this redefinition, parents and educators must interrogate their own frameworks. Many adults, even those with thoughtful intentions, continue to reinforce narrow success scripts through subtle cues: who they admire, what they envy, what they avoid. Children are exquisitely attuned to these signals. They know when admiration masks insecurity, when generosity is performative, when work is treated as a burden or badge. To redefine success, adults must not only *say* different things—they must *become* different models.

There is also a place for contrasting views. Some argue that in a competitive economy, softening the success narrative can backfire—lowering ambition or creating confusion. But this critique misunderstands the aim. Redefining success is not about lowering standards; it's about *recalibrating them to reflect reality and purpose*. A generation raised to pursue wealth without grounding will not be more successful—they will merely be more brittle. What we need is not less ambition, but *smarter ambition*—ambition tethered to contribution, not just accumulation.

One practical implication of this shift is how we structure financial education. Instead of focusing solely on tools—budgeting apps, investment portfolios, debt calculators—we must teach frameworks. What is money for? Who benefits from your spending? How do your values appear in your transactions? These questions are not rhetorical. They are diagnostic. They allow children to interrogate their relationship with money before it calcifies into reflex.

Ultimately, to redefine financial success is to invite children into a larger conversation—not just about what they want to have, but about who they want to be. It is a chance to ask, with seriousness and openness: *What kind of life are you trying to build? What does enough look like? Where does your sense of worth come from?* These questions are not ancillary to financial education. They are its core. And if we can help children grapple with them early—honestly, courageously, without shame—we stand a far better chance of raising adults who use money well, rather than being used by it.

## Intergenerational Repair

Most families inherit more than genes and traditions—they inherit financial patterns. These patterns are rarely acknowledged outright, but they shape the emotional climate of a household as profoundly as love, discipline, or expectations. Whether it's the silence surrounding money, the panic during tax season, the shame about debt, or the overcompensation of conspicuous consumption, these behaviours are passed down, often unintentionally, across generations. The damage isn't always measured in net worth. Sometimes it's in the anxiety a child learns to associate with bills, the inability to ask questions about money without guilt, or the belief that financial security is only for "other people." To repair those patterns takes more than good intentions. It takes skill, clarity, and courage.

For many parents today—particularly those raised amidst economic instability, secrecy, or cultural taboos around money—raising financially aware children represents a kind of generational break. They are doing something their parents did not or could not do: making money discussable, demystified, and, most critically, *de-shamed*. This is not an easy task. It requires unlearning as much as learning. But it may be one of the most powerful forms of inheritance they can offer—not wealth itself, but *the capacity to relate to money with intelligence, dignity, and agency.*

This work often begins with telling the truth. For families coming out of a history of silence, that may involve admitting past mistakes—not performatively, but in a way that models ownership without self-flagellation. A parent who says, "I didn't learn how to manage money until my 30s because we never talked about it growing up," is not simply disclosing failure. They are rewriting the emotional script of financial dialogue. They are making space for a child to do better, *without feeling disloyal.*

Some adults hesitate to be transparent about their financial pasts or current realities out of fear that it will undermine their authority or burden their children. But there is a vital difference between honesty and oversharing. The goal isn't to saddle kids with adult stress; it is to create a climate where money is not a source of fear or shame. A teenager who understands that a parent once carried credit card debt—not because they were irresponsible, but because they were never taught otherwise—gains context. That context builds compassion and wisdom, not judgment.

Repair also means making explicit what was once implicit. Many families operate on unspoken rules: "We don't talk about money," "You never say no to family," "Money is private." These rules often arise out of protection, but they become constraints. They prevent inquiry, block learning, and perpetuate shame. Naming them is the first step toward replacing them. A parent might say, "I was raised to believe that talking about money is rude—but I don't want you to grow up confused the way I did." That single sentence reframes silence as a choice, not a truth. It opens the door.

There is also the more structural work of modelling new behaviours. In families where spending was erratic or unexamined, introducing budgeting—not as punishment, but as a form of stewardship—represents a profound cultural shift. In families where debt was normalised but never discussed, building a plan to repay or avoid it—and involving children in the logic of those decisions—creates new neural pathways, both practically and psychologically. This is not about perfection. It's about *integrity in process*. When children see their caregivers make financial decisions with intention, it teaches them that money is not a minefield. It's a system they can learn, navigate, and eventually master.

Importantly, intergenerational repair is not only about avoiding old mistakes. It's also about amplifying new possibilities. That includes breaking cultural scripts that equate frugality with scarcity or self-worth with financial success. It includes celebrating thoughtful giving, shared decision-making, or saying no to overwork in favour of presence. In many households, success was measured by what was accumulated. Repair means broadening that definition to include *how money is earned, how it's used, and what it enables.* When families start to place value on experiences, wellbeing, and integrity alongside income or assets, they change the gravitational centre of their financial identity.

Sometimes, repair also means confronting ancestral silence—especially in families that experienced systemic economic exclusion. For families from historically marginalised communities, intergenerational repair includes acknowledging how racism, sexism, immigration barriers, or class stratification shaped their financial trajectories. Naming these realities does not breed victimhood—it fosters *historical accuracy*. It explains why certain doors were closed, why certain decisions were made, and why the current generation may face both different challenges and new opportunities. This is not about dwelling in grievance. It's about grounding progress in truth.

It is worth noting that intergenerational repair is not linear. A parent who was never taught to save may overcompensate by becoming rigid. A parent who grew up in poverty may struggle with scarcity mindset even after achieving security. A family that suddenly gains wealth may lack the vocabulary or emotional framework to navigate that change without friction. These tensions are not signs of failure. They are signals that something new is being attempted—something that requires patience, dialogue, and grace.

One of the most powerful tools in this work is language. Even small shifts matter. Changing "We can't afford that" to "That's not how we've chosen to spend our money" reframes constraint as agency. Explaining why a decision is made—not just what it costs—helps children see the logic beneath the choice. Over time, this builds a culture in which money is not a taboo or a weapon, but a teachable, shared domain.

This work also requires *staying power*. A single conversation won't undo decades of inherited dysfunction. Repair happens cumulatively—in monthly budget meetings, in transparent goal setting, in jointly navigating windfalls or disappointments. It happens when children are invited into the process, not merely protected from it. And it deepens when families return to the table after hard conversations, reaffirming that discomfort is not a threat to love or respect. It is part of what transformation looks like.

Critically, this process must be future-facing. Repair is not only about what the current generation corrects—it is about what they equip the next generation to sustain. That means not only resolving their own confusion, but *teaching their children how to adapt, question, and recalibrate*. It means fostering financial thinkers, not just financial followers. And it requires a long view: one that sees each child not just as a recipient of new habits, but as a future teacher of their own children someday.

For families engaged in this work, the gains are rarely dramatic or visible. But they are profound. A child who knows how to ask questions about a loan, decline a bad offer, negotiate a raise, or discuss money without shame is not just financially literate—they are financially free. And that freedom does not emerge from reading a textbook. It emerges from years of subtle, intentional repair—of courageously breaking what needed breaking, and gently building what had never existed before.

That is the real inheritance. Not a trust fund. Not an income bracket. But a lineage of clarity, confidence, and care—one that will long outlast the currency it touches.

## The Long Arc of Stewardship

The most enduring financial legacies are not built on acquisition. They are built on *stewardship*—the capacity to manage resources with clarity, accountability, and care, not just for oneself, but for the generations that follow. Yet modern culture rarely celebrates this mode of thinking. It valorises accumulation over intention, quick gain over sustained trust, and autonomy over interdependence. Wealth, as popularly understood, is framed as a private destination. But true financial wisdom is collective and cumulative. It unfolds not in bursts, but across decades—and it resists being reduced to numbers alone.

To steward money is to treat it as a means, not an end. It is to orient decision-making not around short-term optimisation, but around long-term meaning. This is a conceptual pivot that feels radical in a society saturated with financial content that promotes hyper-individualism, competitive advantage, and the fantasy of total control. Stewardship begins with an acknowledgment of limitation: that we are temporary holders of resources shaped by histories we did not author and futures we will not see. The role is not to dominate money, but to direct it with integrity.

This reframing has direct implications for families trying to cultivate financial literacy that lasts. Teaching a child to save is a tactic. Teaching them to *steward* resources is a worldview. The latter requires helping them understand that their choices ripple outward—into relationships, into systems, into the lives of those who may one day depend on them. It means resisting the lure of the transactional mindset, where money is treated as a private commodity to be maximised at all costs. Instead, *stewardship assumes relationality*: money is always in motion, always shaped by the context in which it moves.

Consider the case of inheritance. A parent who leaves behind wealth without context has passed on assets, not stewardship. The gift becomes fragile—vulnerable to mismanagement, misunderstanding, or disconnection. But when that inheritance is accompanied by conversations, values, and expectations, it becomes more than money. It becomes *a baton, not a bomb*. The difference lies in preparation. Stewardship asks not only, "What are you leaving?" but "Who are you preparing to receive it—and how?"

Stewardship also asks what one is funding—implicitly or explicitly—with their money. Are we enabling dependency, or fostering capacity? Are we reinforcing value, or distorting it? Parents who aim to be stewards must model these questions in their own behaviour. A family that spends generously on experiences but selectively on status items is communicating priorities. A family that discusses the ethical dimensions of investment—not just the returns—is expanding the child's conception of money's role. These are not lectures. They are lived signals.

Importantly, stewardship is not synonymous with conservatism. It does not mean hoarding, nor does it resist risk. It means that risks are taken with eyes open and purpose clear. The entrepreneur who launches a business rooted in community need, rather than trend-chasing opportunism, is a steward. So is the family that uses surplus not only for comfort but for redistribution—whether through charitable giving, community partnerships, or supporting relatives in quiet, dignified ways. *Stewardship rejects the binary of self versus others*. It understands that sustainability is shared.

This is particularly critical in times of volatility. During financial crises—whether personal or global—stewardship offers stability that mere accumulation cannot. A child who has seen their family adjust thoughtfully to downturns, cut expenses with transparency, or delay gratification in service of a long-term goal, is learning how to anchor themselves. They are seeing money not as a fixed symbol of power, but as a variable element in a well-anchored life. This distinction may be the most enduring gift a parent can offer: not a promise of wealth, but a *method of resilience*.

Generationally, this perspective also invites a more inclusive view of what financial contribution means. In many households, especially those with cultural or economic legacies shaped by migration, struggle, or systemic exclusion, stewardship may not mean passing on wealth—it may mean passing on *discipline, dignity, and direction*. The parent who never had savings to invest but modelled rigour, honesty, and generosity is still practising stewardship. That example *is* an inheritance. And it is often more translatable—and more transformational—than any financial asset.

In practical terms, cultivating a culture of stewardship in the home can begin early. It might mean inviting children to participate in discussions about how the family budgets for holidays—not just what they can afford, but why they prioritise certain kinds of spending. It might mean narrating the decision to wait before replacing a car, or choosing a local vendor over a cheaper multinational, as a reflection of family values. These are not abstract ethics. They are decisions made in real time that model *values under constraint*.

Another powerful practice is helping children see the lifecycle of a financial decision. For example, involving them in the process of saving for something meaningful, then later reflecting on whether the purchase lived up to expectation, instils reflective habit. It teaches them that money is not just about acquisition—it's about reflection, adjustment, and alignment. Over time, this develops into financial maturity: *the ability to link one's spending with one's story*, to be accountable not just for what one buys, but for what it represents.

For older children and teens, stewardship can become a more explicit conversation about legacy. Not in the narrow sense of estate planning, but in the expansive sense of impact. Questions like: "What kind of financial example do you want to set?" or "If you were to look back at your financial life in 50 years, what would you be proud of?" move the conversation from compliance to vision. They encourage young people to see themselves not merely as consumers or earners, but as *narrators of an ethical arc*.

It's also worth exploring how digital tools and environments shape—or distort—young people's sense of stewardship. The immediacy of apps, the gamification of spending, and the absence of physical cash all conspire to collapse the temporal gap between desire and decision. Stewardship counters this compression. It stretches the timeline. It asks: not just "Can I buy this now?" but "What am I committing to, and what does it crowd out?" In a culture built for immediacy, *the long arc is itself a radical stance.*

Crucially, stewardship acknowledges the moral dimension of money. Not moralism, but moral consideration. It treats financial decision-making as an extension of one's character, one's commitments, and one's accountability to others. This is not to say that money is inherently virtuous or corrupt. It is neutral—*until it is activated*. And it is that activation—what we do with it, and why—that determines its ethical trajectory. Stewardship is simply the discipline of staying conscious through that activation.

For those seeking to instil this mindset in children, consistency matters more than intensity. A one-off conversation about philanthropy will never compete with years of witnessing whether giving is routine or reactive. A spreadsheet of compound interest will never teach as much as watching a parent delay gratification to pay off a loan or contribute to a family goal. The question is not how much you teach, but *how congruent your habits are with your claims*. Children, as ever, learn by watching—especially when no one is watching them.

The arc of stewardship, then, is less a curriculum than a posture. It asks: What do I want my money to reflect about my values? Who is affected by my choices, and how? How will the people who come after me be shaped by what I've done—or failed to do—with the resources I've managed? These are not questions with fixed answers. They are questions to be lived, revisited, and refined.

And when families take that long view—when they talk not just about what they can afford, but what they stand for—they are not just preparing the next generation to succeed. They are preparing them to *steward*—which is harder, deeper, and infinitely more meaningful. They are teaching them that the point of money is not to prove one's worth, but to live one's worth—with clarity, with consequence, and with care that extends far beyond the present moment.

## Raising Adults, Not Just Kids

The true measure of financial education is not whether a child can recite definitions of compound interest or distinguish between credit and debit. It is whether, years later, they approach money with thoughtfulness, discipline, and values intact—especially when no one is supervising. If financial literacy is about understanding, financial adulthood is about application under pressure, in ambiguity, and often in solitude. The real goal, therefore, is not to raise financially knowledgeable children. It is to raise financially capable, principled adults—individuals equipped not only with the skills to navigate money, but with the inner architecture to do so responsibly.

This reframing matters because it shifts the emphasis from performance to orientation. A child can ace a financial literacy quiz yet falter when faced with real-world dilemmas: Should I lend money to a friend who won't pay it back? Can I afford to move out even if I technically have enough for rent? Do I pursue a higher-paying job that undermines my values? These are not problems solved with formulas. They require judgement, resilience, and a clear sense of self. *Financial adulthood is ethical as much as it is technical.*

And yet, most conventional financial education stops short of this maturity. Schools, apps, and even many family efforts tend to front-load mechanics: budgeting, saving, banking, taxes. Useful, yes. But not transformative. These tools must be nested within deeper questions: *What does money represent to me? How does it connect to my identity, my aspirations, my obligations?* Without this, financial behaviours risk becoming performative or hollow—boxes checked, but not beliefs built.

Raising a financially capable adult starts with modelling, not dictating. Children internalise the lived values of the home far more than they adopt abstract principles. If they witness impulsive spending followed by justification, they will learn that money is about mood management. If they see budgeting handled with anxiety and secrecy, they may associate finance with shame or fear. Conversely, when they observe thoughtful trade-offs, transparent discussions, and decisions aligned with values, they are given a map—a working model of integrity under constraint. *Children build financial maturity by watching adults wrestle honestly with reality.*

This means that even parental imperfection is a teaching tool—if made visible. A parent who says, "I regret that purchase—I made it too quickly and didn't plan ahead" is not diminishing their authority. They are *demonstrating accountability*. They are showing that adults are not immune from financial missteps—but that growth is possible through reflection. Such moments are more potent than lectures. They help normalise the fact that financial adulthood is not about mastery, but about consistent course correction.

Equally important is gradually expanding a child's financial sphere of control. Too many young people reach adulthood having never made a significant money decision. Then, in one dizzying leap, they must manage tuition, rent, credit, work, taxes—often without guidance. This abrupt transition sets them up for mistakes that are not just financially costly, but *identity-shaking*. They begin to define themselves not by their emerging adulthood, but by their perceived failures within it.

To counter this, parents must shift from protectors to partners. Early on, that means letting a child mismanage small amounts. Letting them blow their birthday money on a toy they regret two days later. Allowing them to experience the friction of choosing between wants when they can't afford both. Over time, this expands: contributing to family grocery shopping, managing a mobile phone budget, co-owning the consequences of late payments or overdrawn accounts. The goal is not punitive. It's *formative*. Each misstep is a low-stakes rehearsal for high-stakes adulthood.

But skill-building alone is insufficient without self-awareness. Part of raising a principled adult is helping them understand *what money activates in them*. Do they equate spending with status? Do they feel guilt when they have more than others? Do they fear asking for financial help? These are not irrational feelings. They are shaped by culture, class, trauma, and personality. Parents who can help their children name and interrogate these responses are giving them tools far more powerful than any budgeting app. *They are helping them integrate finance into the broader work of becoming a person*.

This is especially vital during adolescence, when identity and autonomy begin to crystallise. Teenagers often chafe against financial boundaries not out of entitlement, but because money becomes a proxy for freedom, self-definition, or peer belonging. Rather than framing these moments as disciplinary issues, they can be treated as developmental ones. A conversation about a teen's desire for designer clothing, for instance, can open up questions about image, insecurity, and aspiration. The point is not to shame the desire, but to *contextualise it*. To ask: What do you think this represents? How else might you express that? What are the trade-offs?

Such inquiries foster moral reasoning. They help the teen realise that financial decisions are never isolated—they reverberate socially and emotionally. They are not just about what one can afford, but about *what kind of person one is becoming*. That insight—when truly absorbed—becomes a compass. And a young adult with a compass will make better decisions in ambiguity than one with only a rulebook.

Of course, building this moral compass requires parental humility. Many families must unlearn the tendency to treat financial conversations as one-way broadcasts. If a teen never feels safe to ask naïve questions, admit confusion, or disagree with their parents' financial philosophies, they will not develop internal confidence. They will become compliance-driven at best, or rebellious at worst. The alternative is to foster reciprocal dialogue. To treat the child not as a future adult, but as a *developing one,* worthy of engagement today.

This does not mean ceding control or eliminating boundaries. It means inviting thought. For example: "We're deciding how much to spend on holiday gifts this year—what do you think would feel meaningful but reasonable?" Or, "We're rethinking our streaming subscriptions—would you be willing to help us compare what we actually use?" These are small on-ramps. But they signal trust, capability, and inclusion. Over time, they lay the groundwork for independent decision-making rooted in shared logic.

And shared logic matters. Because financial adulthood does not occur in a vacuum. It unfolds within systems—familial, cultural, institutional—that shape possibilities and perceptions. A child raised in a high-income household may struggle with guilt or identity dissonance around privilege. One raised in scarcity may have internalised habits of hyper-control or self-denial. Neither is inherently wrong—but both must be *understood* in order to be matured. Helping a young person identify these inherited scripts, and consciously choose which to revise or retain, is part of the adult-making process.

Another essential shift is teaching young people to think longitudinally. Children are naturally present-oriented. But financial adulthood requires the ability to *stretch time*. To think in months, years, decades. To ask: How will this decision impact Future Me? What will I wish I had done differently? Adults can scaffold this by narrating their own decisions: "We're skipping a new car this year because we're focused on building an emergency fund—just in case." These explanations, repeated over time, teach the child to align money with a broader arc of planning, patience, and purpose.

Ultimately, raising a financially capable adult is less about preparing them to follow instructions, and more about equipping them to write their own. To evaluate competing goals. To discern the difference between freedom and indulgence. To hold ambition in one hand and values in the other. This is not just financial readiness. It is *ethical readiness*—a preparedness to be a full actor in a world where money is not neutral, and where each decision leaves a trace.

The greatest financial compliment a parent can receive is not "You taught me how to save." It's "You helped me understand how money fits into the life I want to live." That is a generative legacy. That is adulthood well-raised.

# About the Author

Eli Shepherd writes with a calm urgency—inviting readers to slow down and think deeper about the choices shaping their lives and families. With a keen interest in how values are formed and passed on, Shepherd explores modern parenting through a lens of intention, empathy, and real-world practicality. Known for distilling big ideas into accessible frameworks, Shepherd is passionate about helping parents raise thoughtful, capable children in an age of distraction and excess. Whether exploring digital boundaries, emotional intelligence, or money habits, his work offers clarity, compassion, and actionable wisdom for the modern household. Eli lives with his partner and two children, where dinner table conversations often spark the next book idea.

www.ingramcontent.com/pod-product-compliance
Lightning Source LLC
Chambersburg PA
CBHW031335230926
51848CB00002B/251
*9789371775946*